China's Footprints in Southeast Asia

China's Footprints in Southeast Asia

Edited by

Maria Serena I. Diokno,
Hsin-Huang Michael Hsiao
and Alan H. Yang

NUS PRESS
SINGAPORE

This book resulted from a project funded by the Japan Foundation.

© 2019 Maria Serena I. Diokno, Hsin-Huang Michael Hsiao and Alan H. Yang

Published by:
NUS Press
National University of Singapore
AS3-01-02, 3 Arts Link
Singapore 117569

Fax: (65) 6774-0652
E-mail: nusbooks@nus.edu.sg
Website: http://nuspress.nus.edu.sg

ISBN 978-981-4722-89-6 (paper)

All rights reserved. This book, or parts thereof, may not be reproduced in any form or by any means, electronic or mechanical, including photocopying, recording or any information storage and retrieval system now known or to be invented, without written permission from the Publisher.

National Library Board, Singapore Cataloguing in Publication Data

Name(s): Diokno, Ma. Serena I., editor. | Xiao, Xinhuang, editor. |
    Yang, Alan H., editor.
Title: China's footprints in Southeast Asia / edited by Maria Serena I. Diokno,
    Hsin-Huang Michael Hsiao and Alan H. Yang.
Description: Singapore: NUS Press, [2019] | Includes bibliographical references
    and index.
Identifier(s): OCN 1046081283 | ISBN 978-981-47-2289-6 (paperback)
Subject(s): LCSH: China--Foreign relations--Southeast Asia. | Southeast Asia--
    Foreign relations--China. | China--Foreign economic relations--Southeast
    Asia. | Southeast Asia--Foreign economic relations--China.
Classification: DDC 327.51059--dc23

Cover background: Maria Skrigan/Shutterstock.com

Printed by: Markono Print Media Pte Ltd

Contents

Chapter 1	China's Soft Footprints in Southeast Asia: Accommodation and Contestation *Maria Serena I. Diokno, H.H. Michael Hsiao, and Alan Hao Yang*	1
Chapter 2	China's Soft Footprint in the Arena of Foreign Policy: Not "Hiding Light" Anymore? *Teng-Chi Chang*	31
Chapter 3	China's Economic Offensive and Its Discontent in Southeast Asia: Diminishing Footprints in Myanmar *Ian Tsung-yen Chen*	63
Chapter 4	The Political Economy of China's Economic Presence in Malaysia *Ngeow Chow Bing*	90
Chapter 5	Producing Power: China-Indonesia Cooperation in the Fast Track Program I *Natalia Soebagjo*	117
Chapter 6	Limits of China's Aid Diplomacy: Lessons from the Philippines *Dennis D. Trinidad*	141
Chapter 7	The Re-recognition of Confucianism in Indonesia: An Example of China's Soft Footprint in Southeast Asia *Yumi Kitamura*	172

Chapter 8 Confucius Institutes in Southeast Asia: Assessing   194
           the New Trends in China's Soft Diplomacy
           H.H. Michael Hsiao and Alan H. Yang

About the Contributors   226

Index   228

CHAPTER 1

China's Soft Footprints in Southeast Asia: Accommodation and Contestation

Maria Serena I. Diokno, H.H. Michael Hsiao, and Alan Hao Yang

In the past decade, an increasing amount of literature has emphasized China's growing quest for "wealth and power" (*fuqiang*) and "rejuvenation" (*fuxing*) (Schell and Delury 2013: 5) and the strategic implications of this quest on neighboring countries (Goldstein 2005; Ross and Zhu 2008; Sutter 2010). The attention has focused largely on Beijing's engagement with its Southeast Asian counterparts through economic favors and investment projects (Hou and Yeoh 2005; Yeoh, Yoo and Liong 2010) on the one hand, and China's central role in disputes with its neighbors on the other (Yahuda 2012; Huang and Billo 2015). New interpretations portray China's involvement in the Southeast Asian region as "the afterlife of tributary relations" (Reilly 2013: 161–2), an "Eastphalian order" (Maogoto and Coleman 2013), and an exercise in "the politics of dependency" (Hsiao and Yang 2014). China has long aimed to loop its Southeast Asian neighbors into its "sphere of influence" (Kang 2010; Reilly 2013), treating the South China Sea today, called by some its "Caribbean" (Holmes and Yoshihara 2006; Kaplan 2014: 32–50), as a platform for staging its influence over its coastal periphery, driven by power shifts in the political, economic and security order (Acharya 2013; Hagström and Jerdén 2014).

Some of the concepts used to explain China's relations with Southeast Asia at present, such as "tributary relations" and "sphere of influence," hark back to ancient times. That these concepts have resurfaced with new meaning is a testament not only to the long continuum of Chinese engagement in Southeast Asia but also to the transformation of Sino-Southeast Asian relations in contemporary times. A brief history is therefore necessary to understand the workings of China's soft power in the region today.

From Mutual Suspicion to Diplomatic Relations, 1950–90

Contemporary relations between China and Southeast Asian countries may be divided into four phases: the period of mutual hostility from 1950 to the 1970s; the opening-up period from the mid-1970s to the early 1990s; the period of transformation from the 1990s to 2012; and the growing assertiveness of China in the region since 2013.

China's influence over Southeast Asia in the first period "waxed and waned" (Tate 1971: 11) according to China's domestic unity and stability but, as Tate points out, China's moments of glory consistently reverberated in the region. With the end of the political struggle between the Chinese Nationalist Party and the Communist Party of China (CPC) in the late 1940s, the new political leadership of China focused inward, consolidating its domestic authority after a long conflict. Only three Southeast Asian countries established formal diplomatic ties with China in 1950: Vietnam, Indonesia, and Myanmar (then Burma). Of the three, the last has had the steadiest relationship with China. Based on Chinese Premier Zhou Enlai's Five Principles of Peaceful Coexistence,[1] Beijing highlighted the importance of Myanmar to its peripheral diplomacy in the 1950s and 1960s (Steinberg and Fan 2012: 7).

Beijing's relations with Vietnam, in contrast, went through highs and lows during this period. Chinese military and economic assistance to the Democratic Republic of Vietnam (DRV) represented the peak of their relations, but after Vietnam invaded Cambodia and adopted a bandwagon policy toward the Soviet Union in the 1970s, Sino-Vietnamese relations deteriorated. For a different reason, Sino-Indonesian diplomatic ties were also battered during this phase. Confronted by a domestic anti-communist movement (Gestok) in 1965 that resulted in the overthrow of Sukarno, the Indonesian government suspended bilateral relations with China in 1967.

In contrast, the rest of the Southeast Asian countries chose to approach Beijing with suspicion, fearful that local communist movements would court Chinese support. Thus while the communist states of Cambodia and Laos established diplomatic ties with China in 1958 and 1961, respectively, the other Southeast Asian countries established relations more than a decade later.

Table 1 Establishment of Diplomatic Relations between China and Southeast Asia

Country	*Start of Diplomatic Ties*
Vietnam	January 18, 1950
Indonesia	April 13, 1950
Myanmar (Burma)	June 8, 1950
Cambodia	July 19, 1958
Laos	April 25, 1961
Malaysia	May 31, 1974
Philippines	June 9, 1975
Thailand	July 1, 1975
Singapore	October 3, 1990
Brunei Darussalam	September 30, 1991

Source: Ministry of Foreign Affairs of the People's Republic of China. Various years. "Asian Countries." <http://www.fmprc.gov.cn/web/gjhdq_676201/gj_676203/yz_676205/> (accessed March 23, 2017).

For its part, during the early phase China applied a "Good Neighbor Policy," which called for a fairly low profile in the region and the avoidance of an adversarial stance with regard to territorial differences with nearby countries. The creation of the Association of Southeast Asian Nations (ASEAN) in 1967 jarred China, however, for it looked upon this new organization as pro-American, with the intent of containing China's influence and role in the region (Sheng 2008: 256).

China's distrust of the ASEAN was eventually overtaken by changes on the home front. Spurred by the reform policies of Deng Xiaoping, the "offensive realism" of Maoist China evolved into the "defensive realist stance" of Deng Xiaoping and his successors (Tang Shiping 2008: 141). In its 3rd Session in 1979, the 11th Central Committee of the CPC established the opening-up policy based upon the rationale of peaceful engagement with external powers (Li 2009: 19). This policy faced a major challenge during the war between China and Vietnam in 1979. By the early 1990s, however, the opening-up period had come full circle, with the last of the Southeast Asian countries, Singapore[2] and Brunei, entering into formal diplomatic relations with China.

From Softening Up to Chinese Assertiveness, 1990s–2012

China re-articulated the new regime of "opening up" diplomacy in terms of four pillars: peaceful co-existence, anti-hegemonic sentiments, development of economic relations and support for the ASEAN. These principles were proposed by Chinese Premier Li Peng when he visited Bangkok in 1989 (Latif 2007: 197), thereby softening earlier decades of mistrust and suspicion.

As in the past, this foreign policy was a byproduct of China's rapid growth following its domestic economic reform policy. Two specific goals were targeted in Beijing's new political discourse: the sustainability of the CPC regime and the mitigation of global concern that China's rising power would destabilize the current world order.

Thus in the early 1990s, Beijing began to consolidate its internal political power and legitimacy, guided by the notion of a "harmonious society" (*hexie shehui*) (Guo and Guo 2008). By giving attention to social equality and justice, Beijing hoped to enhance the state's capacity to deepen public trust and strengthen the legitimacy of the regime (Li, Sato and Sicular 2013). On the external front, Beijing expanded the domestic conception of a harmonious society to a "harmonious world" as a grand strategy to attract regional support for its ascendency (Chen and Yang 2013). Note that by this time, all ASEAN members had individually established diplomatic ties with China, while at the multilateral level, the normalization of China-ASEAN relations was beginning to take shape.

In 1991, Chinese Foreign Minister Qian Qichen wrote to Abdullah Badawi of Malaysia, then chairman of the ASEAN Foreign Ministerial Meeting, expressing the desire of China to establish formal relations with the ASEAN. On June 13, 1991, Badawi replied favorably, inviting Qian to join the ASEAN meeting in Kuala Lumpur (ASEAN 2014). The ASEAN response was a pragmatic one: members believed it was best to engage with China as a "constructive partner" rather than isolate it by keeping a residue of the old "powerful enemy" syndrome (Chin 1997: 157–9).

For its part, Beijing's strategy toward individual Southeast Asian countries and the ASEAN was straightforward—to develop constructive relationships based on the idea of "making friends instead of making enemies" (Lee Khoon Choy 2013: 128). When the financial crisis struck Southeast Asia in 1997, Beijing seized the opportunity to support Southeast Asian countries through a low-profile and soft approach. The Chinese Ministry of Foreign Affairs reported that it gave Thailand and other Asian countries more than US$4 billion in aid via the International Monetary Fund or through direct bilateral channels, and offered Indonesia and other countries export credit and emergency medicine. President Jiang Zemin also proposed a three-point measure at the 6th Informal Leadership Meeting of the Asia-Pacific Economic Cooperation (APEC) on November 18, 1998, to reinforce international cooperation, restructure the international financial system and respect the decisions of nations in dealing with the crisis—a proposal reiterated at the meeting of the ASEAN, China, Japan and Korea (9 plus 3) the following month (Ministry of Foreign Affairs of the People's Republic of China).

In later years, strategic initiatives such as the China-ASEAN Free Trade Agreement (2010), China-ASEAN Expo (since 2004), and related cooperative projects facilitated the realization of China's persuasive soft diplomacy. In addition to trade and business cooperation, Beijing applied a New Security Concept to China-ASEAN relations, showing a more patient attitude toward territorial disputes (Sutter 2010: 213) in order to soften the hard essence of Chinese military predominance and ease the worries this caused in the region.

Aggressive Diplomacy (2013 to the present)

The continuous development of China-ASEAN relations, however, has not sufficed to end tension and confrontation between China and Southeast Asian countries. Territorial disputes over the South China Sea, particularly with the Philippines and Vietnam, became and remain a central point of contention.

China's response of late has been a more aggressive, though Janus-faced, diplomacy. On the one hand, it promotes a moderate, less threatening image of China's "peaceful rise," as shown in Xi Jinping's Maritime Silk Road project between China and Southeast Asia and his emphasis on Good Neighbor Diplomacy in October 2013. On the other hand, Xi is categorical about the imperative of safeguarding

China's national interest in the South China Sea (Nguyen 2013); he also unilaterally declared an Air Defense Identification Zone in the East China Sea (Saunders 2014). In May 2014, China dragged one of its oil rigs to Vietnam's Exclusive Economic Zone, further flexing its muscle in the region.

The 2016 ruling of the Permanent Court of Arbitration in The Hague in favor of the Philippine position with regard to the South China Sea (referred to in the Philippines as the West Philippine Sea) provided yet another opportunity for China to exert its "not so soft" power in the region. The court ruled that "China's claim to historic rights to the living and non-living resources within the 'nine-dash line' [the demarcation line on a 1947 map of the sea] is incompatible with the [UN] Convention [on the Law of the Sea, to which China is a state party] to the extent that it exceeds the limits of China's maritime zones as provided for by the Convention" (PCA Case No. 2013–19, July 12, 2016).

Chinese President Xi has refused to "accept any positions or actions based on the outcome of the arbitration case over the dispute" (quoted in *Euronews*, July 12, 2016). Foreign Minister Wang Yi described the case as "a farce" and asserted that the Hague decision would turn the area into a "dangerous territory of worsening tensions and confrontation" (cited in *Euronews*). To substantiate its position, China continues to build structures in the contested shoal.

Thus despite its avowed policy of maintaining good and stable relations with Southeast Asia, Beijing's hardline position palpably demonstrates the primacy of its core interests, even at the cost of losing international goodwill. As Joseph S. Nye (2014: 21) explains, China's nationalism reduces the universal appeal of Xi's "Chinese Dream" and its threatening policies in the troubled waters are once again antagonizing its neighbors.

China's Economic Role in Southeast Asia

China's influence in the region is backed by its strong economic position. After more than three decades of economic reform of a once isolated and underdeveloped communist country, China for the first time overtook Japan as the world's second-largest economy after the United States at the end of 2010 (Hamlin and Li Yanping 2010). From being a recipient of foreign direct investment, China has become an important source of outward direct investment (ODI) to Africa,

Asia and Latin America. Garcia-Herrero (2015) estimates China's ODI in Asia in 2013 to be US$41 billion, or 49 percent of China's total ODI, followed by Europe (US$13.9 billion or 19 percent), with Africa receiving the lowest amount (US$5.3 billion or 8 percent). Together with Africa, Southeast Asian countries such as Cambodia, Laos, Myanmar, Thailand and Vietnam are perceived as attractive destinations for Chinese investors.

China's ODI to Southeast Asia concentrates on power generation, petrochemical plants, manufacturing and resource extraction. Rubber plantations in Laos and Vietnam, for example, are areas of Chinese investments that have grown tremendously. Since 2003, China has ranked among the nations with the highest investments in Laos. Today China stands as the second-largest trading partner of the Lao republic, accounting for about 25 percent of the latter's total trade, providing capital imports to Laos and taking in a significant chunk of the agricultural and forestry exports of Laos (Verghis et al. 2016). The Chinese projects hire workers recruited from China's mainland, thereby increasing the presence of Chinese workers in the host country.

In the case of Vietnam, Chinese investments, too, have consistently increased. During the 1990s, they amounted to just about US$120 million, increasing to more than US$1.5 billion by 2008, thereby placing China among the top 15 largest investor countries in Vietnam. At present, China is heavily involved in Vietnam's biggest ever bauxite mining plan, with an investment of more than US$1 billion. The project is located in the province of Dak Nong in the Central Highlands, bordering the Moldokiri province of Cambodia. Factory processing of bauxite in Tan Rai is under construction and Chinese involvement in mining bauxite in the Central Highlands will continue until 2025. The Vietnamese government is committed to the project regardless of strong opposition from intellectuals, social activists and the public at large.

Similarly, Southeast Asia has become a vital market for goods made in China as the trade gap widens between China and countries in the region. To offset the gap, these countries tend to extract their natural resources such as minerals, coal, oil and gas, and agro-forestry products for export to China. It should, however, be noted that even as capital flows from China to Southeast Asia, China itself continues to receive foreign aid and more than 100 million of its people live below the poverty line, with an income of less than one dollar a day (Asian Development Bank 2004).

Shifts in Chinese Investment

While there is no doubt about the increasingly important Chinese economic presence in the Mekong region, the trend of the investments has undergone some changes. From investments in the light industrial sector such as garment manufacturing and small-scale processing, which employ cheap labor, China's investments in Southeast Asia have shifted since the 2000s to mining, energy, infrastructure construction, land concession, plantation, and housing projects with long-term land leases. As per the Heinrich Böll Stiftung et al. report (2008), Chinese projects often exhaust natural resources and cause a loss of biological diversity in forests of the Mekong region. Moreover, the concession projects granted to Chinese companies take land away from local farmers, forcing them to leave their ancestral land and resettle in other rural places or migrate to increasingly crowded urban centers.

Furthermore, China's concentration on agro-products for raw materials and the resulting exploitation of natural resources have expanded to now include transportation infrastructure aimed at connecting China to the region from both mainland and maritime areas. With regard to the first, highways and railways linking the economic centers of Guangzhou (Guangxi) and Kunming (Yunnan) with the Mekong region are under construction. In 2011, China announced investments worth RMB15.6 billion (US$3.05 billion) to build a railway linking Nanning and Singapore via Vietnam (*China Daily* 2011) in order to realize China's plan called "Two Corridors, One Economic Belt" (Xinhua News Agency 2007), which was approved and supported by the Asian Development Bank and countries of the Greater Mekong Subregion in 2002 as a "win-win" project for all the parties involved.

As for the maritime corridor, China has paid more attention to the Malacca Straits through which 80 percent of the country's annual oil imports are transported (Reuters March 4, 2010). Concerned about China's vulnerability in the area, then President Hu Jintao claimed in 2003 that "certain major powers" aimed to control the straits. Citing China's "Malacca dilemma," as the Chinese press came to call it, Storey (2006) quotes a statement from the *China Youth Daily* (June 15, 2004), which states: "It is no exaggeration to say that whoever controls the Strait of Malacca will also have a stranglehold on the energy route of China." Now that investments are pouring into the economic corridors of the Mekong and Malacca, the question of who actually benefits from these infrastructure developments will figure more prominently.

China has also emerged as a player in the field of development assistance to the region. Prior to the 1990s, foreign economic aid to Southeast Asia consisted of four major sources: the Soviet Union, which aided Vietnam and Laos; China, which supplied essential economic aid to Cambodia; and the US and Japan, which aided the rest of the region. After 1990, with the collapse of the world communist system and the end of the Cold War as well as the emergence of new centers of conflict in Iraq and the Middle East, China quickly emerged as a potential donor for the Mekong region, as both Russia and the US turned their eyes elsewhere. Although Japan remains the largest provider of official development assistance to Southeast Asia, the relationship between China and the Mekong basin countries—which, at least on paper, emphasizes bilateral cooperation—seems to have opened the door to Chinese economic aid to the region. In practice, China's aid programs are closely tied to economic bilateral cooperation that facilitates the entry of Chinese goods and capital into these poor countries.

Rogue Aid?

Studies of China's role in Southeast Asia generally focus on economic involvement in investments, trade, aid and migration to the region. It is difficult, however, to be precise with the volume of Chinese foreign aid for, as Sven Grimm et al. (2011) and Jonathan Weston et al. (2011) point out, data on China's annual foreign aid is never fully released. There is some evidence that China's aid supports regimes with poor human rights records (such as Myanmar), leading to a perception that China's aid allocation is not determined by results or by the impact of aid on recipient societies, but rather by China's national interest and an ideological agenda. Studies by Moisés Naím (2007) and Sara Lengauer (2011), for example, show how China uses aid as a tool to advance its interests abroad, allocating aid strategically in order to gain easy access to natural resources, and bribing countries, if necessary, to gain their support in international politics.

On the other hand, Axel Dreher and Andreas Fuchs (2011 and 2012) find fault with the verdict that China's foreign aid is "rogue" in the absence of hard evidence on what determines the allocation of China's aid. They argue that Chinese aid on the grounds of national politics is not unusual; in fact, donor states generally use aid for strategic (vested) reasons. The difference with China is that it communicates its intent more openly. Moreover, its aid is sometimes perceived as a welcome alternative to that of Western donors whose meticulous bureaucratic procedures and detailed policy conditionalities pose an obstacle to the admission of aid. China's focus on infrastructure projects also addresses developmental needs that some donor countries tend to neglect.

While all recognize the huge economic role of China in Southeast Asia, views differ with regard to China's effect on individual countries and the region as a whole. Some neighboring countries have expressed anxiety about the strong emergence of China. In 2002, for instance, then Malaysian Prime Minister Mahathir Mohamad, observed: "China is an economic threat for Southeast Asia. It is already a threat in terms of attracting foreign direct investment, and it is going to be a threat to Southeast Asia's world trade" (quoted in Frost 2004: 7).

Others, in contrast, do not feel threatened. Singapore's Tommy Koh, for example, argues:

> China wants to be respected by the world. China wants a seat at the top table. I don't think China is a revolutionary power which is seeking to export Chinese communism or the Chinese model of development (the so-called Beijing Consensus). I do not have the impression that China is seeking hegemony, whether at the global or regional level (Koh 2011: 202).

However it is perceived by its neighbors, within China there is a consensus that not only "hard" (economic and military strength) but also "soft" power (diplomacy, aid and culture) is necessary for China to project itself as a global influence. He Qinglian (2009) points out that this is the position of the CPC. Culture is central to this approach, according to Yu Xintian (2008), who believes that culture influences the entire spectrum of a nation's policies and institutions. The cultural vehicles for exercising soft power, He Qinglian adds, are Chinese language schools, overseas Chinese associations and Chinese language media—the "three precious treasures of the overseas united front" for the Chinese government. She adds:

> Foreign aid and comprehensive, mutually penetrating economic relations are the core of China's "soft power" resources—this, unlike the "soft power" recognized by the international community, is actually the "hard power" of economic strength being peddled by China as "soft power;" and it is, under the promise of "incentives," Chinese Communist cultural values and ideas cloaked in "Confucius Institutes," aimed at getting the world to accept a "Chinese culture" whose flavor has long ago gone bad (He Qinglian 2009).

Cultural Outreach

How "hard," then, is China's "soft" power? Confucius Institutes (CIs) offer a range of answers. At one end of the spectrum is the belief that China's capacity to influence the region is circumscribed by its own need to address domestic poverty and concomitant social problems. Another claim, espoused by Zhe Ren, is that compared to the US and Europe, and even to Japan and Korea, China's "culture industry lags considerably behind" (2012: 20). He adds:

> At a moment when it is not possible to claim in clear and simple language that something in particular stands out in Chinese culture, China would seem to have no choice but to put that aside and instead stress its history and culture in its quest to find words or concepts synonymous with its culture. Finding such a synonym may become more important than increasing the number of institutes as the Confucius Institute undertaking continues to develop (Zhe Ren 2012: 20).

At the other end of the spectrum is the assertion that the CIs are important to China's propaganda abroad (Chey 2008). McDowell points out that "[t]o China observers and counter-intelligence agents, the runaway expansion of Confucius Institutes represents a threat, both as an arm of Chinese 'soft power' abroad and as a potential vehicle for intelligence gathering" (2010). Referred to as a "spiritual high-speed rail" by the CPC's propaganda chief Liu Yunshan (*The Economist* September 13, 2014), the CIs

> devote themselves to satisfying the demands of people from different countries and regions in the world who learn the Chinese language, to enhancing understanding of the Chinese language and culture by these peoples, to strengthening educational and cultural exchange and cooperation between China and other countries, to deepening friendly relationships with other nations, to promoting the development of multi-culturalism, and to construct a harmonious world (Constitution and By-laws of the Confucius Institutes).

As non-profit educational institutions, the CIs are mandated to follow "the principles of mutual respect, friendly negotiations, and mutual benefit," obey the laws of the countries in which they are located, and "respect local cultural and educational traditions and social customs" (Constitution and By-laws). A decade after the CI program began in 2004, 465 institutes were established in 123 countries with an additional 713 Confucius Classrooms set up in middle and primary schools around the world. In 2014 Southeast Asia had 25 Confucius Institutes and 19 Confucius Classrooms, the majority of them in Thailand (Zhao Yanrong 2014).

The quick-paced expansion of CIs worldwide has not taken place, however, without serious problems. In 2013, the Lyon Confucius Institute closed down because as board chairman Gregory B. Lee explained, the institute's director was "taking his instructions directly from Beijing" and "questioned the content of our courses" (quoted in Ching 2014). Later that year, the Canadian Association for University Professors sought the closure of CIs in Canada because the universities that housed them were "compromising their own integrity" (quoted in Ching). In June 2014, the 47,000-strong American Association of University Professors urged American universities to shut down CIs or rework their contracts so as protect the universities' academic freedom. "Confucius Institutes," asserted the association, "function as an arm of the Chinese state and are allowed to ignore academic freedom" (cited in Cai 2014). A month later, the European Association for Chinese Studies (EACS) was appalled when the director-general of the Confucius Institute Headquarters (Hanban), Xu Lin, had pages of the association's conference packet removed because they referred to a conference co-sponsor, the Taiwanese Chiang Ching-kuo Foundation, and the National Central Library of Taiwan. Roger Greatrex, EACS president, stated: "Such interference in the internal organization of the international conference of an independent and democratically non-profitable academic organization is totally unacceptable. It cannot and will never be tolerated by the EACS" (quoted in Cai).

Going Global

The concern over CIs is not only their effect on the academic freedom of host universities. University of Chicago Professor Emeritus Marshall Sahlins stresses their role in China's soft power strategy: "Routinely and assiduously, Hanban [CI Headquarters] wants the Confucius Institutes to hold events and offer instruction under the aegis of host universities that put the PRC in a good light—thus confirming the oft-quoted remark of Politburo member Li Changchun that the Confucius Institutes are 'an important part of China's overseas propaganda set-up'" (Sahlins 2013).

Sahlins refers to an article in the CPC's *The People's Daily* (2011) that affirms the above assertion. The article cites the growth in the number of CIs all over the world alongside other indicators of China's global ascendancy,

> such as its annual growth rate of 8 percent, its technological and military accomplishments, and its newfound status as the second-largest economy in the world. "Why is China receiving so much attention now? It is because of its ever-increasing power ... Today we have a different relationship with the world and the West: we are no longer left to their tender mercies. Instead we have slowly risen and are becoming their equal" (Sahlins 2013).

The achievement of this equality, then, represents the ultimate success of China's "Going Global Strategy," which was officially launched in 1999. This strategy may be related to an earlier concept of a "soft border," according to which China's territory is not limited to its national physical borders but can be expanded to a larger space, including that of neighboring countries where China has national political, economic and security interests (Cui 1991). This point of view could be the root of the perception that wherever Chinese cultural products are, there, too, lie China's borders.

Theories of Old

The idea of "soft borders" is an example of current discursive efforts to explain China's status and global trajectory. One strand is historically oriented; it looks at how, possibly, traditional Chinese thinking has gained new footing and meaning in contemporary Chinese society. Examples would be the concepts of Sino-centralism and Sino-"barbarian" dichotomy (E. Wang 1999; Callahan 2008). Wang, for example, explains (1999: 30):

> The Chinese view of the world was shaped around the axis of Han ethnic culture, which helped grade and hierarchize the rest of the world according to its acceptance of Han culture. As a result, the Han people and their neighbors formed a dichotomous relation. On one hand, the Han people were wary of their less civilized, barbaric neighbors ... but on the other hand, following the Confucian teaching, which was canonized during the early Han dynasty, Han rulers were also supposed to cultivate morals and virtue among barbarians.

Following this hierarchical view of the world, the CI program makes sense; the very name of the institute heightens the ancient notion of Chinese superiority over its "less civilized" neighbors.

Another concept from the past is the tributary system, the foundation of contemporary interpretations of China's peaceful rise (Wang 2011; Wills 2011). Jacques (2009: 291–2; 374–6) directly links China's new diplomacy to the tributary system of old, marked by gift-giving and obeisance (kowtow) of tributary states to the emperor. Higgins (in Borthwick 2014: 25) argues that the economic motive in tribute-giving was secondary to China, its main purpose being to reaffirm China's centrality in the civilized world, both as the wellspring of civilization and the supreme and universal ruler. This system, Kang explains, was built on institutional structures that regulated China's foreign relations in the interest of order and hierarchy (Kang 2010: 81).

Although these ancient structures and practices have long disappeared, some believe that their consequences linger. Some could argue, for instance, that the economic motive behind China's diplomacy today, while important, is perhaps not as crucial to China as its status as a world power. The array of socialist countries along China's southern border, Reilly maintains, is an effect of centuries of China's practice of "lin[ing] its frontiers with friendly supplicant powers" (2013: 162). Maritime Southeast Asia, in contrast, was less affected, in keeping, Reilly asserts, with the traditional effect of geographic proximity on countries within the orbit of China's tributary system.

There is, too, a sense that China continues to maintain an ethnocentric view of the world in which it is not only equal to the rest, but perhaps equally, if not more, powerful than others. Investments, aid, and cultural and language programs are all means to an end, and an affirmation of China's place of privilege in today's global order. Its foreign policy language exemplified by homegrown concepts of "peaceful rise" and "harmonious world" hinge upon the assertion of China's core interests in the region and the acceptance by the region of these interests. As in the case of China's soft power, China's ascendancy as a super power is also viewed negatively by some, who look upon China's new status as a contradiction to its stance of "peaceful rise" (Ikegami 2009; Shirk 2007) and "harmonious" diplomacy (Qian 2012). China's actions, in short, belie its foreign policy rhetoric (Scott 2012).

Sinicizing Western Theories

A second discursive strand is the reformulation, reinterpretation or perhaps "Sinicization" of Western theories and concepts by Chinese intellectuals and policy elites. Their purpose is not only to assert Chinese-ness (Yang, Hsiao and Chao 2013) but also, by so doing, to make the concepts palatable to the Beijing officialdom. Notwithstanding their alien discursive origin, these concepts can then be made to serve China's national interests as well as the political needs of its regime.

For instance, policy elites and academics discussed Nye's concept of soft power in the mid-2000s (Breslin 2011; Wuthnow 2008) and reformulated it as their own, particularly Chinese, brand. Once reinterpreted, the concept was absorbed into China's foreign policy, as evidenced in the Annual Report on China's Cultural Soft Power Research (Zhang 2011), the blue book of cultural soft power. The report explicitly maintains that soft power lies at the core of a nation's ascent or decline, its strength or weakness, and its prosperity or poverty. The document further suggests that as China's overall capability is enhanced, its intellectual and policymaking community should continue to deepen Chinese cultural influence as a principal component of soft power (Zhang 2011). Culture thus emerges as a crucial instrumentality of foreign policy.

Soft power also fits quite neatly into both the domestic and global modalities of a "harmonious" society/world and at the same time improves China's international image as a "benign hegemon." More importantly, in line with China's domestic reform, the concept offers a theoretical foundation for China's project of building the level of trust from the interior to the exterior, thereby achieving a harmonious society and world. In this light the CIs again figure as a logical instrumentality of the state. Grounded on political and strategic objectives, the institutes promote China's diplomatic strategy wherever they are located.

Examining the Footprints

This anthology collectively aims to interrogate some of the theories or frameworks regarding China's engagement in the Southeast Asian region. The focal concept, which this work pursues, is Nye's idea of soft power as it emanates from three main sources: a country's culture, political values and foreign policy (2004). Teng-Chi Chang (Chapter 2) examines the representational dimension of China's soft footprint, namely, foreign policy prior to and during the government of Xi Jinping, and highlights the shift from Deng Xiaoping's policy of "hide our light and bide our time" to a more open and forward policy in the region. As Chang explains, this change in policy did not emerge overnight. It was, rather, a distinct response to a combination of external and internal conditions: China's territorial disputes in the South and East China Seas on the one hand, coupled with then President Barack Obama's "pivot to Asia," and the changing domestic policy discourse about China's place in this new world. China's reformulated foreign policy (no longer "hiding our light") does, however, suffer from what Chang calls a "trust deficit" on the part of its Southeast Asian neighbors.

To conceptualize soft power on the ground, the contributors to this volume have developed the notion of a "footprint," loosely defined as the tangible presence, mark, or effect of China's exercise of soft power in the region. Aside from foreign policy, other footprints of China discussed in this book are trade, foreign aid and cultural programs in Southeast Asia. The questions the authors seek to answer are not only the kinds of imprints China has made in various Southeast Asian countries but the manner in which they produced them with bilateral partner states and, on the part of the latter, the spaces Southeast Asian partners created or negotiated in order to respond to or, in some cases, even challenge, China's soft power. In the course of focusing on soft footprints—the effect of soft power— the authors bring out the nature of soft power as it is exercised by China in the region. Some of the chapters question the effect of China's emergence as a regional and global power. Has it been disruptive and to whom? The answers differ from country to country, but as this volume suggests, where soft power has been more "invasive" than moderate and domestic conditions are at the same time weak or vulnerable (as in the case of Myanmar), a disruptive rather than a benign effect becomes more visible. Hence the footprint, though ostensibly soft, bears a troubling element.

Another framework that the chapters address is the politics of dependency. H.H. Michael Hsiao and Alan Hao Yang aver that owing to a basic disparity in resources, Southeast Asian countries tend to depend on resource-rich China through soft means (2014: 15–7). Xu Yunhong unabashedly emphasizes this dependence in a paper originally published on the website of *Qiushi Journal*, the official publication of the CPC Central Committee, on December 10, 2010:

> China's neighboring countries need China's international trade more than China needs them, with the vast majority of China's trade deficit caused by these countries. Therefore, they, but not China, will suffer greater damage by antagonizing China. China should make good use of these economic advantages and strategic power. This is also the most effective means to avoid a war (trans. into English by Chinascope.org).

China's upper hand appears quite clearly in the case of Cambodia. Acting like "a giant petty-cash box" (Strangio May 16, 2012), China invested some US$10 billion in Cambodia from 1994 to 2013, mainly in agriculture, mining, infrastructure, hydro-power dams and garment manufacturing. Between 1992 and 2016, China also provided about US$3 billion in concessional loans and grants to Cambodia (Var July 9, 2016). Despite the rhetoric of Chinese non-involvement in the domestic affairs of its partners, the overwhelming generosity of China (if one can call it that) bore fruit in Cambodia. Strangio (2012) points out, for instance, that Cambodia used its chairmanship of the ASEAN in 2012 to support China in the South China Sea dispute—this after then President Hu Jintao had just completed his four-day state visit to Cambodia. Four years later, Cambodia once again took up the cudgels for China, blocking the draft joint statement put forward by the Philippines and Vietnam criticizing China because of its newly built military structures in the South China Sea. This was the second time in the life of the ASEAN that it failed to issue a statement after a meeting, the first being in 2012, which was also caused by Cambodia's objection. As an official from the ASEAN Secretariat in Indonesia observed, "It is the same story again, a repeat of the meeting in 2012" (Mogato et al. 2016). Veasna Var thus concludes: "Excessive dependence on China has … placed Cambodian foreign policy firmly under China's influence" (2016).

Footprints as Spaces of Contestation

Yet, acquiescence is not always the result of dependence. This anthology demonstrates that the politics of dependency is not entirely a one-sided matter as one would expect, but is, too, a potential arena of "soft" contestation on the part of the dependent state. Ian Tsung-yen Chen (Chapter 3) notes the local opposition to China's investments in the Myitsone Dam and Letpadaung copper mine projects in Myanmar, China's longest and most stable partner in the region. Both projects—China's visible footprints in the country—alienated the local communities because of environmental issues and the inequitable allocation of benefits that the projects promised to deliver. The opposition originated from the people rather than the state, a development that neither the government of China nor of Myanmar had anticipated. Chen surmises that as Myanmar democratizes and its citizens become free and better informed, domestic opposition will grow and the government will have to listen to its people. In the process, Myanmar's long-standing stance, akin to China's on such issues as human rights, for example, could well change.

China's economic presence in Malaysia also challenges the conventional political dependency framework. In his study of the Malaysia-China Kuantan Industrial Park as an example of China's soft footprint, Ngeow Chow Bing (Chapter 4) finds that domestic elite actors in both politics and business have shaped China's economic presence in Malaysia rather than the other way around. He demonstrates how political dynamics between the federal government and the state of Pahang (where the industrial park is located) and complicity between local political and business elites have influenced the outcome of joint projects between China and Malaysia.

Like the Malaysia-China Kuantan Industrial Park, Indonesia's Fast Track Program Phase I has faced serious delays. Natalia Soebagjo (Chapter 5) focuses on the coal-fired power plants being constructed by Indonesia's state power firm and Chinese contractor companies. The delay, she explains, is traceable to the failure of Indonesian officials to understand the economic and political culture of Chinese construction companies and banks—these are state-owned enterprises (SOEs), not private enterprises—and the absence of what she calls a "robust" oversight process on the part of Indonesia. Because of their nature, Chinese companies have only one accountable shareholder, the Chinese state, which is moved by national political and economic purposes. Thus, while on paper the Chinese-Indonesian cooperation project appears rational and mutually beneficial, Indonesia's failure to understand the nature of SOEs has stood in the way of its working relations with Chinese contractors.

Contrasting Aid Principles

These Chinese contractors came to Indonesia through engineering, procurement and construction (EPC) contracts that are widely used in the region. In his (unpublished) study of China's aid to Vietnam (2014), Nguyen Van Chinh analyzes these contracts in Vietnam, which comprise some 90 percent of all of Vietnam's major EPC contracts. The EPC contract is no ordinary investment for, as in Indonesia and elsewhere in the region, the Chinese contractor is backed by the government of China, by such agencies as the Ministry of Commerce, Ministry of Foreign Affairs, and Chinese financial institutions like the Export-Import Bank of China, China Development Bank, and China Export and Credit Insurance Corporation. China's tangible footprint, Chinh points out, is in Vietnam's highlands, where mining and forestry products abound. The attraction of these natural resources have, in turn, spurred the development of a transport system linking Vietnam's border provinces to China's southern economic center. Apart from the extraction and processing of mining and forestry resources, the EPCs have served as a partner of Chinese aid to Vietnam, much of which comes in the form of concessional loans that benefit China more than Vietnam. Chinh finds that aid from China to Vietnam is primarily motivated by political and economic benefits to the giver and has bound Vietnam more tightly to China's economy instead of enabling the recipient country to develop a more self-reliant economy. For Chinh, the goal of Vietnamese sustainable development therefore "seems to be an unrealistic ambition" (2014).

Dennis D. Trinidad (Chapter 6) pursues Chinh's point by explaining that Chinese aid is different from official development assistance as defined by the Development Assistance Committee (DAC) of the Organisation for Economic Co-operation and Development. It is for this reason, Trinidad elaborates, that China's aid diplomacy in the Philippines has been weak. China's aid institutions have yet to be formed and are still strongly tied to Chinese business, unlike Western counterparts that separate public from private. Different principles therefore govern Chinese aid/business practices, resulting in controversies linked to corruption. In the case of the Philippines, whose legal framework conforms with the DAC model and principles, two high-profile projects funded by China in the early 2000s—the Northrail and the ZTE-National Broadband Network—were eventually scrapped because of legal violations and perceptions of graft at high levels of the Philippine government. The institutional mismatch was inevitable, Trinidad maintains, owing to "conflicting aid systems and processes between a non-DAC aid donor [China] and a DAC-conforming aid recipient [the Philippines]."

Chinese Cultural Footprints

This volume also looks at Chinese culture and education as distinctive footprints in the region. Malaysia presents a rather different situation from the rest of Southeast Asia (except perhaps for Singapore), given its already sizable Chinese Malaysian population, with Chinese schools and Chinese language books and newspapers readily available. Danny Wong (2014) observes a marked shift in recent decades from Taiwan to China as the destination country of choice for Chinese Malaysians wishing to pursue higher education overseas. Interestingly, the shift is caused not by China's initiatives in the country but by local conditions: the fact, for instance, that Malaysia recognizes university degrees from China while giving Taiwan degrees limited recognition; local acknowledgement that China's leading universities are ranked highly in world university rankings; and the attraction of huge markets in China.

The conscious orientation toward China is evident in other aspects of Chinese Malaysian culture. Wong cites as an example the restoration of decrepit Chinese temples and heritage structures by skilled craftsmen from China instead of by Malaysian craftsmen familiar with localized and hybrid forms. The result is a resurgence of traditional Chinese styles in place of Straits Chinese or Nanyang architectural models. Even the simplified script used in China was adopted by Chinese schools in Malaysia starting in 1993, replacing the centuries-old traditional script.

Two chapters in this volume examine the cultural footprints of China: Yumi Kitamura's article on the re-establishment of Confucianism as a state religion in Indonesia after years of Chinese Indonesians being forced to assimilate into Indonesian culture (Chapter 7), and Michael Hsiao's and Alan H. Yang's study of Confucius Institutes in Southeast Asia (Chapter 8). Kitamura situates the official recognition of Confucianism within the context of China's soft power aid in the 2000s and the desire of the post-Suharto government to attract Chinese investment to Indonesia. Chinese Indonesians used the space hitherto closed to them to push for the identification of Confucianism as a state religion from its status as a "delisted" religion. Kitamura frames her narrative of Confucianism's checkered history—from an officially recognized religion to delisted status and back again to state acceptance—within the "strategic mobilization of Chinese soft power by Chinese Indonesians" rather than by China.

If Confucianism in Indonesia has proven to be a resilient cultural imprint of China, the Confucius Institutes (CIs) in Southeast Asia, on the other hand, bear the more straightforward agenda of promoting guanxi (networks) between Chinese and Southeast Asians through the vehicle of Chinese culture and language. Unlike some universities in Europe and North America that approach the CIs from the standpoint of academic freedom, Hsiao and Yang highlight the strategic value of the CI networks in Thailand, Singapore and Cambodia to China as the core component of the latter's "Great External Propaganda" (*dawaixuan*), an instrument of the Chinese state, and the resulting footprint in Southeast Asia. This network, an active footprint, extends to national and local elites, government units, educational institutions, and overseas Chinese groups. Since, as Nye asserts, the purpose of soft power is to persuade or influence the thinking of others, the CIs' connections with highly placed members of Southeast Asian societies become crucial to the operation of China's soft power in the region.

A Footprint of Large Proportions: The Belt and Road Initiative

Recent initiatives suggest that China intends to implant its soft footprint more firmly and more expansively on Southeast Asian ground. The soft component of its Belt and Road Initiative, China explains, is anchored on cultural and people-to-people exchanges, educational cooperation, networks of think tanks, joint development of historical and cultural heritage as "tourist products," exchanges between parliaments, political parties, civil society organizations, and broad sectors of society, all "with a view to achieving inclusive development" (Xi Jinping May 14, 2017). Xi's reference to history—the "chapter of friendship" built along the ancient Silk Road over two millennia (Xi Jinping September 7, 2013)—is especially instructive because it highlights the soft rather than the hard aspect of Chinese efforts in the region, namely: "solidarity, mutual trust, equality, inclusiveness, mutual learning and win-win cooperation" (ibid). Within this China-centered "community of common destiny" (Xi Jinping 2015) belongs Southeast Asia. Xi himself explained the "win-win" pathway to this China-ASEAN community: "The interests of others must be accommodated while pursuing one's own interests, and common development must be promoted while seeking one's own development. The vision of win-win cooperation not only applies to the economic field, but also to the political, security, cultural and many other fields" (Xi Jinping March 28, 2015).

But, in fact, China's self-interest is the main driver here. As *The Economist* points out (May 15, 2017), China seeks to place its foreign exchange reserves in more hospitable and long-lasting ventures than global securities currently offer, as the country is in search of vast, new markets for its high-speed railway and other industries as well as its oversupply of steel and cement. China's desire to develop its coastal and interior regions, which Summers (2016) calls the "sub-national regional dimension," also motivates the Belt and Road Initiative. Linked to Beijing's geopolitical interest is the "geoeconomics" of Chinese strategy, or the pursuit of China's geopolitical interests through trade (Edward Luttwak, cited in Hancock 2017).

In a sense the sheer magnitude of China's 21st-century footprint could become the source of its own weakness (Lu Jianren 2016: 382–5). Already, delays in the implementation of projects, differing bilateral interest across Southeast Asia, domestic investment laws, bureaucratic constraints, and opposition from civil society and non-government organizations—some of which are taken up in this book—could pose even greater problems in the future.

More importantly, at bottom some Southeast Asian countries are not comfortable with China's goals in the region. Then Indonesian Trade Minister Feng Huilan (Mari Pangestu) expressed concern "about China pushing its products, service and even corporations to other countries forcibly" through the Belt and Road Initiative (Lu Jianren 2016: 384). Noting that the Silk Road project is not new, Dr Trinh Van Dinh of the University of Social Sciences and Humanities in Vietnam observed, "History tells us that every new road by the Chinese emperors served the goal of invasion or expansion of the country" (Việt Nam News, November 27, 2015). The issue over the West Philippine/South China Sea, presumably resolved by the 2016 Hague ruling, continues to be rejected by China, apparently owing to its treatment of the area as a "core national interest" like Taiwan, Tibet and Xinjiang (Interview of Hillary Clinton, Department of State, 2010). Adding to the confusion is Philippine President Rodrigo Duterte's retreat from the ruling, preferring instead to engage more closely with China as part of his administration's infrastructure program ("build, build, build").

All these events suggest that China will continue to deboss its soft footprint in the region more deeply and more extensively, even as it faces the challenges posed by the Belt and Road Initiative of connecting China to Asia and the world.

Notes

1. The five principles are mutual respect for each other's territorial integrity and sovereignty, mutual non-aggression, mutual non-interference in each other's domestic affairs, equality and cooperation for mutual benefit, and peaceful co-existence.
2. Singapore had had informal relations with China since 1965 and even set up a representative office of commerce in 1981.

References

"A Message from Confucius: New Ways of Projecting Soft Power." 2009. *The Economist*, October 22. <http://www.economist.com/node/14678507> (accessed October 24, 2009).

Acharya, Amitav. 2013. "Power Shift or Paradigm Shift? China's Rise and Asia's Emerging Security Order." *International Studies Quarterly* 58, 1: 158–73.

ASEAN. 2014. "ASEAN-China Dialogue Relations." <http://www.asean.org/news/item/asean-china-dialogue-relations> (accessed December 5, 2015).

Asian Development Bank. 2004. "Poverty Profile of the People's Republic of China," May. <https://www.adb.org/publications/poverty-profile-peoples-republic-china> (accessed April 2, 2014).

"Beijing Refuses to Accept Hague Ruling over South China Sea Territorial Claims." 2016. *Euronews*, July 12. <http://www.euronews.com/2016/07/12/beijing-refuses-to-accept-hague-ruling-over-south-china-sea-territorial-claims> (accessed July 15, 2016).

Breslin, Shaun. 2011. "The Soft Notion of China's 'Soft Power'." Asia Programme Paper, February. <http://www.chathamhouse.org/sites/files/chathamhouse/public/Research/Asia/0211pp_breslin.pdf> (accessed May 20, 2014).

Cai, Peter. 2014. "China Fails the Soft Power Test," *China Spectator*, August 6. <http://www.businessspectator.com.au/article/2014/8/6/china/chi...t&utm_medium=email&utm_content=850183&utm_campaign=kgb&modapt=> (accessed August 7, 2014).

Callahan, William. 2008. "Chinese Version of World Order: Post-hegemonic or a New Hegemony?" *International Studies Review* 10: 749–61.

Chen, Ian Tsung-yen and Alan Hao Yang. 2013. "A Harmonized Southeast Asia? Explanatory Typologies of ASEAN Countries' Strategies to the Rise of China." *Pacific Review* 26, 3: 265–88.

Chey, Jocelyn. 2008. "Chinese 'Soft Power' – Diplomacy and The Confucius Institute," *Sydney Papers* 20, 1: 33–48.

Chin Kin Wah. 1997. "ASEAN in the New Millennium." In Chia Siow Yue and Marcello Pacini (eds.), *ASEAN in the New Asia: Issues and Trends.* Singapore: Institute of Southeast Asian Studies.

Ching, Frank. 2014. "Growing Influence of Confucius Institutes." *New Straits Times,* October 2. <http://www.nst.com.my/news/2015/09/growing-influence-confucius-institutes> (accessed October 19, 2014).

Chinh, Nguyen Van. 2014. "China's Aid to Vietnam: Between "Politics First" and "Economic Gain," project of the SEASREP Foundation.

Confucius Institutes Headquarters (Hanban). Constitution and By-laws of the Confucius Institutes. <http://english.hanban.org/node_7880.htm> (accessed May 28, 2013).

Cui, Yu-Chen (崔彧臣). 1991. *The Struggle for a Soft Border* (爭奪「軟邊疆」的新角逐). Sichuan: Sichuan Education Publishing House.

Dreher, Axel and Andreas Fuchs. 2012. "Rogue Aid? On the Importance of Political Institutions and Natural Resources for China's Allocation of Foreign Aid," January 27. <http://www.voxeu.org/index.php?q=node/7569> (accessed January 29, 2012).

Dreher, Axel and Andreas Fuchs. 2011. "Rogue Aid? The Determinants of China's Aid Allocation." <http://ncgg.princeton.edu/IPES/2011/papers/F1120_rm3.pdf> (accessed January 8, 2012).

"Experts Sceptical of Maritime Silk Road." 2015. *Việt Nam News,* November 27. <http://vietnamnews.vn/print/experts-sceptical-of-maritime-silk-road/279113.html> (accessed May 17, 2017).

"Factbox – Malacca Strait Is a Strategic 'Chokepoint'." 2010. Reuters, March 4. <http://in.reuters.com/article/idINIndia-46652220100304> (accessed March 9, 2010).

Frost, Stephen. 2004. "Going to Southeast Asia: Chinese Foreign Investment and its Implications," Paper presented at the workshop on China's Overseas Investment, Hong Kong University of Science and Technology.

Garcia-Herrero, Alicia. 2015. "China's Outward Foreign Direct Investment," June 28. <http://bruegel.org/2015/06/chinas-outward-foreign-direct-investment/> (accessed July 10, 2015).

Goldstein, Avery. 2005. *Rising to the Challenge: China's Grand Strategy and International Security.* Stanford: Stanford University Press.

Grimm, Sven et al. 2011. "Transparency of Chinese Aid: An Analysis of the Published Information on Chinese External Financial Flows," Centre for Chinese Studies, Stellenbosh University and Publish What You Fund, August. <http://www.aidtransparency.net/wp-content/uploads/2011/08/Transparency-of-Chinese-Aid_final.pdf> (accessed February 24, 2012).

Guo, Sujian and Baogang Guo (eds.). 2008. *China in Search of a Harmonious Society*. Lanham: Lexington Books.

Hagström, Linus and Björn Jerdén. 2014. "East Asia's Power Shift: The Flaws and Hazards of the Debate and How to Avoid Them." *Asian Perspective* 38: 337–62.

Hamlin, Kevin and Li Yanping. 2010. "China Overtakes Japan as World's Second-Biggest Economy," *Bloomberg News*, August 16.

Hancock, Tom. 2017. "China Encircles the World with One Belt, One Road Strategy," *The Financial Times*, May 4. <https://www.ft.com/content/0714074a-0334-11e7-aa5b-6bb07f5c8e12> (accessed May 17, 2017).

He Qinglian. 2009. "'Soft Power' with Chinese Characteristics Is Changing the World," December 12. <http://www.hrichina.org/en/content/3175> (accessed January 16, 2010).

Heinrich Böll Stiftung, World Wildlife Fund, and International Institute for Sustainable Development. 2008. "Rethinking Investments in Natural Resources: China's Emerging Role in the Mekong Region." <http://www.iisd.org/sites/default/files/publications/trade_chinapolicybrief.pdf> (accessed January 14, 2009).

Higgins, Roland L. 2014. "The Tributary System." In Mark Borthwick (ed.), *Pacific Century: The Emergence of Modern Pacific Asia*. Boulder: Colorado Westview Press.

Holmes, James R. and Toshi Yoshihara. 2006. "China's 'Caribbean' in the South China Sea," *SAIS Review of International Affairs* 26, 1 (Winter–Spring): 79–92.

Hou Kok Chung and Yeoh Kok-Kheng (eds.). 2005. *Malaysia, Southeast Asia and the Emerging China: Political, Economic and Cultural Perspectives*. Kuala Lumpur: Institute for China Studies, University of Malaya.

Hsiao, H.H. Michael and Alan Hao Yang. 2014. "Differentiating the Politics of Dependency: Confucius Institutes in Cambodia and Myanmar." *Issues & Studies* 50, 4: 11–44.

Huang, Jing and Andrew Billo. 2015. *Territorial Disputes in the South China Sea: Navigating Rough Waters*. New York: Palgrave Macmillan.

Ikegami Masak. 2009. "China's Grand Strategy of 'Peaceful Rise'." In H.H. Michael Hsiao and Cheng-Yi Lin (eds.), *Rise of China: Beijing's Strategies and Implication for the Asia-Pacific*. London: Routledge.

Jacques, Martin. 2009. *When China Rules the World*. New York: The Penguin Press.

Jiang Zemin. 1998. Speech at the 6th APEC Informal Leadership Meeting, Kuala Lumpur, Malaysia, November 18. In Ministry of Foreign Affairs. <http://www.fmprc.gov.cn/mfa_eng/wjb_663304/zzjg_663340/gjs_665170/gjzzyhy_665174/2604_665196/2606_665200/t15276.shtml> (accessed May 3, 2012).

Kaplan, Robert D. 2014. *Asia's Cauldron: The South China Sea and the End of a Stable Pacific*. New York: Random House.
Kang, David. 2010. *East Asia Before the West: Five Centuries of Trade and Tribute*. New York: Columbia University Press.
Koh, Tommy. 2011. "21st Century: China and the World." In *China in the Next 30 Years*. Beijing: Central Compilation & Translation Press. <https://lkyspp.nus.edu.sg/wp-content/uploads/2013/04/pa_tk_21st-Century-China-and-the-World_11.pdf> (accessed March 2, 2012).
Latif, Asad-Ul Iqbal. 2007. *Between Rising Powers: China, Singapore and India*. Singapore: Institute of Southeast Asian Studies.
Lee Khoon Choy. 2013. *Golden Dragon and Purple Phoenix: The Chinese and Their Multi-Ethnic Descendants in Southeast Asia*. Singapore: World Scientific Publishing Co. Pte. Ltd.
Lengauer, Sara. 2011. "China's Aid Policy: Motive and Method," Culture Mandala: *Bulletin of the Center for East-West Cultural and Economic Studies* 9, 2 (September–December): 35–81.
Li Mingjiang. 2009. "Explaining China's Proactive Engagement in Asia." In Tang Shiping, Mingjiang Li and Amitav Acharya (eds.), *Living with China: Regional States and China through Crises and Turing Points*. New York: Palgrave Macmillan.
Li Shi, Hiroshi Sato and Terry Sicular (eds.). 2013. *Rising Inequality in China: Challenges to a Harmonious Society*. Cambridge: Cambridge University Press.
Lu Jianren. 2016. "The 21st Century Maritime Silk Road and China-ASEAN Industry Cooperation," *International Journal of China Studies* 7, 3 (December): 375–89.
Maogoto, J. and A. Coleman. 2013. "'Westphalian' Meets 'Eastphalian' Sovereignty: China in A Globalised World." *Asian Journal of International Law* 13, 3: 1–34.
McDowell, Adam. 2010. "Are China's Confucius Institutes in Canada Culture Clubs or Spy Outposts?" *National Post*, Canada, July 9.
Mogato, Manuel, Michael Martina and Ben Blanchard. 2016. "ASEAN Deadlocked on South China Sea, Cambodia Blocks Statement." Reuters, July 26. <http://www.reuters.com/article/us-southchinasea-ruling-asean-idUSKCN1050F6> (accessed July 30, 2016).
Ministry of Foreign Affairs (People's Republic of China). N.d. "Pro-Active Policies by China in Response to Asian Financial Crisis." <http://www.fmprc.gov.cn/mfa_eng/ziliao_665539/3602_665543/3604_665547/t18037.shtml> (accessed July 25, 2012).
Ministry of Foreign Affairs. Various years. "Asian Countries." <http://www.fmprc.gov.cn/web/gjhdq_676201/gj_676203/yz_676205/> (accessed March 23, 2015).

Naím, Moisés. 2007. "Rogue Aid," *Foreign Policy* 159 (March–April): 95–6.
Nguyen, Phuong. 2013. "China's Charm Offensive Signals a New Strategic Era in Southeast Asia." Center for Strategic & International Studies, October 17. <http://csis.org/publication/chinas-charm-offensive-signals-new-strategic-era-southeast-asia> (accessed June 22, 2015).
Nye, Joseph S. 2004. *Soft Power: The Means to Success in World Politics*. New York: PublicAffairs.
Nye, Joseph S. 2014. "The Information Revolution of Power." *Current History* 133: 19–22.
Permanent Court of Arbitration. 2016. "PCA Case No 2013-19 in the Matter of the South China Sea Arbitration before an Arbitral Tribunal Constituted under Annex VII to the 1982 United Nations Convention on the Law of the Sea between the Republic of the Philippines and the People's Republic of China," The Hague, Netherlands, July 12. <https://pca-cpa.org/wp-content/uploads/sites/175/2016/07/PH-CN-20160712-Award.pdf> (accessed November 5, 2016).
Qian, Cheng (Jason). 2012. "Challenges for China's Harmonic Diplomacy." In Hong-Yi Lai and Yi-Yi Lu (eds.), *China's Soft Power and International Relations*. New York: Routledge.
Reilly, Benjamin. 2013. "Southeast Asia: In the Shadow of China." *Journal of Democracy* 24, 1 (January): 156–64.
Ross, Robert S. and Zhu Feng (eds.). 2008. *China's Ascent: Power, Security and the Future of International Politics*. Ithaca: Cornell University Press.
Sahlins, Marshall. 2013. "China U." *The Nation*, October 30. <https://www.thenation.com/article/china-u/> (accessed November 16, 2013).
Saunders, Philip. 2014. "A Guide to Understanding China's Regional Diplomacy." *The National Interest*, April 30. <http://nationalinterest.org/blog/the-buzz/guide-understanding-chinas-regional-diplomacy-10346> (accessed May 20, 2015).
Schell, Orville and John Delury. 2013. *Wealth and Power: China's Long March to the Twenty-First Century*. New York: Random House.
Scott, David. 2012. "Soft Language, Soft Imagery and Soft Power in China's Diplomatic Lexicon." In Hongyi Lai and Yiyi Lu (eds.), *China's Soft Power and International Relations*. London: Routledge.
Sheng, Lijun. 2008. "China and ASEAN in Asian Regional Integration." In Wang Gungwu and Zheng Yongnian (eds.), *China and the New International Order*. London: Routledge.
Sheridan, Greg. 2010. Interview with Hillary Rodham Clinton, Secretary of State, in Melbourne, Australia, November 8, US Department of State. <https://2009-2017.state.gov/secretary/20092013clinton/rm/2010/11/150671.htm> (accessed May 17, 2017).
Shirk, Susan. 2007. *China: Fragile Superpower*. Oxford: Oxford University Press.

"Soft Power: Confucius Says." 2014. *The Economist*, September 13. <http://www.economist.com/news/china/21616988-decade-ago-china-began-opening-centres-abroad-promote-its-culture-some-people-are-pushing> (accessed September 18, 2014).

Steinberg, David I. and Hongwei Fan. 2012. *Modern China-Myanmar Relations: Dilemmas of Mutual Dependence*. Copenhagen: Nordic Institute of Asian Studies.

Storey, Ian. 2006. "China's Malacca Dilemma," *China Brief* 6, 8 (April 12). <https://jamestown.org/program/chinas-malacca-dilemma/> (accessed May 18, 2006).

Strangio, Sebastian. 2012. "China's Aid Emboldens Cambodia." YaleGlobal Online, May 16. <http://yaleglobal.yale.edu/content/chinas-aid-emboldens-cambodia> (accessed May 19, 2012).

Summers, Tim. 2016. "China's 'New Silk Roads': Sub-national Regions and Networks of Global Political Economy," *Third World Quarterly* 37, 9: 1628–43.

Sutter, Robert G. 2010. *Chinese Foreign Relations: Power and Policy since the Cold War*. Maryland: Rowman & Littlefield Publishers, Inc.

Tang Shiping. 2008. "From Offensive to Defensive Realism: A Social Evolutionary Interpretation of China's Security Strategy." In Robert S. Ross and Zhu Feng (eds.), *China's Ascent: Power, Security, and the Future of International Politics*. Ithaca and London: Cornell University Press.

Tate, D.J.M. 1971. *The Making of Modern Southeast Asia. Volume 1: The European Conquest*. Kuala Lumpur: Oxford University Press.

Var, Veasna. 2016. "Cambodia Should Be Cautious When It Comes to Chinese Aid." *East Asia Forum*, July 9. <http://www.eastasiaforum.org/2016/07/09/cambodia-should-be-cautious-when-it-comes-to-chinese-aid/> (accessed July 31, 2016).

Verghis, Mathew, Sally Burningham, et al. 2016. *Lao Economic Monitor: Challenges in Promoting More Inclusive Growth and Shared Prosperity*. Washington, DC: World Bank.

Wang, Edward. 1999. "History, Space, and Ethnicity: The Chinese Worldview." *Journal of World History* 1, 2: 285–305.

Wang, Yuan-Kang. 2011. *Harmony and War: Confucian Culture and Chinese Power Politics*. New York: Columbia University Press.

Weston, Jonathan, Caitlin Campbell, and Katherine Koleski. 2011. *China's Foreign Assistance in Review: Implications for the United States*. Washington, DC: United States – China Economic and Security Review Commission.

"What Is China's Belt and Road Initiative?" 2017. *The Economist*, May 15. <http://www.economist.com/blogs/economist-explains/2017/05/economist-explains-11> (accessed May 20, 2017).

"White Paper: China's Foreign Aid." 2011. *China Daily*," April 22. <http://www.chinadaily.com.cn/cndy/2011-04/22/content_12373944.htm> (accessed April 24, 2011).

Wills, John. 2011. *Past and Present in China's Foreign Policy: From "Tribute System" to "Peaceful Rise."* Portland: Merwin Asia.

Wong, Danny Tze Ken. 2014. "The Shifting Emphasis and Orientation in Malaysian Chinese Education and Chinese Culture," a project of the SEASREP Foundation.

Wuthnow, Joel. 2008. "The Concept of Soft Power in China's Strategic Discourse." *Issues & Studies* 44, 2: 1–23.

Xi Jinping. 2013. "Promote Friendship Between Our People and Work Together to Build a Bright Future," Nazarbayev University, Kazakhstan, September 7, Ministry of Foreign Affairs, People's Republic of China. <http://www.fmprc.gov.cn/mfa_eng/wjdt_665385/zyjh_665391/t1078088.shtml> (accessed November 20, 2014).

Xi Jinping. 2015. "Towards a Community of Common Destiny and A New Future for Asia," Boao Forum for Asia Annual Conference 2015, Boao, Hainan, March 28. <http://news.xinhuanet.com/english/2015-03/29/c_134106145.htm> (accessed May 17, 2017).

Xi Jinping. 2017. "Work Together to Build the Silk Road Economic Belt and the 21st Century Maritime Silk Road," keynote speech at the opening ceremony of the Belt and Road Forum for International Cooperation in Beijing, China, Xinhua News Agency, May 14. <http://news.xinhuanet.com/english/2017-05/14/c_136282982.htm> (accessed May 20, 2017).

Xinhua News Agency. 2007. "China, Vietnam Discuss Economic Corridor Development," December 3. <http://www.china.org.cn/international/2007-12/03/content_1234184.htm> (accessed April 10, 2012).

Xu Yunhong. 2010. "How China Deals with the U.S. Strategy to Contain China," *Seeking Truth*, English version by Chinascope. <http://chinascope.org/archives/6353/92> (accessed February 3, 2013).

Yahuda, Michael. 2012. "China's Recent Relations with Maritime Neighbours." *The International Spectator* 47, 2: 30–44.

Yang, Alan Hao, H.H. Michael Hsiao and Hao-Yu Chao. 2013. "How China's Epistemic Community Remakes Soft Power: A Critical Literature Review." *Mainland China Studies* 55, 4: 59–88.

Yeoh, Emile Kok-Kheng, Im-Soo Yoo and Lionel Wei-Li Liong. 2010. "China and East Asian Regional Integration: Inception of ACFTA and APEC at 20." *International Journal of China Studies* 1, 1: 46–88.

Yu Xintian. 2008. "The Role of Soft Power in China's Foreign Strategy," *Guoji Wenti Yanjiu*, March 13.

Zhang Guo-zuo (ed.). 2011. *Annual Report on China's Cultural Soft Power Research*. Beijing: Social Science Academic Press.

Zhao Yanrong. 2014. "Confucius Institutes Extend Reach," *Asia Weekly*, October 3. <http://epaper.chinadailyasia.com/asia-weekly/article-3358.html> (accessed November 9, 2014).

Zhe Ren. 2012. "The Confucius Institutes and China's Soft Power," Institute of Developing Economies Discussion Paper No. 330, March. <http://ir.ide.go.jp/dspace/bitstream/2344/1119/1/ARRIDE_Discussion_No.330_ren.pdf> (accessed June 19, 2012).

CHAPTER 2

China's Soft Footprint in the Arena of Foreign Policy: Not "Hiding Light" Anymore?

Teng-Chi Chang

> He who has no pleasure in killing can unite it [the under-heaven].
>
> Mencius, "Chapter on King Hui of Liang"
>
> Hence to fight and conquer in all your battles is not supreme excellence; supreme excellence consists in breaking the enemy's resistance without fighting.
>
> Sun Tzu, "Attack by Stratagem," *The Art of War*

Introduction

Shortly after the 1989 Tiananmen Square incident, Deng Xiaoping counseled, "Keep cool-headed to observe, stand firmly, be composed to react. Hide our light [capabilities] and bide our time, never try to take the lead, and be able to accomplish something."[1] The phrase "hide our light and bide our time" became China's foreign policy guideline for more than 20 years. Such thinking is not rare, since the Chinese have traditionally favored political strategies that accomplish goals without fighting.[2] However during Jiang Zemin's and Hu Jintao's years of leadership (2002–13), the question of whether China should amend Deng's "hiding our light" and switch to "accomplishing something" was a fiercely debated issue. Nevertheless, Jiang's willingness to assume the "responsibilities" of his "great power diplomacy" and Hu's "harmonious world" policy generally maintained the foreign policy course set by Deng. It was during the period of Jiang and Hu's leadership that Joseph Nye's conception of "soft power" was adopted as a Chinese foreign policy tool to offset the widespread, negative image of China as a threat. For China, soft power based on cultural attractiveness and institutional legitimacy, according to Nye's definition, would help Beijing win foreign support, which was (and is) crucial for China's political and economic goals. However, as public grievances over inequality and bureaucratic corruption grew in the late 1980s, the legitimacy of the Communist Party of China's (CPC) rule started to be called into question. When the CPC's legitimacy seemed weak, the Party usually tended to strengthen it by nationalistic measures. The Chinese government consequently found it gradually had less space for sophistication, the manipulation of soft power included, in foreign issues.

Words like "assertive," "arrogant" and even "aggressive" have now become common to describe changes in China's foreign policy since 2010. More investment in the PLA (People's Liberation Army) and tougher measures towards neighbors in territorial disputes became easy but costly options. This was the challenging scenario that Hu Jintao left for Xi Jinping.

This chapter argues that China's foreign policy change has shifted directions due to a policy disorder brought about by its territorial disputes with its Southeast Asian neighbors over access to the South and East China Seas, its unrefined "core interests" policy discourse, and the "rebalancing" and "pivot to Asia" strategies of the US. To counterbalance Washington and its allies' economic and military balancing and to redirect domestic discontent with inequality and corruption, Hu's soft power approach to foreign policy began to take on some "hard-balancing" measures in the last two years of his term. The Xi Jinping administration chose to actively assume the responsibility of being a great power, as prescribed by the CPC's 18th Congress Report. This move was remarkable because the policy debate on whether China should shoulder international responsibility had been contested for a decade. To undertake international responsibility, for many Chinese strategists, meant both a distraction from Deng's "hiding light" principle, and a compromise with Western powers, which had urged China to "be responsible." Nevertheless, "responsibility" now does not mean adherence to the established world order. Xi's style has proved that he is a candid and tough rival to the West, and that China's soft power offensive shaped in the decade after the 1997 Asian financial crisis has been significantly reformulated by his new goals of the so-called "Chinese Dream."

This chapter begins by describing the essence of soft power and its Chinese version from a sociological-constructivist perspective. It is followed by a review of how China's foreign policy of soft power evolved before Xi's takeover. An examination of the reformulation of Deng's strategy by Xi Jinping's administration and its relationship with Xi's Chinese Dream will be addressed next. Lastly, the theoretical and practical implications of Xi's readjustment of China's changing soft power policy are summarized.

Soft Power in Debate and Its Sociolinguistic Nature

Debating the Nature and Scope of Power

Any serious discussion on a given country's power, hard or soft, needs to commence from the essence and nature of power. The examination of the foundation and exercise of China's soft power is no exception. This chapter starts with a brief discussion of power and soft power. The style and paradox of China's soft power will be considered accordingly.

There are two main theoretical approaches to defining power.[3] The first approach involves realist and neorealist theories about power. According to Morgenthau, "interest defined in terms of power" makes politics an autonomous discipline.[4] However, the desire to maximize power transforms power into an end in itself, which may lead to irrational and illogical consequences. Kenneth N. Waltz improves this definition by claiming that power should be seen as a tool consisting of combined capabilities including size of population, economic and industrial assets, military strength, and political stability. Among these factors, military capability is the "ultimate ratio."[5] The ultimate concern of states is not power, but security. Excessive power leads other states to pool their strength together to check threatening actors.[6]

The second approach involves institutionalist theories of power. Institutionalist thinkers have criticized efforts to define power merely in terms of material capabilities. Robert O. Keohane points out that theories based solely on capabilities have "proven to be notoriously poor at accounting for political outcomes."[7] The institutionalist criticism of power has raised questions about the scope of power (What effects do actors intend to cause?) and domain of power (What objects can be influenced by actors?).[8] For institutionalists, the study of a state's power should be based on which objects can be affected in which ways. Soft power is no exception.

Human Ideation, Constructivism and Soft Power

The above discussion raises the following question — to what extent the distribution of power is material or non-material (social)?[9] The worldview of realism is mainly a materialist one that stresses the military and economic capabilities of states. Most mainstream international relations theory (IRT) researchers tend to believe that ideational factors, such as discourse and ideological propaganda, are not major causal variables in international politics.[10] For example, Waltz claims that the "War on Terror" launched by the Bush administration would not jeopardize the position of the US, even though the decisions made by Bush might be unwise.[11] Like IRT theorists, some policymakers are also skeptical about the role of soft power in foreign policy. For example, former US Defense Secretary Donald Rumsfeld proclaimed: "I don't know what 'soft power' is."[12] And, some policy-oriented analysts choose not to use the concept of soft power. For example, the famous China expert, David M. Lampton, talks about integrating the "three faces" of Chinese power as the three "M"s: might, money and mind. Apparently the face of "mind" is something that concerns soft power, although Lampton chooses to adopt a broader concept of "mind" instead.[13]

Constructivist theories provide an equally sound picture of power. These theories generally assume that human relations are built mainly with shared ideas about human agency rather than material factors. From this assumption, constructivists argue that international relations are inter-subjective rather than material, and the distribution of power is mainly social rather than primarily material. Because the concept of soft power is defined by an appealing lifestyle and convincing ideas, its social and ideational nature is irreducible.

Constructivists further argue that without human ideation, material forces are simply unable to give a comprehensive account of international politics. Constructivists are not claiming that states do not act on the basis of interests; rather they are arguing that interests are themselves idea-based.[14] Because ideas are social realities that are derived from the interactions among state agents, soft power can be seen as a specific distribution of ideas that favors a specific state or bloc of states. For example, the formal and informal norms that underpinned China's tributary system were widely accepted in ancient Northeast Asia because they helped to stabilize interstate actions and maintain peace.[15] Other Northeast Asian countries recognized China's pre-eminent role as the originator and defender of this system and its norms.

Despite differences in theoretical perspectives noted above, material (hard) power and non-material (soft) power do seem related. Nye concurs with Huntington who observed, "[M]aterial success makes a culture and ideology attractive, and ... economic and military failure lead to self-doubt and crises of identity."[16] Janice B. Mattern offers a shrewd addition by arguing that soft power is not in juxtaposition to hard power, but is "a continuation of it by different means."[17] This raises the question: what makes hard and soft power distinct from each other? An answer can be found in the sociolinguistic nature of soft power.

Soft Power as Sociolinguistically Constructed "Truth"

Nye provides the widely accepted definition of soft power as "the ability to get desired outcomes because others want what you want." That is, "the ability to achieve goals through attraction rather than coercion," which in turn rests on "the appeal of one's culture or the ability to set the agenda through standards and institutions that shape the preferences of others."[18] His remarks sound like those of Mencius from 2,000 years ago. With this kind of ability, a state can make its goals legitimate "in the eyes of others" and eliminate the need to resort to coercion. Furthermore, in the current era of information overload, credibility makes valuable information stand out. Herein lies the focus of the struggle for soft power among nations: to make one's own information and ideas credible and destroy the credibility of enemies' information and ideas.[19]

On the issue of credibility, Nye differs from material-based stances somewhat by arguing that large democratic powers will benefit most from the new, info-tech based trend of soft power because democratic societies see credibility as based on valued characteristics like professionalism, procedural fairness and transparency—features authoritarian states usually lack. Andrew Hurrell further explicates the centrality of the credibility to power from a constructionist point of view: power requires recognition from the "club of great powers" and other weaker countries. Hurrell contends that the BRIC countries (Brazil, Russia, India, China) stand outside the international society of the "Liberal Greater West" because these nations have not sought the approval of the West, but historically have challenged the West's liberalism.[20]

Janice B. Mattern's critique of Nye's notion of soft power sheds light on the nature of soft power. Mattern begins by asking: "What exactly is it that makes an idea attractive or appealing in the first place?"[21] Her answer is that attraction is a "sociolinguistically constructed 'truth' about the appeal of some idea" that has won over other possible interpretations. Such attraction in effect does not rest upon evidence-based reasoning, because social actors often have no common understanding of what counts as evidence. What they care about is the security of their sociolinguistically constructed subjectivity. Consequently, powerful actors tend to portray reality in ways that affirm the existence of their "Self" regardless of evidence demonstrated by others. The capabilities for constructing "truth" statements to defend the Self and destabilize the sociolinguistic realities which comprise the other's Self are what Mattern calls "representational force."

Mattern illustrates the dual function of representational force with an example from the first Iraq war. American authorities spread specific ideas that equated the "War on Terror" as a morally righteous action against the lawless, evil others. The attractive reality of a world-defending America was presented to other international actors with little room for alternative interpretations. "You are either with us or with the terrorists," as President George W. Bush declared.[22] In short, even though such a force may not necessarily be carried out through one's perceivable hard power, this force of attraction is never soft. Soft power can be coercive in nature.

Foreign Policy Discourse as an Expression of China's Soft Footprint

In line with the above theoretical exploration, this chapter focuses on Beijing's foreign policy discourse before and under Xi Jinping as the expression of China's soft footprint in the arena of global engagement. China's style of discourse may look old-fashioned to its Western counterparts. When viewed in combination with its geopolitical manipulation and booming economy, however, some observers believe that China's rising "indirect influence" has become a threat to the West and some of China's neighbors. To date, China's developmental model, the "Beijing Consensus," seems to rival America's "Washington Consensus." As a result, some Western observers note, "the American Dream is not the only vision in town."[23]

In addition, Beijing has put aside its antagonistic revolutionary mode of discourse and switched to new discourses built around the notions of the "peaceful rise" and "harmonious world" to remind the world that it will never repeat the warlike, colonial strategy of the ascending great powers in the past.[24] Tellis and Hawksley both find that Beijing has exerted its own soft power to project itself as a friendly, non-intervening power and has at the same time adroitly exploited some regional discontent toward America. China is also keen to market its culture and language abroad and appears to acknowledge that "a genuine appreciation of Confucian rectitude" can go a long way to water down the perceptional strength of the "China threat." Are these "soft" efforts in the Chinese style effective?[25]

In the 1990s, many observers in the West shared the belief that China had not yet demonstrated that it would comply with international rules. Their comments were built around subtexts like "China is not a civilized state" and "China is a cheater." However, soft power gurus like Nye felt that China was entering the US-dominated global popular culture, with support from its unique traditions and modernized media industry.[26]

A few polls from the early 2000s tend to confirm Nye's judgment. One survey conducted by the University of Maryland in 2004 showed that 48 percent of people interviewed in 22 countries believed that China's role was mainly positive. An average of 38 percent of those interviewed saw America's influence as positive.[27] It was only after Barrack Obama took office that the national image of the US began to be viewed more positively than China's again. According to a June 2014 international poll, 65 percent of the people surveyed favored America while 49 percent favor China.[28]

How should we interpret the above facts? America's popularity seemed at its highest point during the Clinton years, and regained momentum after Obama resumed a multilateralist foreign strategy, replacing Bush's unilateralist one.[29] The once growing positive image and various influences of China became threatening. To alarmists,

China's influence seemed to be in a zero-sum competition with America's primacy, which endangered universal liberal values. In their eyes, Deng Xiaoping and his successors were like Bismarck, rallying the people with xenophobic distrust but hiding these actions from foreigners. They saw China's new developmental model as giving rise to a new ideological competitor to the West. Its large number of overseas descendants could provide a fifth column as Beijing extended its "Sinicized charm offensive."[30] From the alarmists' point of view, China's so-called soft power was not soft.

Chinese Foreign Policy Before Xi Jinping

An "Over-involved" China?

Probably due to its limited hard power, China's engagement with other countries after the end of the Cold War was viewed as cautious, modest and passive. Some of its actions in the UN were seen as benefiting the West because China did not have sufficient military power to actively support its "Stand with the Third World" causes.[31] This inactiveness was particularly salient in the series of UN resolutions toward Iraq, in which China abstained twice from authorizing the use of force.[32] Nevertheless, China successfully cultivated active flexibility and sophistication in its foreign policy. Examples can also be found in China's UN voting pattern: Beijing voted for UN Resolution 1441 on weapons inspections in Iraq (2002), increased its participation in peacekeeping operations, ratified interstate treaties regarding non-proliferation, and declared unilateral adherence to regimes such as the Kyoto Protocol and the Missile Technology Control Regime (MTCR) even though Beijing is not a signatory.[33] During the 2011 Syrian humanitarian crisis, China's vetoes were also the result of careful calculations: Moscow took the lead in the United Nations Security Council, and received most of the criticism.

The above instances may be regarded as strategies of free riding, hiding or buck-passing, due to China's lack of hard power. However, Johnston's detailed study finds that since the 1990s, China has gradually become "over-involved" in international organizations in terms of its level of development.[34] There is little evidence that China was either forced by the US to support its positions in the UN, or is undermining the current capitalist regime by its enthusiastic participation.

Other Chinese strategists have argued that, in the long run, the provision of more regional and global public goods is inevitable if China undertakes the role of a responsible great power (or a "responsible stakeholder," in Robert B. Zoellick's terms). Such an analysis assumes that taking on more responsibility is a positive display of self-expression and representation to the international community that the Chinese have moved past being obsessed by the national disgrace of not being able to counteract negative portrayals of their country since 1840—a situation that recent leaders have pledged to rectify.[35] Hence the impression of a softer, less aggressive, and more responsible major power is part of China's effort to create a new footprint in the world. After almost 18 years of debate, the decision to become a responsible major power was officially endorsed in 2012 in the high-profile report of the CPC's 18th Congress. However, the role of being responsible now was not only about positive national image building abroad; it also reflected Beijing's expectation of just and proportional relationships with the international institutions of which it is a member. Beijing, in short, wanted a part in shaping these institutions' decisions proportional to its level of participation and financial support.

The Trend, the Model and the Way

China's expectations raise the following question: what kind of discourse would be most convincing, and consequently best reflect the aims of Chinese foreign policy? Before Xi Jinping's inauguration in 2012, I contend the answer was a discourse built around three fundamental ideas: multipolarity, China's "peaceful rise" and a "harmonious world."

For the originator of the Chinese version of "multipolarity," Deng Xiaoping, the concept works like "balance of power" in International Relations studies that means both a law-like pattern and a desirable policy. Since Mao and Deng were opponents of so-called hegemonism, a synonym of a bipolar world dominated by the US and the Soviet Union, a world of "multipolarity" implies a balanced world in which power is shared by many nations. In this way, multipolarity was not only a concept promoted by government policymakers; it was also a prediction put forward by many Chinese strategists regarding the future order. It can be argued that Beijing was acting as an agent promoting a multipolar structure and rallying others' support for this law-like pattern. There are some measures Beijing has adopted to facilitate the consolidation of a multipolar world.

One salient example of this is its building of "partnerships" with other major or middle powers. China has tried to enhance its appeal as a "friendly partner," "infrastructure builder," and "capital lender" without aligning with any particular state or bloc of states, thus retaining flexibility and leaving room for its commitment of "always standing by the developing world."[36]

Since 2000, thanks to official support and the work of Chinese academics, the concept of China's "peaceful rise" has been developed as a new way to define the emergence of China and to explain the implications of this peaceful rise for the world. Zheng Bijian is one of the leading academic figures with wide political influence who forged the concept of China's peaceful rise to answer Western proponents of the China threat theory in the early 2000s. Zheng published an article in *Foreign Affairs* elucidating his ideas, in response to the widespread interest generated by his viewpoint. He argued that unlike other emerging powers that have acquired resources through coercion and wars in the past, China can instead obtain the capital, technology and resources it needs by peaceful means, which would further help China to integrate itself into a globalized world and deepen China's domestic reform and marketization. Through this approach, China could transcend the old ways of industrialization and Cold War competition, which would be an unprecedented feat, if successful.[37] Xi Jinping's recently revised principle of "new model of great power relations" is also a logical consequence of the "peaceful rise" rhetoric, which is discussed below.

The notion of a "harmonious world" signified Hu's new efforts in China's soft power building, which demonstrated not only how China could take its place as a major power in the world but also what kind of world order it was pursuing for the foreseeable future. This new concept was first unveiled officially by Hu Jintao in the "Sino-Russian Joint Statement on the International Order for the 21st Century" when Hu met Vladimir Putin in Beijing in October 2004. It appeared again on the 40th anniversary of the Afro-Asian Conference on April 22, 2005 in Indonesia—an occasion that commemorated Third World unity. And it was included in Hu's speech during the summit meeting for the 60th anniversary of the UN in September 2005. At the Asia Pacific Economic Cooperation (APEC) annual summit on November 18, 2005 in South Korea, Hu raised the concept once again.[38]

Hu's repeated mentions of "China's peaceful rise/development" and a "harmonious world" confirmed them as a set of ideas that China would promote abroad as a basis of its foreign policy. It also echoed Hu's call for a domestic "harmonious society." Some Chinese diplomats and researchers contended that the idea of a harmonious world would enhance China's soft power because it transcended the obsolete Chinese principle of "peaceful coexistence" and incorporated the wisdom of traditional Chinese philosophy. In addition, these ideas might be able to compete with Washington's core foreign policy ideas of freedom and democracy that had been "on sale since World War I."[39] Although the harmonious world appeal appears to be raised less often by Xi Jinping, it celebrates the same roots of Chinese traditional thought found in Xi's "Chinese Dream." Thus, the notion of a "harmonious world" will have enduring effects.

In the domain of foreign policy, for example, Zhao Haiqing argued that this ideational innovation of a harmonious world implied that Hu's government had turned to a mild, gradualist approach in order to modify the status quo world order. Jin Canrong, a senior Chinese specialist in American studies, also recognized that "slogan outcry can hardly generate sympathy if your audience is not able to comprehend what you are conveying." Therefore, the Chinese "need to theorize and systematize their concepts in order to enrich them and contribute them to the shared values of all civilizations."[40]

Chinese strategists contended that the concept of harmony can be traced back to Confucianism and Taoism. Before Beijing decided to utilize this idea as a foreign policy tool of soft power, the concept of "harmony" was closely studied by some Sinologists, which resulted in the following insights.

Yao Xinzhong suggests that the Confucian understanding of harmony is basically related to music and the ancient perception of the relationship between heaven and humanity. Generally speaking, unlike the tendency of dualism evident in Western philosophy, there is no definite line between heaven (nature) and human beings in the traditional Chinese way of thinking (especially in Confucianism and Taoism). The relationship between nature and human beings is primarily one of harmony rather than differentiation and conflict. Therefore, the way of heaven (*Tiandao*) and the way of humans (*Rendao*) can be seen as interrelated and complementary.[41]

This kind of philosophy has been shaped by China's physical milieu and historical conditions. In China's large, complex and diverse cultural make-up, substantial flexibility must exist to allow significant discrepancies between belief and ritual, and professed ideals and actual practice. Therefore, for the Chinese, ritual conformity and role adaption are not necessarily hypocrisy, but a hallmark of traditional culture that has held Chinese society, and to a degree, the broader East Asia tributary order together.[42] Underpinning this system is the Confucian idea of harmony that says when all parties perform their roles properly, everyone will gain from this "moral pretension."[43]

From "Multipolarity" to the "Harmonious World": An Uncertain, Evolving Chinese Identity

It is important to acknowledge two points that characterize the move from multipolarity to a harmonious world during the Jiang-Hu period. First of all, accompanying its rising hard power was China's need to revise its foreign policy discourse in order to deflect the notion that its growing strength would harm other nations. However, as Chih-yu Shih and I argue, the puzzle of "how to represent China" is not merely a matter of how to build up soft power outwardly, but also a matter of an inward self-identity reformation.[44] Chinese authorities have never settled on a conceptual framework that describes what kind of state China is or should be in the future. The continuing debate about China as a state indicates a lack of consensus on foreign policy, lack of agreement about the West's ideational influence on China, and a lasting confusion as well as uncertainty about what it means to be "Chinese." This continuing confusion explains why some Chinese thinkers advocate a change of the haunting "victim mentality" in order to facilitate the identity of a "normal China" in the international community. Pro-left, dogmatic sentiment is also held accountable for a biased foreign policy in the past. It is suggested that the required components of the new mentality are positive thinking and self-confidence, which will help expel the "China-in-siege mentality."[45] It is believed that this way of self-reformation will enable China to complete its transition to a real, responsible great power.

However, the issue is more complex than we have discussed. For example, there is a significant contradiction between the ideas of the harmonious society/world and the orthodox ideology of the CPC. Marxism–Leninism and Maoism stress that struggle and confrontation are necessary and inevitable in human history. To date, communist elites have hedged this problem. Such unresolved ideas, ideology and problems of identity have seriously impeded the smooth exercise of Chinese soft power. Consequently, the image of China that Beijing has tried to promote internally and internationally has always seemed suspicious. When serious strategic challenges loom, such as the maritime disputes in the South China Sea, Beijing's soft approach hardens into more unyielding positions. Washington's "rebalancing" and "pivot to Asia" policies have further encouraged China to respond with hard measures.

China's Hard Balancing Against America's "Rebalancing"

On the eve of Barack Obama's overhaul of foreign strategy—the US having been trapped both by the costly Afghanistan and Iraq wars and the global financial crisis—Beijing's Hu-Wen administration had enjoyed a period of more than six years of opportunities for "peaceful rise." Their "four-frontier strategy" revealed in 2004, which emphasized managing relations with great powers, prioritizing China's cooperation with its neighbors, consolidating friendship with developing countries, and improving multilateral diplomacy, was generally deemed successful.[46] Important policy tools employed in the four frontiers to smoothen China's image included foreign aid and language and culture exchanges (for example, the Confucius Institutes), which can be seen as Beijing's deployment of soft power.

Confronted by several major domestic and external challenges, such as the severe acute respiratory syndrome (SARS) outbreak, the unrest in Tibet and Xinjiang, and the global financial crisis, the Chinese government stood steady and outperformed the economies of Germany and Japan. The concept of the so-called "G2" was then forged, and unprecedented expectations were attributed to China, as were responsibilities.[47] The Western conception of responsibility required China to support the established Western regimes. However, the Chinese government felt these requirements were imposed without consultation and fair reward. As a consequence, the debate about whether to insist on Deng's doctrine of "hiding light" reignited when nationalist critics on the Internet and Chinese social media like Weibo and WeChat criticized Hu-Wen's "soft image" as too submissive to defend China's national interests.

Unsurprisingly, one factor driving Washington to introduce its "rebalancing" strategy was the desire to check China's successful soft power and "Good Neighbor Policy" in East Asia and elsewhere in the developing world.⁴⁸ Empowered by its fast and strong economic growth, China was not only becoming the top trading partner of its neighboring countries, but also its investments in raw material mining and infrastructure constructions were outpacing those of Western democracies.

This strategy is ongoing, so its full components are still in the making. Nevertheless, given several clarifications offered by senior US policymakers on the subject of how to be "rebalanced," I maintain that rising China is squarely Washington's target. It was not a coincidence that Washington rapidly reduced its military presence in the Afghan-Iraq theater and started to "pivot to Asia." As Ben Rhodes elaborated, the "pivot" was made possible by the winding down of the "two wars," allowing more focus on "the fastest-growing economic region in the world."⁴⁹ Several salient diplomatic measures that exemplify the vigorous nature of America's "rebalancing" China strategy will be briefly discussed next.

Washington: Rebalancing and "Forward Deployment"

The Obama administration, from the moment of assuming office, took Asia seriously. After Obama briefly unveiled the idea of "back to Asia" at the 2009 Bali Summit of APEC, identifying himself as the first "Asia-Pacific President," Hillary Clinton reiterated and reinforced the idea in Hawaii less than two months later.⁵⁰ Most observers were skeptical of this policy change at the time, and some even concluded that the US had lost Asia forever.⁵¹ Nevertheless, the decision makers at the White House began to implement this new policy change with diplomatic and military initiatives. Clinton's "forward deployed diplomacy" and Leon Panetta's "rebalancing" have been the most critical and far-reaching of these until now.

"Forward deployed diplomacy" was aimed at countering China's fruitful "Good Neighbor Policy" and other soft power measures in Asia. Of note is Secretary Clinton's "forward deployed diplomacy" in a nine-nation trip in July 2012. Clinton made three stops in the Middle East and Europe and six stops in countries that are China's key neighbors: Afghanistan, Japan, Mongolia, Vietnam, Laos and Cambodia. Clinton proclaimed that support for democracy and human rights was at the heart of American strategy. She told reporters in Mongolia that beyond democracy and human rights, the strategic priority of American foreign policy was now to make substantially increased investments in various diplomatic, economic and strategic areas in Asia, that is, to "pivot to Asia."[52]

Meanwhile, Washington successfully encouraged Mongolia's "Third Neighbor Diplomacy" that aimed to lessen Russia's and China's influence over Mongolia. Washington also reassured Japanese Prime Minister Yoshihiko Noda's cabinet of its support as the Diaoyu (Senkaku) Islands dispute was escalating. The US reopened high-level exchanges with Laos, the first since John Foster Dulles' 1955 visit. The most prominent part of Clinton's 2012 itinerary was her tour to Hanoi, demonstrating that iron-fisted communist rule was not necessarily an obstacle to specific US-Vietnam cooperation.[53] Although Clinton nominally voiced concerns over Hanoi's "peaceful expression of ideas" and detention of bloggers, the US still agreed to provide Hanoi with military equipment. The US-Vietnam ties tightened more in 2016, when President Obama lifted a decades-long embargo on arms sales to Vietnam, a significant countermeasure against China's growing military presence in the South China Sea.[54]

Beijing: Defending "Core Interests," Not Hiding Light?

While it seems clear that Washington intended to counterbalance China's expanding influence in Southeast Asia,[55] Washington's success cannot solely be attributed to its well-organized policy strategy. I argue that Beijing's foreign policy and its hard and soft power tools unintentionally aided America's pivot to Asia. Events in the South China Sea and the Korean Peninsula further worsened Beijing's geopolitical standing after 2012.

China's response to Washington's new policy initiatives was a gradual readjustment of the proportion between Deng's principles of "hiding light" and "being able to accomplish something." This readjustment can be dated from Jiang Zemin's Great Power Diplomacy in the late 1990s, the aim of which was to strengthen China's image and identity as a "great power" that would be recognized as such at home and abroad. For this reason, Beijing reassured the ASEAN countries after the 1997 Asian financial crisis that China would be responsible and would not depreciate its currency. The discourse around the idea of responsibility reflected notions of soft power in key bilateral diplomatic documents and remarks. However, what it means to be a responsible and great power was, and has always been problematic for China, not only because it is the West that has depicted and defined "responsibility," but also because China's qualification as a "great" power continues to be questioned.[56]

The growth of China's economy has been accompanied by an increase in the number of public complaints of inequality and corruption, a crisis of legitimacy that President Xi Jinping has been compelled to address. However, his readjustment of "hiding light" and "accomplishing something" has taken a different, more risky track. Because the ruling elites of the CPC did not adopt more far-reaching political and economic reforms, the CPC became potentially vulnerable and lost the ability to be diplomatically flexible. This subtle change explains China's increasing unwillingness to shift its position in disputes with its Southeast Asian neighbors and Japan over island territories. One serious result is that its softly constructed "truth" about China's peaceful rise to power has lost credit.

At the center of the policy change was China's unspoken assumption that the South China Sea is part of China's "core interests." When this assumption became public in 2010, debates intensified over whether Beijing would place the Spratly Islands on par with other sovereignty issues that could justify military intervention, like Taiwan, Tibet and Xinjiang. Notwithstanding the 2002 Declaration on the Conduct of Parties in the South China Sea (DOC), viewed as a milestone of China's soft discourse and Good Neighbor Policy, suspicion grew that a rising China was simply biding its time and would face its neighbors down when strong enough to impose its will on them. The appeal of the Philippines to the Hague tribunal for a resolution of differences in the South China Sea represents the pinnacle of this suspicion.

One can also find provocative editorials in state-run Chinese papers saying, "If these countries do not want to change their ways with China, they will need to prepare for the sound of cannons. It may be the only way for the dispute in the sea to be resolved."[57] The Chinese blockade of the Huangyan/Scarborough Shoal, aggressive patrolling around the Japan-controlled Diaoyu Islands, and announcing the East China Sea ADIZ (Air Defense Identification Zone) only reinforced Tokyo's and Manila's support of more US involvement, further undermining ten years of Beijing's soft foreign policy. As China was planting a soft footprint on the ground, therefore, the recourse to strong measures remained firmly by its side.

The "Chinese Dream": A Soft or Hard Footprint?
China Facing Up to "Increasing Hegemonism"

The differences between Hu's and Xi's style of leadership strengthened Xi's hard adjustments. Hu did not take control of the PLA immediately after the CPC's 2002 Congress. By contrast, Xi assumed all three powerful posts and was endorsed by the 2012 CPC Congress and the 2013 National People's Congress less than half a year later. As a descendant of the PLA's top brass and a victim of the Great Cultural Revolution, Xi enjoyed the blessings of the party's seniors, the Red Second Generation in particular, on his rise to power.[58] For these reasons, Xi appeared confident and affable, or in Leon Panetta's words, "frank and candid."[59]

The CPC's 18th Congress report represents to a fair degree the new agenda to be achieved by the Xi-Li administration. In the sections covering world politics and foreign policy, the report recognized "increasing hegemonism, power politics and neo-interventionism." It further condemned the "law of the jungle" and "arbitrary use of force," strong words not found in the previous two party congress reports coordinated by Jiang and Hu.[60] America's pivot to Asia and forward deployment diplomacy to Asia were depicted as hegemonic without being named.

Facing up to pressing challenges like "increasing hegemonism," Xi's public speeches on China's goals and the CPC's mission were also frank, brief and bold, a sharp contrast to Hu Jintao, who usually expressed his ideas in socialist jargon. The party pledged to completely build "a moderately prosperous society" in which the per capita Chinese income could reach as high as US$12,000, allowing the Chinese GDP to possibly overtake the US by 2020.[61] On other occasions, Xi outlined the concept of the "Chinese Dream" and rallied support for a "great renaissance of the Chinese nation."[62]

With its goal of China's "great renaissance" in mind, it seems that Xi and his followers are marching away from "hiding light" and towards "accomplishing" the Chinese Dream. Nevertheless we should bear in mind that Xi's hardening approach does not downplay the use of China's soft tools. On the contrary, Xi has re-emphasized that China should improve its use of soft power by "telling a good story of China." In one internal high-level meeting of the CPC propaganda leaders in mid-2013 he instructed:

> Propaganda that elaborates on Chinese characteristics must make clear that the historical traditions, cultural achievements and basic national circumstances of all countries and nations are different, their development path inevitably has its own characteristics as well ... [that] make clear that China's excellent traditional culture is a prominent superiority of the Chinese nation, and is an important spiritual pillar for the Chinese nation to constantly strive to renew itself, unite and struggle, it is our most profound "cultural soft power ...."
>
> We must strive to move international communications capacity construction forward, innovate foreign propaganda methods, strengthen discourse system construction, strive to forge new concepts, new categories and new expressions that circulate between China and the outside world, tell China's story well, disseminate China's voice well, and strengthen our "discourse power" internationally.[63]

The "Chinese Dream" and Its "Discourse Power"

The "Chinese Dream" is about "realizing a prosperous and strong country, the rejuvenation of the nation and the well-being of the people" to meet the "Two 100s" goals of China becoming a "moderately well-off society" by 2020, the 100th anniversary of the CPC, and a modernized nation by 2049, the 100th anniversary of the People's Republic.

Xi's Chinese Dream discourse has four parts: Strong China (economically, politically, diplomatically, scientifically and militarily); Civilized China (equity and fairness, rich culture, and high morals); Harmonious China (amity among the social classes); and Beautiful China (a healthy environment and low pollution). The goal of a "moderately well-off society" is where all citizens, rural and urban, enjoy high standards of living. This includes doubling the 2010 GDP per capita by about 2020 and completing urbanization (roughly 70 percent of China's population will be living in cities) by about 2030. The eventual goal of a modernized China is to regain its position as a world leader participating actively in all areas of human endeavor.

According to the state-run news agency Xinhua, the regime calls for all workers to "combin[e] their personal dreams ... with the national dream and fulfill their obligations to the country."[64] But, the Chinese Dream is not about abandoning communist rule for constitutionalism, Western-style human rights or democracy. The "American

Dream" celebrates individualism (work hard and you will reap the rewards) while Xi's "Chinese Dream" celebrates collectivism (work hard and your nation will be better off). Many officially printed posters now ubiquitous in streets, parks and public sites read, "The China Dream, my dream," "The China Dream: the dream of a powerful nation," "Fulfill the China Dream with intelligence and hard work." Chinese diplomats abroad are also commissioned to elaborate on how the Chinese Dream is compatible with the dreams of the people in the countries where they serve. Xi himself addressed the Brazilian Parliament saying the Chinese Dream and "Latin American Dream" are closely linked.[65] Another example is the "shared future" of the "Chinese Dream" and the "Korean Dream." Interviewed by Beijing's state-run TV in 2014, Korean President Park Geun-hye agreed that the "Korean Dream" shares the same goal of peace and common prosperity with the "Chinese Dream," and the convergence of the two dreams will reach a further "Dream of Northeast Asia."[66] Whether for instrumentalist purposes or not, Park's remarks indicate the degree to which Xi's dream can influence the shape of discourse in Asia.

Not surprisingly, the response from Obama and Joe Biden to such a candid, confident "dream" was that China should put more emphasis on "fairness" and "rules" (that is, individual rights), whereas the Chinese believe that "fairness" and "rules" should emphasize the promotion of equality based on stability, collectivism and conformity. As Elizabeth Economy observes, trust is only built over time.[67] Xi's several exchanges with Obama and other Washington leaders since 2012 might have been frank and constructive, but were far too little to bridge the trust deficit between China as a "rising power" and the United States as an "established power."

Xi's New Leverage: Hard or Soft?

One of Xi's countermeasures to deal with Washington's rebalancing and the prospect of cooling Sino-US relations has been to revive China's traditional strategies dating back to the Cold War era. Two traditional Chinese counterweights against foreign economic and military containment were the Soviet Union (and Russia after the collapse of the Soviet Union) and the Third World.

Moscow's nationalist elites have long been discontented with the reluctant economic support from the West and the West's active involvement in various "color revolutions" that aim to further break up Russia. China and Russia share a fear of being marginalized by a unipolar world. This fear explains various consecutive Russo-Chinese joint statements calling for multi-polarization and a just political and economic world order that echo the key ideas driving Chinese foreign policy discourse reviewed above. Certainly, China's partnership with the Russians is not new. Xi's choice of Russia as the first stop of his maiden overseas trip in March 2013 reflects this partnership. Xi stressed that the two countries are each other's "most important strategic cooperative partner," and that he was determined to deepen their comprehensive strategic partnership in their foreign policy.[68]

Xi's first joint statement with Vladimir Putin further celebrates "a good example for the harmonious coexistence between the great powers" because the two powers lend "support to each other in the 'core interests' involved in each other's sovereignty," oppose "unlimited anti-missile strategy" at the expense of other countries, observe the "indivisible principles of security architecture" in the Asia-Pacific region, and reject a "zero-sum game and bloc politics" way of thinking.[69] Here I contend that the original Chinese idea about a new model of great power relations solely designed to amend the US-China stalemate has been partly abandoned. Xi also seemed to be suggesting that a classic balance of power, and not a "new model" of great power relations, was the best way to deal with the US. In this way, Beijing and Moscow have now found common ground as they each seek to claim a place as a respected great power.

Although the idea of the existence of a Third World is passé today, non-Western countries with large markets that are growing larger (for example, BRICs) do share similar ideas with China about amending the rules of international trade and finance. Deng once taught his followers that China should stand with the Third World forever. Although the CPC regime has downplayed Deng's original notion, its stand against established Western institutions is still visible. Moreover, the growing diversity of issues of global governance, like international terrorism, climate change, and the reform of the International Monetary Fund (IMF) provides new opportunities for blocs of non-Western countries to put forward various ideas for alternative ways of governing the world. For Beijing, the BRIC bloc could evolve into a tangible organizational force pooling together renewed elements of anti-imperialism traditionally embedded in the idea of the Third World.

The BRIC bloc has not yet evolved into an all-powerful anti-West body as predicted by some observers. This is partially due to worries in India and Russia that China's economic strength could overwhelm the bloc. For example, there are reports claiming that China will finance 41 percent of the BRICs' planned currency reserve assets.[70] It is now at least a loose coalition of convenience to which China can contribute financial help, and in return other BRIC members can offer China support in international forums on issues like emissions, international finance and debts. Another similar mechanism for Beijing to try a formulation combining its hard and soft power is the Asian Infrastructure Investment Bank (AIIB) launched in 2015. China's leadership in the BRICs and AIIB is also a good opportunity to test the competitiveness of China's proposals for global governance. Injecting new vigor into the BRICs and AIIB could help China to break out of the emerging American net of military-economic containment.

Conclusion: Chinese Foreign Policy at a Crossroads

This chapter has provided a general picture of the development and discourse of Chinese foreign policy as the representational dimension of its soft footprint in the world. I argue that China constructed sophisticated soft power foreign policy discourses around conceptual frameworks like multi-polarity, peaceful rise and the "harmonious world" to improve its standing and image in the world. These soft power initiatives were successful to a certain extent. However, in the last few years of Hu's presidency, China's policymakers gradually stopped framing foreign policy in favor of soft power, because of the country's souring relations with its Southeast Asian neighbors and Washington's "rebalancing" strategy aimed at constraining the rising China. Another reason for this change is growing domestic problems like stagnated growth and widespread corruption, which have eroded the legitimacy of the CPC. Since President Xi took power, traditional Chinese culture and socialist ideas like the Third World were enlisted to replace old soft power concepts of "responsibility" and "harmony."

The Chinese Dream has replaced Hu Jintao's "harmonious world" as the conceptual basis of Xi's core discourse. As a consequence, Deng's teaching of "hiding light" has largely yielded to Xi's hard version of "responsible great power"—being responsible for accomplishing the "Chinese Dream," and an order in which no hegemon could dominate the international society. However, given that the Chinese are still obsessed with a crisis of identity about what kind of great power China can and should be,[71] they are carefully learning the lessons taught by the history of the West, and reminding themselves not to be trapped by a great power rivalry or "Thucydides Trap."

In sum, at this moment we probably cannot answer the question of whether Xi's Chinese Dream will end up an outright revisionist foreign policy no longer appealing to "soft" image building. Xi may not have determined the best way to respond to this question. He still needs Deng's wisdom of gradualism: "When confronted by mountains, one finds a way through. When blocked by a river, one finds a way to bridge to the other side."[72] Given various domestic challenges and the "trust deficit" haunting China and its rivals, Xi is at the crossroads of China's own rebalancing: to reformulate a tangible balance between a more assertive mark in the world and a more restrained, soft footprint. For all "dreamers" concerned, the rising, the established, and others, it is also a test of strategic prudence.

Notes

1. Qu Xing, then vice dean of the University of Diplomacy (Beijing), indicated that the 28-character strategy was first raised by Deng several months after the Tiananmen Square incident in 1989. Then deputy chief of staff of the PLA, Gen. Xiong Guangkai, contended that the translation of "hide our capabilities" was too "narrow" to demonstrate Deng's teaching. His suggestion instead was "hide our light" which echoed the usage of Fareed Zakaria's book, *The Post-American World*. The author adopts Zakaria and Xiong's translation. Please refer to Zhai Hua, "How to Explain to Foreigners that We are 'Hiding Light'?" *China Daily*, June 25, 2010, <http://www.chinadaily.com.cn/language_tips/trans/2010-06/25/content_10020700.htm> and Fareed Zakaria, *The Post-American World* (New York: W.W. Norton & Company, 2008).
2. Yan Xuetong, *Ancient Chinese Thought, Modern Chinese Power* (Princeton: Princeton University Press, 2011), 23–69.
3. Robert O. Keohane, "International Institutions: Two Approaches," *International Studies Quarterly* 32, no. 4 (1988): 379–96.
4. Hans J. Morgenthau, *Politics Among Nations*, 5th ed. (New York: Alfred A. Knopf, 1978), 5.
5. Kenneth N. Waltz, *Theory of International Politics* (Reading, Mass.: Addison-Wesley Press, 1979), 113–31.
6. Kenneth N. Waltz, "Realist Thought and Neorealist Theory," *Journal of International Affairs* 44, no. 1 (1990): 36; Glenn H. Snyder, "Mearsheimer's

World: Offensive Realism and the Struggle for Security," *International Security* 27, no. 1 (2002): 151.
7. Robert O. Keohane, ed., *Neorealism and Its Critics* (New York: Columbia University Press, 1986), 10–11. Joseph S. Nye is more concerned with "soft power" and its effect and implications for the US and world politics. To be concise, soft power consists of culture, thought and institutions by which the preferences and identities of other countries are reshaped in accordance with the powerful. He concludes soft power is a "co-optive behavioural power" which concerns "whose story wins." See Joseph S. Nye, *Bound to Lead: The Changing Nature of American Power* (New York: Basic Books, 1990); *The Paradox of American Power: Why the World's Only Superpower Can't Go Alone* (Oxford: Oxford University Press, 2002); "The Rise of China's Soft Power," *Wall Street Journal Asia*, Hong Kong, December 29, 2005, <http://www.ksg.harvard.edu/ksgnews/Features/opeds/122905_nye.htm> (accessed March 3, 2013).
8. David A. Baldwin, ed., *Neorealism and Neoliberalism: The Contemporary Debate* (New York: Columbia University Press, 1993), 3–17.
9. "Social" refers to the shared ideas embedded in an inter-subjective setting like regimes, institutions, etc. See Alexander E. Wendt and Daniel Friedheim, "Hierarchy under Anarchy: Informal Empire and the East German State," in *State Sovereignty as Social Construct*, ed. Thomas Biersteker and Cynthia Weber (Cambridge: Cambridge University Press, 1996), 242.
10. For example, see John J. Mearsheimer, *The Tragedy of Great Power Politics* (New York: W.W. Norton Press, 2001), 145–6.
11. See Kenneth N. Waltz, "The Continuality of International Politics," in *World in Collision: Terror and the Future of Global Order*, ed. Ken Booth and Tim Dunne (New York: Palgrave Macmillan, 2002), 348–53.
12. See James Traub, "The New Hard-Soft Power," *The New York Times*, January 30, 2005, <http://www.nytimes.com/2005/01/30/magazine/30IDEA.html?pagewanted=print&position=&_r=0> (accessed July 12, 2016).
13. David M. Lampton, *The Three Faces of Chinese Power: Might, Money, and Minds* (Berkeley: University of California Press, 2008), 10–1; 117.
14. Alexander E. Wendt, *Social Theory of International Politics* (Cambridge: Cambridge University Press, 1999), 41.
15. See Robert E. Kelly, "A 'Confucian Long Peace' in Pre-Western East Asia?" *European Journal of International Relations* 18, no. 3 (2012): 407–30; David Kang, "International Relations Theory and East Asian History: An Overview," *Journal of East Asian Studies* 13 (2013): 181–205.
16. Joseph S. Nye, "Power and Interdependence in the Information Age," *Foreign Affairs* 77, no. 5 (1998): 86; Samuel P. Huntington, *The Clash of Civilizations and the Remarking of World Order* (New York: Simon & Schuster Press, 1996).

17. Janice B. Mattern, "Why 'Soft Power' Isn't So Soft: Representational Forces and the Sociolinguistic Construction of Attraction in World Politics," *Millennium* 33, no. 3 (2005): 583.
18. Nye, "Power and Interdependence in the Information Age," 86.
19. See Joseph S. Nye, and William A. Owen, "America's Information Edge," *Foreign Affairs* 75, no. 2 (1996): 20–36; Michael Beckley, "China's Century? Why America's Edge Will Endure," *International Security* 36, no. 3 (2011): 41–78.
20. Nye, "Power and Interdependence in the Information Age," 90–4; Andrew Hurrell, "Hegemony, Liberalism and Global Order: What Space for Would-Be Great Powers?" *International Affairs* 82, no. 1 (2006): 1–19.
21. Because attraction is a subjective experience, according to Mattern, two further questions arise: what makes something or someone alluring to some and not to others; and how does attraction happen? See Mattern, "Why 'Soft Power' Isn't So Soft," 584–6.
22. George W. Bush, Address to a Joint Session of Congress and the American People, September 20, 2001. See Mattern, "Why 'Soft Power' Isn't So Soft," 604–9.
23. For more information, please see Joshua Cooper Ramo, *The Beijing Consensus* (London: The Foreign Policy Centre, 2004), 5–6; Robert D. Kaplan, "How We Would Fight China?" *The Atlantic Monthly* 29, no. 5 (2005): 49–64; Ken Miller, "Coping With China's Financial Power: Beijing's Financial Foreign Policy," *Foreign Affairs* 89, no. 4 (2010): 96–109; Martin Jacques, *When China Rules the World* (London: Penguin Publisher, 2012).
24. See Zheng Bijian, "A New Path for China's Peaceful Rise and the Future of Asia," Bo'ao Forum for Asia, Bo'ao, Hainan, China, The Secretariat of Bo'ao Forum, 2003, <http://www.brookings.edu/fp/events/20050616 bijianlunch.pdf> (accessed July 13, 2016); "China's 'Peaceful Rise' to Great-Power Status," *Foreign Affairs* 84, no. 5 (2005): 18–25; Humphrey Hawksley, "Chinese Influence in Brazil Worries US," *BBC*, London, April 3, 2006, <http://news.bbc.co.uk/2/hi/americas/4872522.stm> (accessed July 9, 2016).
25. Ashley J. Tellis, "A Grand Chessboard," *Foreign Policy*, Special Report (2005): 52–4.
26. See Alastair Iain Johnston, "Is China a Status Quo Power?" *International Security* 27, no. 4 (2003): 5; Nye, "The Rise of China's Soft Power."
27. See *BBC*, "China's Influence Seen Positive," <http://news.bbc.co.uk/1/hi/world/asia-pacific/4318551.stm> (accessed December 29, 2014). The poll was conducted from November 15, 2004 to January 5, 2005.
28. See *The Wall Street Journal*, "Asian Nations' Fears of War Elevated as China Flexes Muscle," <http://online.wsj.com/articles/asian-nations-fears-

of-war-elevated-as-china-flexes-muscle-study-finds-1405361047> (accessed July 13, 2016).
29. Joshua Kurlantzick, "The Decline of American Soft Power," *Current History* 104 (2005): 420.
30. Various related comments, such as Bill Gertz, *The China Threat* (Washington DC: Regnery Publishing, 2000); Emma V. Broomfield, "Perceptions of Danger: The China Threat Theory," *Journal of Contemporary China* 35, no. 12 (2003): 265.
31. See Rosemary Foot, *The Practice of Power: U.S. Relations with China since 1949* (Oxford: Oxford University, 1995), 22–51; James R. Lilley, "Crossing the River by Feeling One's Way along the Bottom Stone by Stone: China's Greater China Strategy," in *Greater China and US Foreign Policy*, ed. Thomas A. Metzger and Ramon H. Myers (Stanford CA: Stanford University, 1996), 29–40.
32. David M. Lampton, "The Stealth Normalization of US-China Relations," *National Interests* 73 (2003): 40.
33. Evan S. Mederios and M. Taylor Fravel, "China's New Diplomacy," *Foreign Affairs* 82, no. 6 (2003): 22–35.
34. Johnston, "Is China a Status Quo Power?" 11–5.
35. Wang Yiwei, "Zhongguo Heping Jueqi De Cangchong Jeidu" [Three Interpretations of China's Peaceful Rise], *Da Guo* [*Major Power Quarterly*], 2007, <http://www.blogchina.com/new/display/78900.html> (accessed March 9, 2013); Men Honghua, "Peaceful Rise: A Framework for China's International Strategy," *World Economics and Politics* 286 (2004): 16–9.
36. See Lowell Dittmer, "Reform and Chinese Foreign Policy," in *Remaking the Chinese State: Strategies, Society and Security*, ed. Chien-min Chao and Bruce J. Dickson (London: Routledge, 2001), 187; Deborah Brautigam, *The Dragon's Gift: The Real Story of China in Africa* (Oxford: Oxford University Press, 2009).
37. See Zheng, "A New Path for China's Peaceful Rise and the Future of Asia"; "China's 'Peaceful Rise' to Great-Power Status;" and "China's Development and Her New Path to a Peaceful Rise," Speech given at the Villa d'Este Forum, Paris, 2004, <http://www.brookings.edu/fp/events/20050616bijianlunch.pdf.> (accessed March 6, 2013).
38. The title of Hu's speech was "Deepen Cooperation in the Asia-Pacific Region, Construct a Harmonious Future in Joint Force," see Hu Jintao, "Deepen Cooperation in the Asia-Pacific Region, Construct a Harmonious Future in Joint Force," *Xinhuanet*, November 18, 2005, <http://politics.people.com.cn/BIG5/1024/3866673.html> (accessed June 26, 2016).
39. See an interview of several Chinese senior scholars of diplomacy, Jin Canron et al. "To Build a 'Harmonious World': A New Development

of Chinese Foreign Policy Thought," September 25, 2012, <http://big5.huaxia.com/zt/tbgz/12-039/3015968_7.html> (accessed June 26, 2016).
40. Zhao Haiqing, "Con Heping Gongchu Wuxiang Yuanze Dao Hexei Shijei Xinlinien" [From the Five Principles of Co-Existence to the New Idea of a Harmonious World], *Banyuetan* [*Fortnight Talks*], 2006, <http://www.banyuetan.org/> (accessed March 11, 2013).
41. See Yao Xinzhong, *An Introduction to Confucianism* (Cambridge: Cambridge University Press, 2000), 169–79.
42. Steve Chan, "Chinese Perspectives on International Order," in *International Order and the Future of World Politics*, ed. T.V. Paul and Johan A. Hall (Cambridge: Cambridge University Press, 1999), 197–212; Teng-chi Chang and Yin-si Chen, "Chaogong tixi zaixian yu 'tianxia tixi' xingqi? Zhongguo waijiao de anli yanjiu yu lilun fansi" [Tribute System Revitalized and the Rise of the "Under-Heaven System?" Case Studies and Reflections on China's Diplomacy]. *Mainland China Studies* 55, no. 4 (2012): 89–123.
43. Chih-yu Shih, *China's Just World: The Morality of Chinese Foreign Policy* (Boulder: Lynne Rienner, 1993), 31–2; "Assigning Role Characteristics to China: The Role State Versus The Ego State," *Foreign Policy Analysis* 8, no. 1 (2012): 71–91.
44. Chih-yu Shih, "Breeding a Reluctant Dragon: Can China Rise into Partnership and Away from Antagonism?" *Review of International Studies* 31 (2005): 757–8; Teng-chi Chang, "Debating the Chinese School of IR: A Reflective Review from Taiwan," in *Constructing a Chinese School of International Relations: Ongoing Debates and Sociological Realities*, ed. Yongjin Zhang and Teng-chi Chang (London: Routledge, 2016), 81–97.
45. See Ye Zicheng and Yin Li, "Jianguo Daguo Waijiao Zhi Huen: Zhenchangxin, Zixinxin, Leguanxin" [Constructing the Soul of a Great Power Diplomacy: Mentality of a Normal State, Self-Confidence, and Optimistic Thinking], *Zhongguo Waijiao* [*Chinese Diplomacy*] 2001): 66–73; Wu Jianmin, "Ruoguo Xintai Bixu Baituo" [The Mentality of "Weak State" Must Be Expelled] *Banyuetan* (*Fortnight Talks*), August 23, 2006, <http://www.banyuetan.org/> (accessed March 12, 2013).
46. Zhang Minqing, "Liushinienlai Zhongguo Waijiao de Fazhan" [The Development of Chinese Foreign Policy], *Waijiao Pinglun* [*Foreign Affairs Review*] 4 (2009): 32–42.
47. C. Fred Bergsten, "A Partnership of Equals: How Washington Should Respond to China's Economic Challenge," *Foreign Affairs* 87, no. 4 (2008): 57–69.
48. Chin-hao Huang, "China's Soft Power in East Asia: A Quest for Status or Influence?" *NBR Special Report No. 42*, The National Bureau of Asian Research, January 2013.

49. George E. Condon Jr., "Obama Ends Remarkable Summit Run with 'Pivot' to Asia," *National Journal*, November 11, 2011, <http://www.nationaljournal.com/whitehouse/obama-ends-remarkable-summit-run-with-pivot-to-asia-2011> (accessed April 2, 2013).
50. Hillary R. Clinton, "Remarks on Regional Architecture in Asia: Principles and Priorities," *U.S. Department of State*, January 12, 2010, <http://www.state.gov/secretary/rm/2010/01/135090.htm> (accessed July 9, 2016).
51. See Evan A. Feigenbaum, "Why America No longer Gets Asia?" *The Washington Quarterly* 34, no. 2 (2011): 25–43.
52. "US Secretary of State Hillary Clinton on Historic Laos Visit," *BBC*, July 11, 2012, <http://www.bbc.co.uk/news/world-asia-18792282> (accessed July 14, 2016).
53. Tatiana Avery, "Vietnamese Distinguished Visitors Tour George Washington," *America's Navy*, October 20, 2012, <http://www.navy.mil/submit/display.asp?story_id=70263> (accessed July 13, 2016).
54. "US Lifts Decades-long Embargo on Arms Sales to Vietnam," *Guardian*, May 23, 2016, <https://www.theguardian.com/world/2016/may/23/us-lifts-decades-long-embargo-on-arms-sales-to-vietnam> (accessed July 12, 2016).
55. Simon Teng-Chi Chang, "The Strategic Implications of Hillary Clinton's Visits to China's Neighbouring Countries: An Offensive Realist Perspective," *Zhanwang yu Tansuo* [*Prospect & Exploration* (Taipei)] 10, no. 8, (2012): 11–6.
56. See David Shambaugh, "Coping with a Conflicted China," *Washington Quarterly* 34 no. 1 (2011): 7–27.
57. "China Paper Warns of Sound of Gun and Cannon," *Reuters*, October 25, 2011, <http://www.reuters.com/article/2011/10/25/us-china-seas-idUSTRE79O1MV20111025> (accessed March 11, 2013).
58. The term "Red Second Generation" in China refers to sons and daughters of the founders of the CPC and PRC. Regarding Xi's tight grip on power and his personality, see Elisabeth Economy, "China's Imperial President: Xi Jinping Tightens His Grip," *Foreign Affairs* (2014 November/December), <http://www.foreignaffairs.com/articles/142201/elizabeth-c-economy/chinas-imperial-president> (accessed April 22, 2016).
59. Karen Parrish, "Panetta Calls Beijing Meetings 'Substantive, Productive'," *U.S. Department of Defense*, September 20, 2012, <http://www.defense.gov/news/newsarticle.aspx?id=117935> (accessed March 9, 2013).
60. Hu Jingtao, "Report to the 18th Party Congress of the Communist Party of China (full text)," *Xinhua News Agency*, November 17, 2012, <http://news.xinhuanet.com/english/special/18cpcnc/2012-11/17/c_131981259.ht> (accessed February 23, 2013).
61. The timetable for "completing" these goals has never been directly mentioned in previous party documents. The personal income estimation

was made by Lin Yifu, former vice president of the World Bank. Please refer to *Xinhuanet*, March 5, 2013, <http://news.xinhuanet.com/2013lh/2013-03/05/c_124416625.htm> (accessed May 1, 2013).
62. David Cohen, "Xi Jinping's Chinese Dream," *The Diplomat*, December 7, 2012, <http://thediplomat.com/china-power/xi-jinpings-chinese-dream/> (accessed June 29, 2016).
63. Xi Jinping, "Speech at the National Propaganda and Ideology Work Conference," November 12, 2013, <http://chinacopyrightandmedia.wordpress.com/2013/11/12/xi-jinpings-19-august-speech-revealed-translation/> (accessed July 12, 2016).
64. "Salute the Builders of Chinese Dream," *Xinhua News Agency*, April 26, 2013, <http://news.xinhuanet.com/english/indepth/2013-04/29/c_132349167.htm> (accessed July 13, 2016).
65. Xi Jinping, "Carry Forward Traditional Friendship and Jointly Open up New Chapter of Cooperation," MOFA website of the PRC, July 17, 2014, <http://www.fmprc.gov.cn/mfa_eng/zxxx_662805/t1176214.shtml> (accessed July 12, 2016).
66. See "President Park Holds Interview with CCTV," *Korea Net*, July 3, 2014, <http://www.korea.net/NewsFocus/Policies/view?articleId=120388> (accessed July 9, 2016).
67. Elizabeth Economy, "Xi's Tour Won't Fix the US-China Trust Deficit," *Foreign Affairs*, February 14, 2012, <http://www.foreignaffairs.com/articles/137236/elizabeth-economy/xis-tour-wont-fix-the-us-chinese-trust-deficit> (accessed March 7, 2013).
68. See David M. Herszenhorn and Chris Buckley, "China's Leader Argues for Cooperation with Russia," *The New York Times*, March 23, 2013, <http://www.nytimes.com/2013/03/24/world/europe/chinas-leader-argues-for-cooperation-with-russia.html>; Elizabeth Wishnick, "China and the Two Pivots," *Ponars Euroasia*, July 2015, <http://www.ponarseurasia.org/sites/default/files/policy-memos-pdf/Pepm365_Wishnick_July2015.pdf> (accessed June 22, 2016).
69. "Joint Statement of the People's Republic of China and the Russian Federation on the win-win cooperation and deepen the comprehensive strategic partnership of cooperation," *Comprehensive News*, March 23, 2013, <http://www.comprehensivenews.us/news-4150601-Joint-Statement-of-the-People-39s-Republic-of-China-and-the-Russian-Federation-on-the-win-win-cooperation-and-deepen-the-comprehensive-strategic-partnership-of-cooperation.html> (accessed May 1, 2013).
70. Graham Allison argues that it is more appropriate to consider China separately from other BRICs, which, "if an acronym is called for, can be called: 'RIBS'." See Graham Allison, "China Doesn't Belong in the BRICS," *The Atlantic*, March 26, 2013, <http://www.theatlantic.com/china/

archive/2013/03/china-doesnt-belong-in-the-brics/274363/> (accessed July 13, 2016).
71. See Simon Teng-chi Chang, *Writing China: Identity Formation and Great Power Diplomacy* (Taipei: Yangzhi Publisher, 2003), in Chinese; Shambaugh, "Coping with a Conflicted China."
72. "We Welcome Your Rise (sort of)," *The Economist*, February 15, 2012, <http://www.economist.com/blogs/lexington/2012/02/xi-jinping> (accessed July 11, 2016).

References

Baldwin, David A., ed. *Neorealism and Neoliberalism: The Contemporary Debate*. New York: Columbia University Press, 1993.
Beckley, Michael. "China's Century? Why America's Edge Will Endure." *International Security* 36, no. 3 (2011): 41–78.
Bergsten, C. Fred. "A Partnership of Equals: How Washington Should Respond to China's Economic Challenge." *Foreign Affairs* 87, no. 4 (2008): 57–69.
Brautigam, Deborah. *The Dragon's Gift: The Real Story of China in Africa*. Oxford: Oxford University Press, 2009.
Broomfield, Emma V. "Perceptions of Danger: The China Threat Theory." *Journal of Contemporary China* 35, no. 12 (2003): 265–84.
Chan, Steve (1999). "Chinese Perspectives on International Order." In *International Order and the Future of World Politics*, edited by T.V. Paul and Johan A. Hall, 197–212. Cambridge: Cambridge University Press.
Chang, Teng-chi. *Writing China: Identity Formation and Great Power Diplomacy*, (in Chinese). Taipei: Yangzhi Publisher, 2003.
———. "The Strategic Implications of Hillary Clinton's Visits to China's Neighbouring Countries: An Offensive Realist Perspective." *Zhanwang yu Tansuo* [*Prospect & Exploration* (Taipei)] 10, no. 8 (August 2012): 11–6.
———. "Debating the Chinese School of IR: A Reflective review from Taiwan." In *Constructing a Chinese School of International Relations: Ongoing Debates and Sociological Realities*, edited by Yongjin Zhang and Teng-chi Chang, 81–97. London: Routledge, 2016.
Chang, Teng-chi and Chen Yin-si. "Chaogong tixi zaixian yu 'tianxia tixi' xingqi? Zhongguo waijiao de anli yanjiu yu lilun fansi" [Tribute System revitalized and the rise of the "Under-Heaven System? Case Studies and Reflections on China's Diplomacy]. *Mainland China Studies* 55, no. 4 (2012): 89–123.
Dittmer, Lowell. "Reform and Chinese Foreign Policy." In *Remaking the Chinese State: Strategies, Society and Security*, edited by Chien-min Chao and Bruce J. Dickson, 171–89. London: Routledge, 2001.

Feigenbaum, Evan A. "Why America No longer Gets Asia?" *The Washington Quarterly* 34, no. 2 (2011): 25–43.
Foot, Rosemary. *The Practice of Power: U.S. Relations with China since 1949.* Oxford: Oxford University, 1995.
Gertz, Bill. *The China Threat.* Washington D.C.: Regnery Publishing, 2000.
Huang, Chin-hao. *China's Soft Power in East Asia: A Quest for Status or Influence?* NBR Special Report No. 42, The National Bureau of Asian Research, January 2013.
Huntington, Samuel P. *The Clash of Civilizations and the Remarking of World Order.* New York: Simon & Schuster Press, 1996.
Hurrell, Andrew. "Hegemony, Liberalism and Global Order: What Space for Would-Be Great Powers?" *International Affairs* 82, no. 1 (2006): 1–19.
Jacques, Martin. *When China Rules the World.* London: Penguin, 2012.
Johnston, Alastair Iain. "Is China a Status Quo Power?" *International Security* 27, no. 4 (2003): 5–56.
Johnston, Alastair Iain. *Social States: China in International Institutions, 1980-2000.* Princeton: Princeton University Press, 2008.
Kang, David. "International Relations Theory and East Asian History: An Overview." *Journal of East Asian Studies* 13 (2013): 181–205.
Kaplan, Robert D. "How We Would Fight China?" *The Atlantic Monthly* 29, no. 5 (2005): 49–64.
Kelly, Robert E. "A 'Confucian Long Peace' in Pre-Western East Asia?" *European Journal of International Relations* 18, no. 3 (2012): 407–30.
Keohane, Robert O., ed. *Neorealism and Its Critics.* New York: Columbia University Press, 1986.
_____. "International Institutions: Two Approaches." *International Studies Quarterly* 32, no. 4 (1988): 379–96.
Kurlantzick, Joshua. "The Decline of American Soft Power." *Current History* 104 (2005): 419–24.
Lamptom, David M. "The Stealth Normalization of U.S.-China Relations." *National Interests* 73 (2003): 37–49.
Lampton, David. *The Three Faces of Chinese Power: Might, Money, and Minds.* Berkeley: University of California Press, 2008.
Lilley, James R. "Crossing the River by Feeling One's Way along the Bottom Stone by Stone: China's Greater China Strategy." In *Greater China and US Foreign Policy*, edited by Thomas A. Metzger and Ramon H. Myers, 29–40. Stanford: Stanford University, 1996.
Mattern, Janice Bially. "Why 'Soft Power' Isn't So Soft: Representational Forces and the Sociolinguistic Construction of Attraction in World Politics." *Millennium*, 33, no. 3 (2005): 583–612.
Mearsheimer, John J. *The Tragedy of Great Power Politics.* New York: W.W. Norton Press, 2001.

Mederios, Evan S. and M. Taylor Fravel. "China's New Diplomacy." *Foreign Affairs* 82, no. 6 (2003): 22–35.
Men, Honghua. "Peaceful Rise: A Framework for China's International Strategy." *World Economics and Politics* 286 (2004): 14–9.
Miller, Ken. "Coping With China's Financial Power: Beijing's Financial Foreign Policy" *Foreign Affairs* 89, no. 4 (2010): 96–109.
Morgenthau, Hans J. *Politics among Nations.* 5th ed. New York: Alfred A. Knopf, 1978.
Nye, Joseph S. *Bound to Lead: The Changing Nature of American Power.* New York: Basic Books, 1990.
———. "Power and Interdependence in the Information Age," *Foreign Affairs* 77, no. 5 (1998): 81–94.
———. *The Paradox of American Power: Why the World's Only Superpower Can't Go Alone.* Oxford: Oxford University Press, 2002.
Nye, Joseph S. and William A. Owen. "America's Information Edge." *Foreign Affairs* 75, no. 2 (1996): 20–36.
Ramo, Joshua Cooper. *The Beijing Consensus.* London: The Foreign Policy Centre, 2004.
Shambaugh, David. "Coping with a Conflicted China." *Washington Quarterly* 34, no. 1 (2011): 7–27.
———. *China Goes Global: The Partial Power.* Oxford: Oxford University Press, 2013.
Shih, Chih-yu. *China's Just World: The Morality of Chinese Foreign Policy.* Boulder: Lynne Rienner, 1993.
———. "Breeding a Reluctant Dragon: Can China Rise into Partnership and Away from Antagonism?" *Review of International Studies* 31 (2005): 755–74.
———. "Assigning Role Characteristics to China: The Role State Versus The Ego State." *Foreign Policy Analysis* 8, no. 1 (2012) 71–91.
Snyder, Glenn H. (2002). "Mearsheimer's World: Offensive Realism and the Struggle for Security." *International Security* 27, no. 1 (2002): 149–73.
Tellis, Ashley J. "A Grand Chessboard." Special Report, *Foreign Policy* (2005): 51–3.
Waltz, Kenneth N. *Man, the State and War.* New York: Columbia University Press, 1959.
———. *Theory of International Politics.* Reading, Mass.: Addison-Wesley Press, 1979.
———. "Realist Thought and Neorealist Theory." *Journal of International Affairs* 44, no. 1 (1990): 21–37.
———. "The Continuality of International Politics." In *World in Collision: Terror and the Future of Global Order,* edited by Ken Booth and Tim Dunne, 348–54. New York: Palgrave Macmillan, 2002.

Wendt, Alexander E. *Social Theory of International Politics*. Cambridge: Cambridge University Press, 1999.
Wendt, Alexander E. and Daniel Friedheim. "Hierarchy under Anarchy: Informal Empire and the East German State." In *State Sovereignty as Social Construct*, edited by Thomas Biersteker and Cynthia Weber, 240–72. Cambridge: Cambridge University Press, 1996.
Yan, Xuetong. *Ancient Chinese Thought, Modern Chinese Power*. Princeton: Princeton University Press, 2011.
Yao, Xinzhong. *An Introduction to Confucianism*. Cambridge: Cambridge University Press, 2000.
Ye Zicheng and Yin Li. "Jianguo Daguo Waijiao Zhi Huen: Zhenchangxin, Zixinxin, Leguanxin" [Constructing the Soul of a Great Power Diplomacy: Mentality of a Normal State, Self-Confidence, and Optimistic Thinking]. *Zhongguo Waijiao* [Chinese Diplomacy] (2001): 66–73.
Zakaria, Fareed. *The Post-American World*. New York: W.W. Norton & Company, 2008.
Zhang, Minqing. "Liushinienlai Zhongguo Waijiao de Fazhan" [The Development of Chinese Foreign Policy]. *Waijiao Pinglun* [*Foreign Affairs Review*] 4 (2009): 32–42.
Zheng, Bijian. "China's 'Peaceful Rise' to Great-Power Status." *Foreign Affairs* 84, no. 5 (2005): 18–25.

CHAPTER 3

China's Economic Offensive and Its Discontent in Southeast Asia: Diminishing Footprints in Myanmar

Ian Tsung-yen Chen

Introduction

Some Southeast Asians welcome what they see as the economic benefits of China's investments and aid for their country's development projects. Other Southeast Asians worry about what they see as China's exploitation of Southeast Asia's natural resources under the cover of economic cooperation and development. However, China insists that its investments and aid to Southeast Asia and elsewhere are designed to reflect its pursuit of soft power or the power of attraction, which uses investments and aid as part of a larger strategy to attract other nations to willingly support its economic and political goals internationally. This difference of opinion raises two questions:

- Has China managed to effectively translate its investments and economic aid to Southeast Asia into political influence?
- Have the Southeast Asian region and its local communities become more cooperative and compliant with China's requests?

It is not possible to present answers in a single chapter that cover all of Southeast Asia. However, a crucial-case research design can suggest what these answers might be. In this chapter, I use a most-likely crucial-case research design of Sino-Myanmar relations to present my analysis. If the analysis of a most-likely situation clearly disconfirms arguments about the crucial situation, it would suggest that analyses of similar or less-likely situations will probably also fail to support these arguments. This, in turn, creates a need to formulate new arguments that can be tested for their descriptive, explanatory and predictive adequacy. Because of the high-level connections between the two countries, Myanmar should be very easily influenced by China and respond to what it asks. If this is not true, then the argument of China's undeniable soft footprints in Southeast Asia and their subsequent political influence require alternative explanations.

The evidence presented in this chapter suggests that China's investments and economic aid may have been necessary means for creating influence over Myanmar. However, they have not been sufficient to maintain this influence. Since Myanmar started political reform in 2011, its support for China's positions on human rights issues and a nuclear-weapon-free world has begun to weaken. In addition, China's influence has not been well received by local Myanmar communities due to what these communities see as China's exploitative economic adventurism. The level of dissatisfaction with China's investments is illustrated in this study by a description of local communities' opposition to the Myitsone Dam and Letpadaung copper mine projects. The study suggests that same situation might occur in other Southeast Asian nations with which China has weaker economic ties. As a result, China's soft footprints do not appear as deep and welcome as one might think. The power of interdependent relationships might require political and social cohesion to take hold.

Economic Offensive and Influence

Perhaps the most relevant argument that links China's soft footprints to Southeast Asia is Joseph Nye's concept of soft power. At the core of soft power is the ability to influence through one's attraction instead of coercion or payments. Nye identifies the three main sources of soft power as a country's culture, political values and foreign policies.[1] Although he touches upon the relevance of commercial instruments, Nye treats them as useful intermediaries for creating soft power. For example, more personal contacts or exchanges through cross-border economic activities between China and its Southeast Asian counterparts would make it easier for China to create attraction and then exert influence on Southeast Asian nations. In other words, when discussing

China's soft power infuence, it is the chance of improving attraction through commercial activities that makes economic incentives matter, rather than the number of commercial activities per se. Many works have provided evidence that China's way of doing business and its experience of economic development are more desirable and popular in Southeast Asia than those of Western countries. China's external economic incentives, such as foreign direct investment (FDI) or foreign aid, feature fewer restrictions and conditions. Moreover, the Chinese seem to be more willing to sharetheir knowledge.[2] In addition, Beijing's success in separating the market economy from democracy is particularly attractive to developing countries, the majority of which remain non-democracies.[3] This line of argument depicts the attractive nature of China's economic resources. In brief, the deepening of a bilateral economic relationship creates more opportunities for exchanging each other's views and experiences, which can be beneficial in generating attraction. Such attraction can be further developed into actual influence.

Since this book focuses on the idea of "footprints" as the tangible outcome of China's application of soft power in the region, it makes more sense to discuss sunk economic involvement than mere attraction, the former being more concrete than the latter. Therefore, it is necessary to create a more direct link between economic incentives and influence. The theory of commercial liberalism suggests that a dyad of countries can promote mutual communication between various kinds of actors by deeper economic engagement. With such tight economic bonds, cooperative political behavior is more likely to be realized.[4] Economic interdependence, in other scholars' views, creates mutual economic benefits; thus, domestic actors will urge their governments to maintain stable and cooperative conditions that foster further economic interests.[5] Should the interdependence become unbalanced, however, the more dependent state is more likely to be influenced by the less dependent one, especially when the latter threatens to cut the supply of economic resources or stop buying goods from the former.[6] This line of argument suggests that economic incentives can be used to generate influence by both attractive and coercive means. In short, when compared with a dyad of low economic interdependence, a dyad of higher economic exchanges is more likely to be more cooperative with each other. In addition, the less dependent country might be more able to generate influence. One should observe less political discordance under such a situation.

If we treat China's economic offensive as a key dimension of its soft footprint in Southeast Asia, we should take into account the possibility that economic interdependence can be both soft, in the sense that Nye describes soft power, and coercive. Beijing can use its policymaking process and abundant economic resources to foster deeper trade relationships, provide attractive foreign direct investment (FDI), grant large and generous loans, and give financial aid to its Southeast Asian neighbors. Greater personal and economic exchanges can be facilitated, which can heighten China's attraction in the region. In addition, higher economic interdependence can be made at the expense of other powers' economic relationships in the region. Since China is the less dependent party in most cases, its influence in the region can be increased through either attractive or coercive instruments. Should this argument be true, one should observe empirically that China's influence in the region increases as its investment and aid to the region increase. Local communities, industries and businesses should welcome China's large-scale presence. Likewise, we should see evidence of the governments of China and Southeast Asia acting to support each other in international forums as their economic relationships deepen. In the following sections, I will assess whether or not China's influence has increased by examining the Sino-Myanmar economic relationship and its political effects.

A Crucial-Case Research Design

I have used the crucial-case method[7] to investigate the most-likely case of the Sino-Myanmar economic relationship. Although the use of a single case to test a theory or an argument might be risky, it can be very illustrative if the case is a crucial one, that is, a situation that is generally seen as clearly confirming or disconfirming a theoretical proposition. To select the pertinent case, two approaches can be applied. The first is to select a case that would be the least likely to confirm a theory or an argument. Except for the dimension focused on in the theory, if other less relevant dimensions in the case are the least supportive of the theory but the case fits into the theory, then this least-likely case confirms the validity of that theory. For example, if we want to argue that China's economic offensive is active and visibly influences the region, then one can select a Southeast Asian country that is inimical to China in many aspects but experiences a high economic exchange with China. If this country, which seems unlikely to follow what China says because of a bitter relationship, nevertheless regards China's economic engagement as attractive and responds favorably to Beijing, then this case confirms the argument that China's economic offensive in the region is successful. Vietnam might be an appropriate case.

For this paper, I use the second approach, a most-likely crucial-case research design,[8] to test the following proposition: China's investments and aid to Southeast Asian nations will increase China's influence in those nations that are more dependent on China to meet their economic and political needs, rather than in those nations upon which China depends.[9] Except for the dimensions of theoretical interests, other dimensions of the case are supportive of the prediction of theory. In such a setting, if the case eventually fails to follow the theoretical prediction, then the theory is disconfirmed because other less-likely cases should be even more unlikely to be fully explained. This approach is treated as more powerful than the least-likely case.[10] For example, the most-likely case for the argument of China's successful economic offensive can be a country that is highly connected to China in aspects other than the economic dimension, such as a security partnership. If the case shows that a country's society resents China's presence and its domestic policies are discordant with China, then the argument for China's economic offensive should be disconfirmed, or at least considered doubtful. In such a situation, one should then look for alternative explanations. Most-likely crucial cases seek to disconfirm theoretical propositions by identifying a case that is generally regarded as providing strong evidence in support of the proposition. However, a close analysis of the case produces facts that disconfirm one or more aspects of the proposition. The success of most-likely crucial-case studies depends on being able to find a case. The China-Myanmar relationship provides a most-likely case for disconfirming the above proposition.

To test the proposition, I have selected a single crucial case of the Sino-Myanmar relationship as the most-likely case for China to achieve successful economic diplomacy. Regardless of its bilateral economic relationship with China, which is the core of the proposition, at least two dimensions make Myanmar a crucial case.

First, Myanmar and China share an interdependent security relationship. When Myanmar was sanctioned and isolated by the international community for its human rights violations, its military-backed regime sought China's support to ensure its continued survival.

China defended the regime from criticism more strongly than other states based on its non-intervention policy, probably the most important principle by which China abides. China may have been the staunchest international ally of the Myanmar military junta. From 2006 to 2011, China continuously voted against United Nations General Assembly (UNGA) resolutions that condemned Myanmar's poor human right records.[11] It also vetoed United Nations Security Council (UNSC) resolutions that requested Myanmar release political prisoners and end its military attacks and human rights abuses against ethnic minorities.[12] In fact, among Southeast Asian countries, Myanmar's voting record in the UNGA was the second closest to China.[13] The closest was Vietnam, although China and Vietnam have been historically hostile to each other. In addition, China was the most important supplier of military equipment and training to Myanmar.[14] However, China also needed Myanmar's cooperation to meet its security needs. China has been building port facilities in Myanmar, which are strategically important for China to enter the Indian Ocean.

Second, both China and the Myanmar's military regime were autocracies. Nye points out that "when our policies are seen as legitimate in the eyes of others, our soft power is enhanced."[15] The preference for repressive policies shared by both autocratic regimes, such as imprisoning political foes, quelling the press or suppressing the minority's social movements, may have contributed to creating an interdependent relationship between China and Myanmar resulting from the sense of legitimacy and need for support.

Due to the two factors discussed above, Myanmar should be the country in Southeast Asia most easily influenced by China. Thus in Myanmar's case, one should observe the military-backed government increasing its support for China's policies when Beijing increased its economic aid to Myanmar. If Myanmar did not support China's positions, then the argument that China increased influence by means of economic incentives is disconfirmed. Alternative explanations or possible intervening variables should be presented.

The Sino-Myanmar Interdependent Relationship

The previous section indicated that China and Myanmar developed an interdependent relationship in which both governments helped to meet each other's needs for external and internal security and supported each other against the critics of their political policies in the international society. In this section, I investigate their bilateral economic relationship to see whether a more politically dependent Myanmar was influenced by China's strong economic presence.

China's Economic Presence in Myanmar

Due to Myanmar's repression of domestic opposition parties that began in the late 1980s, the US government implemented economic sanctions in May 1997. In 1998, the military junta-led State Peace and Development Council (SPDC) secured political power. Later it refused to transfer power to the National League for Democracy (NLD) led by Aung San Suu Kyi, which had won a majority of seats in the 1990 general election. The repression resulted in increasing international economic sanctions against Myanmar. In 2003, the Burmese Freedom and Democracy Act, which banned Myanmar's exports to the US, was signed and implemented by Washington. The law also prohibited the exportation or re-exportation of financial services from the US directly or indirectly to Myanmar. Furthermore, the sanctions blocked targeted Myanmar citizens' access to their properties in the US.[16]

Table 1 shows that the effects of the economic sanctions and political isolation by the international community caused Myanmar-US bilateral trade to plummet between 2003 and 2004, from US$303 million to US$13 million. The UK followed suit one year later, albeit on a smaller scale. While Washington urged the boycott of international trade with Myanmar, its traditional Asia-Pacific allies did not respond. For example, Australia did not decrease its trade with Myanmar. Thailand and Singapore, which were (and are) Myanmar's most important ASEAN trading partners, increased their trade with the military regime. Myanmar's total intra-ASEAN trade volume increased from US$3.92 million in 2004 to US$15 billion in 2011.[17] Outside ASEAN, China, India, Japan and South Korea increased their bilateral trade with Myanmar, with China becoming Myanmar's most important trading partner. Although Thailand continued to be Myanmar's largest exporting destination, China became Myanmar's overall largest partner in 2011. Data collected for 2011 suggests that 31.8 percent of Myanmar's total imports came from China while 21.3 percent of Myanmar's total exports went to China,[18] which made China Myanmar's second-largest exporting outlet after Thailand. As a result, Myanmar's domestic consumption relied heavily on products

Table 1 Myanmar's Major Trading Partners, 1991–2013 (USD million)

Year	China*	Thai.	SG	Japan	ROK	India	USA	AU	UK
1998	647.8	0.0	621.3	294.9	176.9	224.7	210.0	21.1	51.8
1999	653.7	548.1	559.5	304.9	221.5	208.6	257.7	21.6	51.7
2000	798.0	810.9	589.4	334.9	340.9	232.0	505.8	23.1	88.5
2001	777.2	1199.5	577.9	307.4	305.9	256.2	514.5	33.8	111.1
2002	1027.0	1270.2	683.6	237.2	214.0	424.3	391.5	20.7	108.7
2003	1242.7	1393.0	799.8	276.5	231.7	485.4	303.0	19.8	110.9
2004	1321.6	2019.2	788.0	295.7	208.3	515.2	12.7	35.7	139.2
2005	1386.1	2562.6	764.5	304.3	188.3	615.9	5.8	46.0	83.2
2006	1673.9	3185.7	689.1	362.3	232.7	761.2	8.4	46.2	56.5
2007	2438.8	3370.0	917.0	490.1	401.9	994.2	9.5	52.5	69.5
2008	3017.8	5239.9	1503.0	524.7	384.5	1153.5	11.8	49.4	68.6
2009	3314.8	4497.5	1096.1	562.5	525.1	1426.0	7.8	73.1	55.9
2010	3349.8	3795.1	1398.9	451.2	378.0	1388.3	27.5	80.4	47.6
2011	5052.3	4515.0	3058.9	822.4	666.8	1371.4	293.1	n.a.	43.7
2012	4984.8	4697.4	2826.8	1498.2	624.0	1320.3	122.8	n.a.	42.0
2103	6930.7	5195.2	3273.3	1655.0	1494.2	1362.6	97.5	n.a.	67.7

Sources: 1991–2009 data is from *Conflict Management and Peace Science*; 2010 data is from the UN Commodity Trade Statistics Database; and 2011-3 data is from Myanmar's Ministry of National Planning and Economic Development.[19]

*The Chinese statistics include both Mainland China and Hong Kong.

or services imported from China. Japan and India also expanded their trade relationships with Myanmar, but on a smaller scale than China.In summary, the data indicates that although the US-led global economic sanctions hampered trade relationships between Myanmar and its key Western partners, the gap was filled by Asian countries with China, Thailand, Singapore, Japan, South Korea and India becoming the military junta's major trading partners.

If we further analyze the top import and export goods, as shown in Table 2, Myanmar's key export goods were natural resources and crops. Of these goods, China was a key importer, especially of precious stones and rough wood. Myanmar's top imports were processed industrial materials and vehicles. On the other hand, China's top exports to Myanmar were motorcycles, delivery trucks, large construction vehicles and refined petroleum that were needed by the domestic transport and manufacturing industries. Because the Western countries' ban included critical commodities for economic development, which China was able to supply to Myanmar, China emerged as the military junta's most important trading partner in the 2000–10 decade.

Table 2 Top Goods in Myanmar and Sino-Myanmar trade (2010)

Rank	MM Exports to All Countries	MM Exports to CN	MM Imports to All Countries	CN Exports to MM
1	Petroleum gas	Precious stones	Construction vehicles	Motorcycles
2	Dried legumes	Rough wood	Motorcycles	Iron structures
3	Rough wood	Iron ore	Delivery trucks	Delivery trucks
4	Rubber	Rubber	Palm oil	Refined petroleum
5	Precious stones	Manganese ore	Iron structures	Synthetic fabrics
6	Crustaceans	Dried legumes	Refined petroleum	Construction vehicles

Source: MIT Media Lab's Macro Connections, available at <http://atlas.media.mit.edu/> (accessed June 26, 2014).

The FDI dimension is presented in Table 3. Before international sanctions started to harm Myanmar in the early 2000s, Western countries and Japan were Myanmar's main investors. In 2004, China's FDI in Myanmar constituted only 1.9 percent of its total global investment. After Western countries applied economic sanctions against the repressive regime in the early 2000s, however, China began to invest substantially in Myanmar and it became the country's largest investor by 2011.[20] In 2012, China's FDI in Myanmar accounted for 33.4 percent of its total worldwide direct investment. From 2004 to 2011, the total FDI volume from China (including Hong Kong) amounted to about US$2.13 billion, followed by Asia's newly industrialized economies' US$1.18 billion and the European Union's US$841.4 million.[21] In terms of FDI stock (the cumulative amounts of FDI in a given year), China contributed a mere 0.4 percent of the total 2004 sunk investments in Myanmar. As China increased its economic engagement starting in 2007, its share of FDI stock surged rapidly. In 2012, China's share of sunk investments in Myanmar amounted to 26 percent. According to the ASEAN-Japan Centre, China's FDI stock from 1988 to 2011 amounted to US$13.9 billion, including 33 approved investment projects.[22] China's FDI stock was the largest amount, followed by Thailand's. Top Western FDI stock contributions during the same period came from the UK, France and the US. However, they only invested US$2.66 million, US$469 million, and US$243.6 million, respectively. The investments of Japan and India amounted to US$211.9 million and US$189 million, respectively. These figures indicate that

Table 3 Myanmar's Inward FDI from the World and China (USD million)

Year	FDI to Myanmar			FDI Stock in Myanmar		
	China	World	%	China	World	%
2000	2.3	258.3	0.9	n.a.	3211	n.a.
2001	2.3	210.3	1.1	n.a.	3305	n.a.
2002	16.8	152.1	11.0	n.a.	3735	n.a.
2003	n.a.	251.5	n.a.	10.22	4393	0.2
2004	4.1	213.5	1.9	20.18	4815	0.4
2005	11.5	234.9	4.9	23.59	4686	0.5
2006	12.6	275.8	4.6	163.12	5191	3.1
2007	92.3	709.9	13.0	261.77	6088	4.3
2008	232.5	863.9	26.9	499.71	6809	7.3
2009	376.7	1079.0	34.9	929.88	7958	11.7
2010	875.6	901.1	97.2	1946.75	8752	22.2
2011	217.8	1000.6	21.8	2181.52	9667	22.6
2012	749.0	2243.0	33.4	3093.72	11910	26.0

Sources: Data on China's FDI (stock) to Myanmar is from the *Statistical Bulletin of China's Outward Foreign Direct Investment* published by the Ministry of Commerce of the People's Republic of China; the total global inward FDI is from the World Bank; and the total global inward FDI stock is from the United Nations Conference on Trade and Development.[23]

China's FDI was undoubtedly the most important source of support for Myanmar's economy and the military junta's political survival.

When Myanmar's inward FDI is broken down by sector, it can be seen that almost all investments concentrated on extractive industries. From 2005 to 2011, approved investments in the oil, gas and mining sectors amounted to 47.7 percent of total investments, while the electricity/hydropower sectors attracted 51.4 percent.[24] In 2010 alone, 13 investments in the power, oil and gas, and mining industries were approved, which constituted 99.6 percent of total investments.[25] A large portion of the investments came from China, which potentially gave it the power to exert control over crucial infrastructure projects in Myanmar.[26] One could therefore conclude that China had become a very influential investor.

Development aid is another source of influence on recipient countries. However, the use of different calculations and definitions by different countries or international organizations makes the China-Myanmar aid relationship less clear.[27] Nevertheless, several studies indicate that China has been a major donor to Myanmar. For example, in the 1970s and 1980s China offered interest-free loans that contributed to the building of power plants and textile factories.

Since the mid-2000s China's aid projects have become more diversified. China has assisted in several huge national projects, including building hydroelectric dams. It also helped Myanmar hold the 2013 Southeast Asian Games. Whether or not such projects can be counted as official aid, Beijing has indeed offered generous deals to Myanmar. In return, China hopes that its investments will yield strategic assets and goods that it needs for its domestic economic development. Therefore, China's aid to Myanmar is sometimes seen as a strategic rather than altruistic act. Regardless of the nature of China's intentions, the Myanmar government has relied heavily on concessional loans and free financial transfers. Since China is Myanmar's largest trading partner and investor, a major aid donor, and a supporter of the Myanmar government, one could expect China's economic presence in Myanmar to dispose the country to support China's economic and political goals.

Composite Index of Economic Influence

China-Myanmar bilateral economic ties suggest a strong interdependent relationship, but to what extent has Myanmar become dependent on China versus its other trading partners, and what changes, if any, have occurred in Myanmar's dependence on China versus its other trading partners? To answer these questions, I have developed the Composite Index of Economic Influence (CIEI), which captures a country's relative interdependent status. The index is calculated in a way that is similar to the well-known Composite Index of National Capability (CINC), which calculates the average of percentages of world totals a country possesses in six dimensions relevant to material power, such as the total and urban population, iron and steel production, primary energy consumption, military expenditure, and military personnel.[28]

The CIEI is composed of four dimensions that include a country's proportion of Myanmar's total trade volume, total inward FDI, total external debts owed, and total foreign visitors. A country's CIEI is the average of these four dimensional proportions. A high CIEI indicates that Myanmar trades more with, secures more investments from, owes more to, and engages in more personal exchanges as measured by the number visitors from a given country. All four

Table 4 Top Ten Countries' CIEI Relative to Myanmar, 2010 and 2013

#	Country	2013 CIEI	TD	FDI	DEBT	VIS	2010 CIEI	TD	FDI	DEBT	VIS
1	China	28.4	27.6	54.0	21.0	11.0	28.1	25.5	50.1	21.0	15.8
2	Thailand	15.5	26.0	20.6	0.0	15.5	19.4	34.6	23.7	0.0	19.2
3	Japan	14.9	8.3	0.6	43.0	7.6	13.3	4.3	0.5	43.0	5.2
4	Singapore	6.1	15.7	4.1	0.0	4.4	4.2	8.4	4.5	0.0	3.9
5	S. Korea	4.0	3.5	6.5	0.0	6.1	4.4	4.0	7.3	0.0	6.1
6	India	2.5	7.3	0.4	0.0	2.3	3.7	11.0	0.5	0.0	3.2
7	Malaysia	2.3	2.5	2.2	0.0	4.4	2.6	2.9	2.4	0.0	5.2
8	UK	2.1	0.2	1.7	2.6	3.7	3.0	0.4	6.6	2.6	2.4
9	US	1.8	0.7	0.5	0.0	6.0	1.5	0.1	0.6	0.0	5.3

Sources: FDI data is from Myanmar's Ministry of National Planning and Economic Development; tourism statistics are from Myanmar's Ministry of Hotels and Tourism; and the data on Myanmar's debt is from *Eurodad Briefing* and the *Financial Times*.[29]

Note: TD, FDI, DEBT and VIS represent total trade, inward FDI, external debt and foreign visitors, respectively.

dimensions are relevant to economic influence from, and cultural exchanges with, other countries that constitute the core of economic interdependent relationships.

In 2010, for example, China accounted for 25.5 percent of Myanmar's total trade with the world, 50.1 percent of China's total foreign investment in Myanmar, 21 percent of Myanmar's total external debts, and 15.8 percent of total foreign visitors to Myanmar. The average of these four figures is 28.1, which is China's 2010 CIEI. In other words, on average China provided about 28.1 percent of meaningful assets that Myanmar needed from the world. However, the CIEI does not indicate one country's influence on Myanmar relative to the influence of other countries. For example, one should not divide China's 2010 CIEI (28.1) by the US's 1.5 and argue that Myanmar depended 18.7 times more on China than it did on the US. The CIEI merely shows that for Myanmar, China is much more important than the US in terms of external economic relationships.

Table 4 shows that China not only launched an ambitious economic campaign in Myanmar, but also successfully outperformed Myanmar's other major partners. A comparison of the 2010 and

2013 CIEIs shows that China remained Myanmar's most influential economic partner followed by Thailand and Japan, with Japan starting to catch up with Thailand. To Myanmar, its neighbor and other regional powers like Japan, South Korea and India, are more important than their Western counterparts. Although the 2013 US CIEI shows an increase, the gap between the CIEIs of the US and Asian countries remains huge. From the above evidence, one cannot deny the potential of China's influence on Myanmar. For those who regard economic interdependency as critical to the nature of power, China would undoubtedly be the country with the most influence on Myanmar. However, is this the case?

Growing Divergence between China and Myanmar

Thus far, we have seen evidence that China and Myanmar have had an interdependent relationship, with Myanmar being markedly more dependent on China than vice-versa. If China has successfully translated its investments and foreign aid into influence, we should see (1) the government of Myanmar demonstrating a willingness to support the economic and political goals of China because Myanmar is attracted to Chinese culture and policies and believes that China's culture and policies are worthy of emulation; and (2) the citizens of Myanmar welcoming China's economic presence in their communities because they believe this presence has more benefits than costs.

There is evidence that this was the case until around 2011 when the military junta and later a civilian-led government began to institute democratic reforms that led to a backlash against Chinese-financed projects in Myanmar. This chapter highlights the weakening of Myanmar's support for China's positions on human rights and a nuclear-weapon-free world in the UN General Assembly, and citizen concerns over two Chinese-financed projects—the Myitsone Dam and the Letpadaung copper mine.

China and Myanmar Voting Patterns in the UN General Assembly

The affinity score I adopt was developed by Anton Strezhnev and Erik Voeten.[30] "0" is assigned to instances when both countries voted the same way on all resolutions in the UN General Assembly (UNGA),

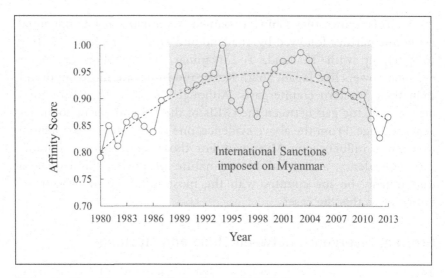

Figure 1 Sino-Myanmar Affinity Score, 1980–2013

and "1" is assigned when they voted differently in all cases. I use this score to determine the degree of similarity between the perspectives of China and Myanmar on global affairs based on their voting patterns in the UNGA. A higher voting similarity indicates higher chances of cooperation between a pair of countries. As Figure 1 shows, the Sino-Myanmar affinity score follows an inverse U-shaped curve from 1980 to 2013. When the international community imposed economic sanctions on Myanmar after the military junta violently cracked down on the nationwide pro-democracy protests in 1988, China and Myanmar acted in concert in the UNGA. Before 1988 and after 2010 as Myanmar began to open up to the outside world, both countries had less similar voting records in the UNGA.

If we further trace China and Myanmar's voting patterns for the UNGA resolutions about which they disagreed, Myanmar has departed more from the role of an obedient partner since 2011 over two issues: human rights and a nuclear-weapon-free world. From 2006 to 2011 in the 61st to 66th UNGA sessions, member countries voted on the resolution "Situation of Human Rights in Myanmar," which strongly condemned the systematic violation of human rights and fundamental freedoms of the people of Myanmar.[31] China stood by the military junta in voting against the resolution in all six sessions. China and Myanmar were also staunch allies in blocking human rights resolutions

Table 5 Voting Behavior of China and Myanmar in the UNGA

Resolution	Session	61st	62nd	63rd	64th	65th	66th	67th	68th
	Year	2006	2007	2008	2009	2010	2011	2012	2013
Nuclear-weapon-free world	China	Y	Y	Y	Y	Y	A	A	A
	Myanmar	Y	Y	Y	Y	Y	Y	Y	Y
Human rights in Iran	China	N	N	N	N	N	A	N	N
	Myanmar	N	N	N	N	N	N	NP	NP
Human rights in Syria	China	N	N	N	N	N	N	N	N
	Myanmar	N	N	N	N	N	N	NP	NP

Source: General Assembly of the United Nations, Voting Records <http://www.un.org/en/ga/documents/voting.asp>.

Note: Y = Yes; N = No; A = Abstention; NP = Not Participating

on Iran and Syria; both countries voted against "Situation of Human Rights in the Islamic Republic of Iran." However, in the 67th session of 2012, the Myanmar representative chose not to participate in the voting. During the 66th Session in 2011, China abstained from voting on the resolution "Situation of Human Rights in the Syrian Arab Republic," that strongly condemned the Syrian government for human rights violations. Myanmar voted "no." In the following two years, China and Myanmar split further over Syria's human rights problems. In the next two years, China rejected the resolution by voting "no," while Myanmar changed from rejection to "no comment" by not participating in the vote. The resolution was approved by 127 countries in the 68th Session and rejected by 13, while only 6 countries did not participate. Of those 13 countries, many were China's staunchest authoritarian allies, such as Belarus, North Korea, Cuba, Iran, Uzbekistan, Venezuela and Zimbabwe. They criticized the UN's human rights resolutions on the grounds that these resolutions constituted interference in other countries' domestic affairs.

In the 66th General Assembly meeting when a UNGA resolution condemning Myanmar was still being tabled, the representative of Myanmar "accused its main sponsor, the European Union, of exploiting human rights for political purposes." He argued that

Myanmar was working hard to build a democratic society and it deserved the "kind understanding and sincere encouragements of the international community, rather than an unconstructive approach by adopting such a resolution."[32] When the international community saw political reform in Myanmar during the 67th Session of 2012, UNGA representatives toned down the criticism of Myanmar. The subsequent drafts of the resolution were unanimously tabled without harsh criticism of Myanmar's human rights situation. Eventually the UNGA ceased drafting the resolution. The Myanmar UNGA representative commented during the meeting that the country "had reached out to the international community and engaged in bilateral dialogues with the United States, Japan and the European Union, based on the principles of cooperation and genuine dialogue. We [Myanmar] have opted for cooperation rather than confrontation."[33] Unlike other countries that congratulated Myanmar for its new position, the representative of China stated that the "international community should let Myanmar choose its own path and refrain from adopting a country-specific text."[34]

Since 1998, China and Myanmar had cast the same votes on the resolution, "Towards a Nuclear-Weapon-Free World." Both countries abstained in the first two years, and then both voted for the resolution until 2010.[35] Starting in 2011, China abstained on the resolution, arguing that Russia and the United States should reduce their nuclear weapons significantly before requesting other countries do so. China's hesitation came from its anticipation that it would have a need for more nuclear power in the future. Beijing's new position, however, was not shared by Myanmar, which continued to vote for a nuclear-weapon-free world.

The above evidence shows that in terms of human rights protection, Myanmar started to move away from China's position in 2012 even though China was its largest economic partner. Myanmar began to adopt the pro-human rights position favored by the democratic world. In addition, Myanmar's perspective on nuclear weapons has diverged from that of China. The changes in the voting patterns of China and Myanmar suggest that China's economic presence in Myanmar did not make it a staunch ally, at least not on the issues of human rights and nuclear weapons. With Myanmar pursuing democratization, the two countries may continue to diverge more on global issues in the future.

Community-based Opposition to China's Presence in Myanmar

Discontent with China's presence also rose among Myanmar's local communities that were affected by Chinese projects. President Thein Sein suspended the Myitsone Dam project in September 2011. In November 2012, local protests against the Letpadaung copper mine project led to its temporary suspension. The railway construction that linked Myanmar's west coast to Kunming in southern China was stopped. On May 31, 2011, China Mobile and the UK's Vodafone announced that they had withdrawn their joint bid for telecommunications licenses in Myanmar.[36] Myanmar's official statistics show that China's direct investments (including Hong Kong) to Myanmar plummeted from US$4.3 billion in 2011 to US$488.1 million in 2012; it further dropped to US$176 million in 2013. China's percentage of its total FDI to Myanmar subsequently dropped from 93.6 percent to 34.4 percent (2011) and to 4.3 percent (2012). In 2013, Singapore became Myanmar's largest investor while South Korea, Thailand, the UK and Vietnam invested more than China. It seems that the Sino-Myanmar interdependent relationship has not increased Myanmar's attraction to China and that the large scale of China's economic presence has not translated into a lasting influence over Myanmar. Aside from the Myanmar government's political reforms and its subsequent tilt towards countries other than China discussed above, the explanation for this seems to lie in a widespread community-level perception that China's projects are exploitative.

In the case of the Myitsone Dam project, the China Power Investment Corporation (CPIC) signed a memorandum of understanding with Myanmar's Ministry of Electric Power No. 1 in December 2006 stating its intention to build a hydroelectric power plant. In May 2007, the two countries concluded an agreement to build seven dams for a total of US$3.7 billion. The project was scheduled to finish in 2017. The CPIC would manage the project for 50 years and then turn it over to Myanmar. During the period of CPIC's franchise, 90 percent of the electricity produced would go to China while Myanmar would benefit from dividends and bonuses, free electricity and taxes. Although the central government supported the Myitsone Dam project, the people in Kachin State, where the dam is located, opposed it from the day the project started. These objections did not only result from a long-standing conflict between the ethnic Kachin people and the military government. It was also because of the project's environmental impact, possible damage to cultural sites, and the perceived unequal distribution of interests prescribed by the contract.

As local protests peaked, Myanmar's political situation started to change. In March 2011, Thein Sein was sworn in as the president of a civilian government, which completed a transfer of power from the military junta to itself. In May, thousands of political prisoners were released and the opposition leader, Aung San Suu Kyi, was allowed to leave Yangon on a political visit to Thein Sein. These actions demonstrated Myanmar's intention to embrace a more open political regime. On November 11, 2011, U Zaw Min, Minister of Electric Power No. 1, stated that both countries would still continue with the Myitsone Dam project according to the contract. Twenty days later, however, President Thein Sein announced the suspension of the project, emphasizing that the government had to address the people's concerns because the Myanmar government was now elected by the people.[37]

Several Chinese studies, some of which suspect the US' hand behind local opposition, attribute local discontent to at least two aspects. First, local inhabitants and the ecosystem may have been harmed by the dam construction at the time because Myanmar lacked effective environmental regulations to manage such risks. This finding reflects the opinion of most Kachin people. Second, local people considered the project to be beneficial only to China while local interests were sacrificed. For example, the deal stipulated that 90 percent of the electricity would be exported to China. In addition, the Kachin Independence Army (KIA) has been fighting against the government since 1962; thus, it does not trust government-backed projects. Aung San Suu Kyi, who was released from prison as a result of political reforms, strongly opposed the project and enabled the media to report the objections to the project. As a result, people became more aware of the negative impact caused by the Myitsone Dam project.[38]

A similar situation occurred over the Letpadaung copper mine project, a US$1.65 billion joint venture by China's Wanbao Mining, a subsidiary of China North Industries Corporation, and the Union of Myanmar Economic Holdings Limited (UMEHL), run by Myanmar's military. In order to attract foreign investments, the Myanmar government grabbed land from local people without appropriate compensation. Displaced people lost about 7,000 acres of land in 26 villages. Public protests peaked in November 2012 when protestors blocked construction and forced a temporary halt to the project. A standoff between protestors and police occurred outside China's embassy in Yangon. On December 2, the authorities formed an investigatory committee chaired by Aung San Suu Kyi. The committee's final report concluded that the project should continue.[39] The official investigation, however, was not well received by the protestors. When Aung San Suu Kyi visited Letpadaung, furious local people criticized her involvement when she called for a peaceful resolution and suggested that breaking an international contract would harm Myanmar's reputation. Continuing sporadic protests led the authorities to open fire on the protesters and detain several of them.[40]

The cases of Myitsone and Letpadaung illustrate the discontent over China's presence in Myanmar. When the military regime was isolated by international sanctions, China had more leverage over Myanmar. However, this leverage lessened as Myanmar began to democratize. Chinese companies had been able to rely on Myanmar's authorities to repress local resentment during military rule. Research shows that most of China's investments were concentrated on projects that provided jobs mostly for workers from China; extracted and processed Myanmar's natural resources; caused damage to the environment; and provided only limited benefits to local communities in which they were located.[41] The research also shows that, in contrast, investments from Japan put more resources in manufacturing sectors that rely heavily on local people and were welcomed because they created more job opportunities.[42] A poor record in environmental protection and an unequal distribution of interests has alienated China from Myanmar's citizens, a situation which is only likely to intensify as Myanmar democratizes and its people become better informed and able to express their discontent.

Myanmar's civilian government has become more sensitive to its citizens' demands. It also acknowledges the importance of diverse external economic engagements for economic growth. Thus, China is no longer the only major power to please. Myanmar is reaching out to India, Japan and the US. For example, India has carried out several infrastructure projects that not only benefit the local people, but have also strengthened the connectivity between India and Myanmar. These projects include the construction of the 160-kilometer Tamu–Kalewa road with 71 bridges, the Rhi–Tiddim and Rhi–Falam roads, and the Yangon–Mandalay railway; an upgrade of the Sittwe port; and the construction of a 1,360-kilometer highway project linking

India, Myanmar and Thailand. Additionally, several Indian private companies are setting up branches or subsidiaries in Myanmar to increase bilateral trade, technological development and financing.[43]

The Japanese government pledged JPY800 million in foreign aid in 2011 and promised a further JPY1.6 billion during the 2012 parliamentary by-elections. During President Thein Sein's visit to Japan, Prime Minister Noda Yoshihiko pledged another JPY1.65 billion in aid. Both leaders promised that all funding would be directed to building infrastructure.[44]

The US lowered the level of its economic sanctions after Myanmar's political reform. President Barack Obama announced in May 2012 that Washington would lift certain financial and investment sanctions on Myanmar. In July 2012, the US permitted its financial services to operate in Myanmar, which led to the first American investment project in the country in 15 years. In November 2012, the importation of Myanmar's goods to the US was authorized, and in February 2013 US citizens were allowed to conduct transactions with four of Myanmar's major financial institutions.[45] The US State Department's former Assistant Secretary for East Asian and Pacific Affairs, Kurt Campbell, played an important role in helping an unnamed American businessman win contracts to expand Yangon's international airport and build roads between Yangon and Mandalay. His consulting team successfully bid for more infrastructure projects than business rivals from other countries.[46] It is clear that the balance of economic influence in Myanmar is shifting away from China.

Conclusion

This chapter has presented a most-likely case study of the Sino-Myanmar economic relationship to test whether China's economic presence has successfully increased its influence over Myanmar. Because the Myanmar military junta depended heavily on China's support for political survival and economic development, it is reasonable to conclude that Myanmar would be the least likely Southeast Asian country to resist China's expectations that Myanmar would support Chinese positions taken on UN resolutions. However, despite all measures indicating Myanmar's dependency on China, China quickly lost its influence over Myanmar after the latter started to democratize its political system. This study suggests, however, that it was not only Myanmar's reforms or its democratic orientation that led to China's loss of influence. Rather, it has also been the people's opposition to what they see as the exploitative nature of China's economic presence and the environmental damage done by Chinese-funded projects. These factors might reduce the effectiveness of China's economic presence around the world.

Theoretically speaking, this case casts doubt on the connection between interdependent economic relationships and power. It shows that even though two countries are interdependent, the less dependent country cannot take its power over the more dependent partner for granted, even as it exercises that power through soft economic means. This case suggests that a successful interdependent connection requires political and social cohesion for further strengthening; that is, the more dependent partner in an interdependent economic relationship confers on (or withholds from) its less dependent partner the right to be regarded as a legitimate facilitator of soft power. As demonstrated in this chapter, the depth and sustainability of China's soft footprint in Myanmar rest on questions of political and economic legitimacy.

Notes

1. Joseph S. Nye, *Soft Power: The Means to Success in World Politics* (New York: PublicAffairs, 2004).
2. Joshua Kurlantzick, *Charm Offensive: How China's Soft Power Is Transforming the World* (New Haven: Yale University Press, 2007).
3. Ignatius Wibowo, "China's Soft Power and Neoliberal Agenda in Southeast Asia," in *Soft Power: China's Emerging Strategy in International Politics*, ed. M. Li, 207–23 (Lanham, Md.: Lexington Books, 2009).
4. Edward D. Mansfield and Brian M. Pollins, "The Study of Interdependence and Conflict Recent Advances, Open Questions, and Directions for Future Research," *Journal of Conflict Resolution* 45, no. 6 (2001): 834–59; Arthur A. Stein, "Governments, Economic Interdependence, and International Cooperation," in *Behavior, Society, and Nuclear War*, vol. 3, ed. P.E. Tetlock, J.L. Husbands, R. Jervis, P.C. Stern, and C. Tilly, 241–324 (New York: Oxford University Press, 1993).
5. Albert O. Hirschman, *The Passions and the Interests: Political Arguments for Capitalism before Its Triumph* (Princeton NJ: Princeton University Press, 1977).
6. Ian Chen Tsung-yen, "Balance of Payments and Power: Assessing China's Global and Regional Interdependence Relationship," *International Relations of the Asia-Pacific* 14, no. 2 (2014): 239–69; Robert O. Keohane and Joseph S. Nye, *Power and Interdependence: World Politics in Transition* (Boston: Little, Brown, 1977).

7. Harry Eckstein, "Case Study and Theory in Political Science," in *Handbook of Political Science: Political Science – Scope and Theory*, vol. 7, ed. F.I. Greenstein and N.W. Polsby, 94–137 (Reading: Addison-Wesley, 1975); John Gerring, "Is There a (Viable) Crucial-Case Method?" *Comparative Political Studies*, 40, no. 3 (2007): 231–53; Colin Howson and Peter Urbach, *Scientific Reasoning: The Bayesian Approach* (La Salle, Ill.: Open Court, 1989).
8. Gerring, "Is There a (Viable) Crucial-Case Method?" 237–8.
9. Alice D. Ba, "China and Asean: Renavigating Relations for a 21st-Century Asia," *Asian Survey* 43 (2003): 622–47; Kurlantzick, *Charm Offensive*; Walter Lohman, "More Charm Than Harm: Lessons from China's Economic Offensive in Southeast Asia," *Heritage Lectures #1149* (Washington DC: The Heritage Foundation, 2010); Wibowo, "China's Soft Power and Neoliberal Agenda in Southeast Asia."
10. Gerring, "Is There a (Viable) Crucial-Case Method?" 237–8.
11. The UN Resolution Symbols for UNGA resolutions regarding Myanmar's human rights are A/RES/65/241, A/RES/64/238, A/RES/63/245, A/RES/62/222, and A/RES/61/232. See <http://www.un.org/en/ga/documents/voting.asp> (accessed June 5, 2014).
12. United Nations, "China and Russia Veto US/UK-Backed Security Council Draft Resolution on Myanmar," *UN News Centre*, January 12, 2007, <http://www.un.org/apps/news/story.asp?NewsID=21228> (accessed March 25, 2016).
13. The affinity score developed by Strezhnev and Voeten (2013) seeks to approximate the voting similarity between each dyad in the UNGA. I use the variable "s3un" where "1" means both countries vote the same on all resolutions while "0" means they vote differently in all cases. China-Myanmar dyad scores an average of 0.963 from 2003 to 2011 and China-Vietnam dyad gets 0.966.
14. Niklas Swanström, *Sino-Myanmar Relations: Security and Beyond (Asia Paper)* (Stockholm: Institute for Security and Development Policy, 2012).
15. Nye, *Soft Power: The Means to Success in World Politics*, x.
16. Office of Foreign Assets Control, *Burma Sanctions Program* (Washington, DC: US Department of the Treasury, 2014).
17. Association of Southeast Asian Nations, *Asean Statistical Yearbook 2012* (Jakarta, Indonesia: ASEAN Secretariat, 2013), 56.
18. For more information, refer to the Observatory of Economic Complexity, developed by The MIT Media Lab Macro Connections group at <http://atlas.media.mit.edu/> (accessed June 26, 2014).
19. Time series data comes from three sources, which may have slight discrepancies but allow a consistent cross-sectional comparison to be made. Data from 1991 to 2009 was retrieved from Katherine Barbieri, Omar M.G. Keshk, and Brian Pollins, "Trading Data: Evaluating Our

Assumptions and Coding Rules," *Conflict Management and Peace Science* 26, no. 5 (2009): 471–93. The 2010 data was retrieved from the United Nations Commodity Trade Statistics Database. The 2011–3 data was retrieved from Myanmar's official statistics, <https://www.mnped.gov.mm/html_file/foreign_trade/s09MA0201.htm.> (accessed June 26, 2014).
20. "China Tops Thailand as Biggest Investor in Myanmar," *Bloomberg Businessweek*, February 21, 2011, <http://www.businessweek.com/ap/financialnews/D9LH8K880.htm> (accessed March 25, 2016).
21. Association of Southeast Asian Nations, *Asean Statistical Yearbook 2012*.
22. Data is available from ASEAN-Japan Centre, <http://www.asean.or.jp/en/asean/know/statistics/5.html> (accessed April 1, 2015).
23. Statistics from different sources may have discrepancies, although I have tried to keep the data as consistent as possible for higher validity.
24. Jared Bissinger, "Foreign Investment in Myanmar: A Resource Boom but a Development Bust?" *Contemporary Southeast Asia* 34, no. 1 (2012): 41.
25. See the data from Table 3.
26. The International Monetary Fund's (IMF) description of balance of payments defines FDI as investments that have a lasting influence on the management of foreign assets, where investors have over a 10 percent share of the decision-making power in certain foreign enterprises. See Chen, "Balance of Payments and Power," 239–69.
27. The Organisation for Economic Co-operation and Development (OECD) uses the term official development aid (ODA), which is defined as official concessional deals on development projects. However, as the literature points out, China's development aid around the world is defined by wider (and vaguer) terms that sometimes include unofficial infrastructure investments or low-interest loans. For example, see Song Lianghe and Wu Yijun, "Zhongguo Dui Miandian Yuanzhu De Xianzhuang Ji Jianyi" [Current Situation of China's Aid to Myanmar and Its Recommendations], *Xiamen daxue guoji fazhan luntan* [Xiamen University Forum on International Development] 7 (2013): 64–7.
28. J. David Singer, Stuart Bremer, and John Stuckey, "Capability Distribution, Uncertainty, and Major Power War, 1820–1965," in *Peace, War, and Numbers*, ed. B.M. Russet, 19–48 (Beverly Hills: Sage, 1972).
29. China's trade data includes Hong Kong. The UK's investment data includes the British Virgin Islands and Bermuda. Please refer to Table 3 for trade data. For FDI data, see the data published by Myanmar's Ministry of National Planning and Economic Development, which can be accessed at <http://www.mnped.gov.mm>. For tourism statistics, see data published by Myanmar's Ministry of Hotels and Tourism, which can be accessed at <http://www.myanmartourism.org/>. The estimate of Myanmar's external debt is subject to the problem of data availability. I have relied mainly on analysis, which estimates Myanmar's debts

owed to China, Japan and the Paris Club members. Hulova estimates that the Paris Club members, excluding Japan, were owed 24 percent of Myanmar's external debts. See Diana Hulova, "Myanmar's Debt: What's Behind the Speedy Efforts to Restructure It?" *Eurodad Briefing* (2013), <http://eurodad.org/files/integration/2013/02/Myanmar_debt_briefing_FINALweb1.pdf> (accessed March 25, 2016). The *Financial Times* reported that Myanmar had nine Paris Club members as creditors, including the UK. See Gwen Robinson, "Myanmar Signs Deal with Foreign Creditors." *Financial Times*, January 28, 2013, <http://www.ft.com/intl/cms/s/0/9b2d6e4c-68b2-11e2-9a3f-00144feab49a.html> (accessed March 25, 2016). Therefore, I have estimated the UK's debt share using the average of the nine Paris Club members. For other countries, the available information indicates that Myanmar's debts to other countries amounted to no more than one percent of Myanmar's external debt; therefore, I have used 0.0 to estimate other countries' proportions of debts.

30. Anton Strezhnev and Erik Voeten, *United Nations General Assembly Voting Data* (2013), <http://hdl.handle.net/1902.1/12379> (accessed May 25, 2014).
31. See Note 11.
32. United Nations General Assembly, *Third Committee Approves Draft Resolutions on Human Rights Situations in Iran, Democratic People's Republic of Korea, Myanmar* (New York: United Nations, 2011), <http://www.un.org/press/en/2011/gashc4032.doc.htm> (accessed March 25, 2016).
33. United Nations General Assembly, *Delegates Hail Human Rights Improvements in Myanmar as Third Committee Approves 8 Draft Resolutions, Including 4 Country-Specific Texts* (New York: United Nations, 2013), <http://www.un.org/press/en/2013/gashc4091.doc.htm> (accessed March 25, 2016).
34. Ibid.
35. For details of the resolution, go to the United Nations Library website <http://www.un.org/Depts/dhl/> and search "Towards a nuclear-weapon-free world" (accessed June 6, 2014).
36. Jacob Gronholt-Pedersen, "Chinese Investment in Myanmar Falls Sharply," *Wall Street Journal*, June 4, 2013, <http://www.wsj.com/articles/SB10001424127887324063304578525021254736996> (accessed March 25, 2016).
37. Li Chenyang, "Miandian Zhengfu Weihe Gezhi Misong Shuidianzhan Jianshe" [Why Does Myanmar Suspend the Myitsone Dam Project], *Shijie zhishi* [*World Affairs*] 21 (2011): 24–6.
38. Jiang Heng, "Gaochongtu Diqu Touzi Fengxian Zai Renshi: Zhongguo Touzi Miandian Anli Diaoyan" [Re-Acknowledging Investment Risks in High Conflict Zones: A Case of China's Investments in Myanmar], *Guoji jingji hezuo* [*International Economic Cooperation*] 11 (2011): 9–12; Li,

"Miandian Zhengfu Weihe Gezhi Misong Shuidianzhan Jianshe" [Why Does Myanmar Suspend the Myitsone Dam Project]: 24–6; Song and Wu, "Zhongguo Dui Miandian Yuanzhu De Xianzhuang Ji Jianyi [Current Situation of China's Aid to Myanmar and Its Recommendations]: 64–7; Wang Wei, Zhao Yuanxiang, and Gui Wei, "Miandian Yijiang Shangyou Shuidian Kaifa Yimin Anzhi Guihua Tansuo" [Discussion on Immigrant Resettlement for Hydropower Development of Upper Irrawaddy River in Burma], *Renmin changjiang* [*Yangtze River*] 44, no. 2 (2013): 46–53.
39. Liao Yahui, "Miandian: Zhongzi Laibitang Tongkuang Weihe Zao Fandui" [Myanmar: Why China's Letpadaung Investment Project Confronts Rejection], *Shijie zhishi* [*World Affairs*] 9 (2013): 26–7.
40. Zarni Mann, "Eight Detained as Opposition to Burma's Letpadaung Copper Mine Continues," *The Irrawaddy*, February 5, 2014, <http://www.irrawaddy.com/burma/eight-detained-opposition-burmas-letpadaung-copper-mine-continues.html> (accessed March 25, 2016); Khin Pyae Son, "Authorities Open Fire on Myanmar Copper Mine Protesters," *Radio Free Asia*, November 15, 2013, <http://www.rfa.org/english/news/myanmar/mine-11152013160128.html> (accessed March 25, 2016).
41. Thomas Fuller, "Long Reliant on China, Myanmar Now Looks to Japan," *New York Times*, October 12, 2012, <http://www.nytimes.com/2012/10/11/world/asia/long-reliant-on-china-myanmar-now-turns-to-japan-for-help.html> (accessed March 25, 2016).
42. Ibid.
43. Ranjit Gupta, "China, Myanmar and India: A Strategic Perspective," *Indian Foreign Affairs Journal* 8 (2013): 80–92.
44. James Reilly, "China and Japan in Myanmar: Aid, Natural Resources and Influence," *Asian Studies Review* 37, no. 2 (2013): 141–57.
45. Jane Perlez, "U.S. and China Press for Influence in Myanmar," *New York Times*, March 31, 2012, <http://www.nytimes.com/2012/03/31/world/asia/myanmar-reforms-set-us-and-china-in-race-for-sway.html> (accessed March 25, 2016).
46. William Boot, "Trade with Myanmar Key Part of Us Pivot to Asia," *The Irrawaddy*, July 25, 2013.

References

Association of Southeast Asian Nations. *Asean Statistical Yearbook 2012*. Jakarta, Indonesia: ASEAN Secretariat, 2013.
Ba, Alice D. "China and Asean: Renavigating Relations for a 21st-Century Asia." *Asian Survey* 43, no. 4 (2003): 622–47.
Barbieri, Katherine, Omar M.G. Keshk, and Brian Pollins. "Trading Data: Evaluating Our Assumptions and Coding Rules." *Conflict Management and Peace Science* 26, no. 5 (2009): 471–93.

Bissinger, Jared. "Foreign Investment in Myanmar: A Resource Boom but a Development Bust?" *Contemporary Southeast Asia* 34, no. 1 (2012): 23–52.

Chen, Ian Tsung-yen. "Balance of Payments and Power: Assessing China's Global and Regional Interdependence Relationship." *International Relations of the Asia-Pacific* 14, no. 2 (2014): 239–69.

Eckstein, Harry. "Case Study and Theory in Political Science." In *Handbook of Political Science: Political Science – Scope and Theory*, vol. 7, edited by F.I. Greenstein and N.W. Polsby, 94–137. Reading: Addison-Wesley, 1975.

Gerring, John. "Is There a (Viable) Crucial-Case Method?" *Comparative Political Studies* 40, no. 3 (2007): 231–53.

Gupta, Ranjit. "China, Myanmar and India: A Strategic Perspective." *Indian Foreign Affairs Journal* 8, no. 1 (2013): 80–92.

Hirschman, Albert O. *The Passions and the Interests: Political Arguments for Capitalism before Its Triumph*. Princeton, NJ: Princeton University Press, 1977.

Howson, Colin and Peter Urbach. *Scientific Reasoning: The Bayesian Approach*. La Salle, IL: Open Court, 1989.

Hulova, Diana. "Myanmar's Debt: What's Behind the Speedy Efforts to Restructure It?" *Eurodad Briefing* 2013. <http://eurodad.org/files/integration/2013/02/Myanmar_debt_briefing_FINALweb1.pdf> (accessed March 25, 2016).

Jiang Heng. "Gaochongtu Diqu Touzi Fengxian Zai Renshi: Zhongguo Touzi Miandian Anli Diaoyan" [Re-Acknowledging Investment Risks in High Conflict Zones: A Case of China's Investments in Myanmar]. *Guoji jingji hezuo* [*International Economic Cooperation*] 11 (2011): 9–12.

Keohane, Robert O. and Joseph S. Nye. *Power and Interdependence: World Politics in Transition*. Boston: Little, Brown, 1977.

Kurlantzick, Joshua. *Charm Offensive: How China's Soft Power Is Transforming the World*. New Haven: Yale University Press, 2007.

Li Chenyang. "Miandian Zhengfu Weihe Gezhi Misong Shuidianzhan Jianshe?" [Why Does Myanmar Suspend the Myitsone Dam Project?]. *Shijie zhishi* [*World Affairs*] 21 (2011): 24–6.

Liao Yahui. "Miandian: Zhongzi Laibitang Tongkuang Weihe Zao Fandui" [Myanmar: Why China's Letpadaung Investment Project Confronts Rejection]. *Shijie zhishi* [*World Affairs*] 9 (2013): 26–7.

Lohman, Walter. (2010). "More Charm Than Harm: Lessons from China's Economic Offensive in Southeast Asia." *Heritage Lectures #1149*. Washington DC: The Heritage Foundation.

Mansfield, Edward D. and Brian M. Pollins,. "The Study of Interdependence and Conflict Recent Advances, Open Questions, and Directions for Future Research." *Journal of Conflict Resolution* 45, no. 6 (2001): 834–59.

Ministry of Commerce of the People's Republic of China, National Bureau of Statistics of the People's Republic of China, and the State Administration of Foreign Exchange. *2008 Statistical Bulletin of China's Outward Foreign Direct Investment*. Beijing: China Statistics Press, 2009.

_____. *2012 Statistical Bulletin of China's Outward Foreign Direct Investment*. Beijing, China: China Statistics Press, 2013.

Nye, Joseph S. *Soft Power: The Means to Success in World Politics*. New York: PublicAffairs, 2004.

Office of Foreign Assets Control. *Burma Sanctions Program*. Washington, DC: US Department of the Treasury, 2014.

Reilly, James. "China and Japan in Myanmar: Aid, Natural Resources and Influence." *Asian Studies Review* 37, no. 2 (2013): 141–57.

Singer, J. David, Stuart Bremer, and John Stuckey. "Capability Distribution, Uncertainty, and Major Power War, 1820–1965." In *Peace, War, and Numbers*, edited by B. M. Russet, 19–48. Beverly Hills: Sage, 1972.

Song Lianghe and Wu Yijun. "Zhongguo Dui Miandian Yuanzhu De Xianzhuang Ji Jianyi" [Current Situation of China's Aid to Myanmar and Its Recommendations]. *Xiamen daxue guoji fazhan luntan* [*Xiamen University Forum on International Development*] 7 (2013): 64–7.

Stein, Arthur A. "Governments, Economic Interdependence, and International Cooperation." In *Behavior, Society, and Nuclear War*, vol. 3, edited by P.E. Tetlock, J.L. Husbands, R. Jervis, P.C. Stern, and C. Tilly, 241–324. New York: Oxford University Press, 1993.

Strezhnev, Anton and Erik Voeten. *United Nations General Assembly Voting Data* 2013. <http://hdl.handle.net/1902.1/12379> (accessed May 25, 2014).

Swanström, Niklas. *Sino-Myanmar Relations: Security and Beyond (Asia Paper)*. Stockholm: Institute for Security and Development Policy, 2012.

United Nations General Assembly. *Third Committee Approves Draft Resolutions on Human Rights Situations in Iran, Democratic People's Republic of Korea, Myanmar*. New York: United Nations, 2011. <http://www.un.org/press/en/2011/gashc4032.doc.htm> (accessed March 25, 2016).

Wang Wei, Zhao Yuanxiang, and Gui Wei. "Miandian Yijiang Shangyou Shuidian Kaifa Yimin Anzhi Guihua Tansuo" [Discussion on Immigrant Resettlement for Hydropower Development of Upper Irrawaddy River in Burma]. *Renmin changjiang* [*Yangtze River*] 44, no. 2 (2013): 46–53.

Wibowo, Ignatius. "China's Soft Power and Neoliberal Agenda in Southest Asia." In *Soft Power: China's Emerging Strategy in International Politics*, edited by M. Li, 207–23. Lanham, Md.: Lexington Books, 2009.

Zhang Yichuan. "Daxing Guoyou Qiye Zaimian Touzi Mianlin De Gonggong Guanxi Wenti Yanjiu" [Study of Public Relations Issue Confronted by Large State Owned Enterprise's Investments in Myanmar]. *Fazhi yu shehui* [*Legal System and Society*] 29 (2012): 165–6.

CHAPTER 4

The Political Economy of China's Economic Presence in Malaysia

Ngeow Chow Bing

Introduction

In a book published in 1999, then Prime Minister of Malaysia Mahathir Mohamad wrote that "[e]ven though China is growing rapidly and may already possess more political clout than Japan, several decades will pass before China's economy can hope to equal that of Japan's."[1] As astute a politician as Mahathir is, he seriously underestimated the speed and magnitude of China's growth. The "several decades" have been reduced to one decade. In 2009–10 China surpassed Japan as the world's second-largest economy. China is now one of the most important economic partners of Malaysia.

This chapter examines China's economic presence in Malaysia as a case of China's soft footprint in a Southeast Asian country. Ever since the notion of "soft power" was introduced into China, many of the country's policymakers and scholars have enthusiastically explored the meaning and application of the concept to enhance China's foreign policy goals. However, China's use of the concept generally has more emphasis on the economic elements than that of Joseph Nye, the originator of the concept. Economic policies are seen to be the "soft" foreign policy tools for the Chinese government to exercise influence and gain support in a mutually "win-win" way. Soft footprints also convey the sense that there is an actual presence of China on the ground, but because it is "soft," the presence is not coercive nor does it undermine the security of the host country.

While there are several studies on China-Malaysia economic relations, those focusing on China's investment in Malaysia are scarce. Khor Yu Leng's report on the Malaysia-China Kuantan Industrial Park (MCKIP) and the China-Malaysia Qinzhou Industrial Park (CMQIP) was one of the first to explore the state of China's investment in Malaysia and the factors (geopolitical as well as Malaysia's domestic political factors) underlying the establishment of the MCKIP, which aims to draw more Chinese investment into Malaysia.[2] Based on extensive interviews and analysis of secondary data, Guanie Lim's article examines how Chinese firms choose Malaysian partners when they invest in the country.[3] In general, Lim found that these firms prefer not to partner with ethnic Chinese Malaysian companies (except in certain sectors); they are more likely to choose government-linked companies (GLCs) in Malaysia as their investment partners, especially in the construction sector. This is due to the nature of Malaysia's government policy wherein GLCs are heavily favored in the construction sector and, therefore, it is rational for Chinese firms to partner with them. In sectors with less government involvement, ethnic Chinese firms can prosper and emerge as the likely partners for foreign investors, including China's investors.

This chapter attempts to build on these studies in three ways. First, it provides an overview of China's economic presence in Malaysia, which neither Khor nor Lim have done. Second, since the MCKIP has been promoted as the showcase project for enhancing China's investment in Malaysia and it symbolizes Malaysia-China friendship, a more detailed and updated examination of the MCKIP than what Khor has reported is warranted. Third, an analytical dimension of this chapter draws attention to the Malaysian domestic bureaucratic and political factors shaping and influencing the outcome of China's economic footprint. Following the theoretical insight of Andrew Mertha's work,[4] which contends that a powerful country's foreign aid policy towards a small country does not necessarily translate into direct policy influence because of the way the local political-bureaucratic nexus shapes policy outcomes, this paper argues that China's investment in Malaysia is also shaped by the domestic political and bureaucratic environments.

In the following sections, an overview of the economic relationship between Malaysia and China in recent years is first presented.

This is followed by a discussion of China's economic presence in Malaysia, an examination of the MCKIP and, finally, an analysis of China's economic presence in Malaysia from a domestic bureaucratic-political perspective.

Malaysia-China Economic Relations

While official diplomatic relations between Malaysia and China were established in 1974, substantial bilateral economic relations occurred only much later. Mahathir's 1985 visit to China is generally seen as the turning point in Sino-Malaysia relations.[5] During this visit, the first of seven visits during his tenure as Malaysia's fourth prime minister, Mahathir "was convinced ... [that] economic issues should be the basis of a bilateral relationship."[6] The visit ushered in a new era of Malaysia-China economic relations in the 1990s. Malaysia saw China's emerging economy as possessing challenges as well as opportunities. Nevertheless, Malaysia capitalized on China's growth.

China's own economy-based diplomatic charm offensive was also a key factor in drawing the Malaysian and other ASEAN economies closer to itself. The 1997 Asian financial crisis was a critical turning point for many ASEAN capitals. The crisis revealed that economic security was not possible without the participation, or even leadership, of China. On more than one occasion, Mahathir himself mentioned his appreciation of the positive role played by China during the crisis. He regarded China's behavior favorably as compared to that of governments and financial speculators from the West. Successive generations of Malaysia's leadership have remained committed to building strong economic ties with China.

Trade

Bilateral trade is the highlight of economic ties between Malaysia and China. In calculating the total volume of the Malaysia-China trade, the governments of Malaysia and China generate different numbers. The government of Malaysia calculates only direct trade between China and Malaysia and uses the Malaysian currency (ringgit [MYR]) as the main unit of calculation. In contrast, China's official statistics of the Malaysia-China trade come from the Chinese customs authorities, which not only calculate direct trade between Malaysia and China but

Table 1 Malaysian Statistics of Malaysia's Trade with China, 2008–15

Year	Import (MYR billions)	Export (MYR billions)	Total (MYR/USD billions)
2008	66.89	63.21	130.10/35.77
2009	60.66	67.24	127.90/38.51
2010	66.43	80.60	147.03/46.31
2011	75.61	91.25	166.86/52.50
2012	91.86	88.75	180.61/59.39
2013	106.26	96.97	203.23/64.09
2014	115.51	92.35	207.86/61.22
2015	129.36	101.53	230.89/53.63

Source: Malaysia External Trade Development Corporation.

also indirect trade (via Hong Kong, Singapore and other places), and use the US dollar (USD) as the main unit of calculation. Therefore, the Chinese figures tend to be higher than the figures generated by the Malaysian side. Table 1 presents the Malaysian statistics of the volume of Malaysia-China trade from 2008 to 2015. These statistics show that Malaysia-China trade grew substantially in recent years. It should be noted that the negative growth in USD terms from 2013 to 2015 was due to the depreciation of the ringgit, not a decrease in the actual trade volume.

Table 2 presents the Chinese figures from 2009 to 2015. As can be seen in this table, the Chinese statistics register substantially larger volumes of trade throughout this period. Based on the USD calculation,

Table 2 Chinese Statistics of Malaysia's Trade with China, 2009–15

Year	Import (USD billions)	Export (USD billions)	Total (USD billions)
2009	19.63	32.33	51.96
2010	23.81	50.41	74.22
2011	27.90	62.10	90.00
2012	36.50	58.30	94.80
2013	45.93	60.14	106.07
2014	46.36	55.66	102.02
2015	44.06	53.30	97.36

Source: Ministry of Commerce, People's Republic of China.

the Chinese statistics also portray the declining trend of Malaysia-China trade since 2013, although this declining trend has to be understood in the context of the depreciating ringgit. Tables 1 and 2 show that while the recent downturn of China's economy is definitely having a negative impact on Malaysia's trade with China, it has not actually contributed to negative growth in ringgit terms. Nonetheless, since 2009, China has been the largest trade partner of Malaysia, and among all the ASEAN countries, Malaysia has been the largest trade partner of China since 2009.

Bilateral trade has contributed much to the economic growth of both countries.[7] In the 1990s, trade primarily consisted of agricultural products. More recent trade, however, has featured more value-added goods that are capital-intensive,[8] although raw materials, such as palm oil and rubber, remain essential. The main products that Malaysia exports to China today are electrical and electronics products, refined petroleum products, machinery, palm oil, chemicals and chemical products, and rubber products, while the main imports from China include electrical and electronics products, machinery, appliances, furniture, textiles, and chemicals and chemical products. The overlap in the imported and exported categories of goods testifies to the growing phenomenon of intra-industry trade.[9]

Finance

In the financial sector, the Bank of China and the Industrial and Commercial Bank of China opened their branches in Malaysia in 2000 and 2010, respectively. In June 2010, the China Banking Regulatory Commission signed an agreement with the Securities Commission of Malaysia. The agreement designated Malaysia as the 11th country to receive China's financial investment in its capital market under China's Qualified Domestic Institutional Investor (QDII) scheme. Two Chinese funds subsequently entered Malaysia's capital market.[10] In November 2014, Chinese Premier Li Keqiang announced during his visit to Malaysia that the country would receive a RMB50 billion quota under the Renminbi Qualified Foreign Institutional Investor (RQFII) scheme, which allows Malaysian institutional funds to invest in China's capital market. During the same visit, Li also announced plans for China to purchase Malaysia's government bonds and issue RMB bonds.[11] These announcements, together with the decision by a Chinese state-owned enterprise (SOE) to buy the power assets of the troubled 1Malaysia Development Berhad (1MDB), came at a particularly difficult period for the Malaysian economy. Thus, this decision was seen as China extending a helping hand to the Malaysian government.

Another development since 2010 has been the increasing participation of China's enterprises in the Malaysia Stock Exchange. In February 2010, four Chinese enterprises became the first from China to offer initial public offerings (IPOs) in Malaysia.[12] Subsequently, more Chinese companies were listed on the Malaysia Stock Exchange before an IPO freeze was ordered by China's authorities in 2012 (the freeze ended in December 2013). A currency swap agreement was also signed in 2009 and renewed in 2012 and 2015 between Bank Negara Malaysia, the country's central bank, and its Chinese counterpart, the People's Bank of China. In November 2013, Bank Negara opened an office in Beijing and announced several new measures aiming to facilitate bilateral trade and investment, including the signing of a memorandum of understanding (MOU) to establish a Cross-Border Collateral Agreement.[13] In November 2014, Bank Negara Malaysia and the People's Bank of China signed an MOU on RMB clearing bank arrangements in Kuala Lumpur.[14] In January 2015, the Bank of China in Malaysia was appointed as the RMB clearing bank.[15] Recognizing the increasing importance of the Chinese currency, many Malaysian officials, politicians and businessmen have called for greater use of the RMB in the bilateral trade between Malaysia and China.[16]

Tourism

The number of Chinese tourists visiting Malaysia has been growing steadily in recent years. From around 1.2 million in 2011,[17] it increased to 1.56 million in 2012, making China the third-largest contributor to Malaysia's tourist arrivals, after Singapore (13.01 million) and Indonesia (2.38 million). In 2013, 2014 and 2015, the numbers of Chinese tourists visiting Malaysia were 1.6 million, 1 million and 1.3 million, respectively.[18] The decline of Chinese tourists in 2014 and 2015 was largely due to the unfortunate MH370 incident (a China-bound Malaysia Airlines aircraft, carrying 227 passengers including more than 150 Chinese nationals, went missing soon after takeoff from Malaysia) in March 2014, and the kidnapping of a Chinese tourist in the eastern state of Sabah in the following month. Consequently, since late 2015 the Malaysian government has experimented with a visa-waiver policy in an attempt to boost the number of Chinese visitors to Malaysia. However, the policy has suffered from a lack of coordination (for example, between the Ministry of Tourism and the Ministry of Home Affairs, which runs the immigration agency, and between the Malaysian Embassy in China and the privatized visa-processing center in Beijing), which created much confusion for potential Chinese visitors about the fees and requirements for a visa waiver from the Malaysian authorities.[19]

Malaysia's Investment in China

Malaysian businesses began investing in China in 1984. Among the ASEAN countries, Malaysia is generally recognized as the second-largest investor in China, after Singapore. Like the different calculations of official statistics on bilateral trade, China and Malaysia do not have the same figure pertaining to the total amount of Malaysian investment in China. China's figure tends to be larger because the Malaysian investment through Hong Kong into China is included, which is not the case in the figure provided by the Malaysian government.[20] In general, the Chinese figure puts Malaysia's investment in China in the range of US$6–7 billion. Table 3 shows the annual and accumulated Malaysian investments in China from 2009 to 2015 according to the data from the Ministry of Commerce in China.

Table 3 Annual and Accumulated Malaysian Investments in China, 2009–15

Year	Annual Investment (USD billions)	Total Investment (USD billions)
2009	0.43	5.36
2010	0.29	5.65
2011	0.36	6.01
2012	0.32	6.33
2013	0.28	6.61
2014	0.19	6.77
2015	0.48	7.25

Source: Ministry of Commerce, People's Republic of China; Zheng Da, 2011, p. 66.

The main investors include some ethnic Chinese tycoons (for example, Robert Kuok of Shangri-La Hotels and William Cheng of Parkson retail chain stores) as well as GLCs (for example, Sime Darby's huge construction project in Weifang City, Shandong Province). In addition to these big players, a substantial number of small and medium enterprises (SMEs), mostly ethnic Chinese-owned, also invest in China. These investments tend to concentrate in the manufacturing sector for Chinese domestic consumption and export, and they are reactions to the structural problems in Malaysia's economy.[21] The domestic Malaysian market has been increasingly dominated by bumiputra firms that are supported by the government. Thus venturing into the Chinese market has become an increasingly attractive option, especially for Chinese-owned companies.[22]

Five-Year Program for Economic and Trade Cooperation between China and Malaysia

Both the Chinese and Malaysian governments have expressed strong interest in further deepening existing bilateral economic relations. Xi Jinping, the current Chinese leader, paid his first visit to Malaysia in October 2013, whereupon he signed four bilateral agreements with Malaysia. Among them was the Five-Year Program for Economic and Trade Cooperation between China and Malaysia (2013–17), which identifies 11 sectors for cooperation: agriculture; manufacturing and industrial parks; infrastructure construction; natural resources; information and communications technology; tourism; project services; the Halal food industry; SMEs; logistics; and retail. Using Chinese statistics for projection, the program aims to achieve a bilateral trade amounting to US$160 billion by 2017. However, it was soon realized that this target, announced in 2013, would be difficult to achieve, given China's slowing economic growth and the depreciating ringgit (mentioned above). Committed as it was to achieving this target, Malaysia failed to meet it. In March 2015, a government special committee was formed to strategize economic ties with China.[23]

China's Economic Presence in Malaysia

There are two main manifestations of China's economic presence in Malaysia. One is China's foreign direct investment (FDI), which

Table 4 China's Annual Investment in Malaysia, 2010–5 (Malaysian Data)

Year	Investment (MYR millions)	Investment (USD millions)
2010	639.5	207.6
2011	1,194.2	373.6
2012	1,977.8	646.3
2013	3,017.6	920.0
2014	4,751.7	1,357.6
2015	1,872.0	436.4

Source: Malaysian Investment Development Authority.

involves Chinese companies transferring capital from China to Malaysia in order to set up plants, factories, and corporations; to merge with Malaysia's enterprises; and to set up joint ventures. The second manifestation involves Chinese companies bidding for and winning construction projects offered in Malaysia. In this case, there may not be a large-scale capital inflow from China and the financing comes from the local government or private sectors. Short-term investment in capital markets is not considered part of China's economic presence in Malaysia.

China's Economic Presence in Malaysia: Statistical Data

The Malaysian Investment Development Authority (MIDA) keeps track of China's investments in Malaysia. However, the MIDA data covers only the manufacturing sector; it does not include investments in other sectors, such as real estate and banking. Table 4 provides the value of approved investment projects from China from 2010 to 2015; Table 5 shows the accumulated approved projects invested by Chinese companies in various manufacturing sectors in Malaysia.

Once again, Malaysian official data does not coincide with the Chinese official data. Table 6 presents China's Ministry of Commerce data on the annual and accumulated investment by China in Malaysia. It is not clear if China's data covers the manufacturing sector only or all sectors (excluding short-term portfolio investment).

It appears that there is a wide discrepancy in the two sets of data provided by the Malaysian and Chinese governments. The MIDA's data appears to give much higher figures compared to the data provided

Table 5 Projects Approved and Implemented, 1987–2015 (Malaysian Data)

Industry	Number	Employment	Investment (MYR)	Investment (USD)
Food Manufacturing	16	720	50,097,425	13,807,887
Beverage and Tobacco	2	347	41,535,128	11,024,734
Textiles and Textile Products	18	1,974	568,024,934	173,671,387
Wood and Wood Products	15	1,370	108,836,800	32,209,507
Furniture and Fixtures	6	475	16,283,474	4,506,254
Paper, Printing and Publishing	6	309	13,437,021	3,892,542
Chemicals and Chemical Products	36	2,555	256,579,480	72,489,319
Petroleum Products (incl. Petrochemicals)	4	319	16,390,765	5,861,559
Rubber Products	20	1,708	112,652,004	35,519,653
Plastic Products	20	1,424	180,826,418	51,422,177
Non-metallic Mineral Products	16	1,585	759,834,245	193,090,003
Basic Metal Products	39	16,874	10,674,383,426	3,211,398,544
Fabricated Metal Products	20	1,764	195,720,381	58,363,051
Machinery and Equipment	38	1,869	184,908,789	57,395,167
Electronics and Electrical Products	30	9,108	3,715,795,564	1,082,210,414
Transport Equipment	26	3,542	228,679,857	65,068,765
Scientific and Measuring Equipment	5	441	111,804,000	33,930,239
Miscellaneous	12	769	22,975,500	6,842,199
Total	329	47,153	17,258,765,211	5,112,703,401

Source: Malaysian Investment Development Authority.

Table 6 China's Investment in Malaysia, 2012–5 (Chinese Data)

Year	Annual Investment (USD billions)	Accumulated Investment (USD billions)
2012	0.07	1.46
2013	0.21	1.67
2014	0.12	1.79
2015	0.41	2.19

Source: Ministry of Commerce, People's Republic of China.

Table 7 Chinese Companies' Construction Projects in Malaysia, 2013–5

Year	Annual Contract Value (USD billions)	Annual Turnover Value (USD billions)	Accumulated Contract Value (USD billions)	Accumulated Turnover Value (USD billions)
2012	3.6	2.37	17	10.9
2013	2.47	2.53	19.47	13.43
2014	4.33	3.07	23.8	16.5
2015	7.26	3.56	31.06	20.06

Source: Ministry of Commerce, People's Republic of China.

by China's Ministry of Commerce (US$5.11 billion versus US$2.19 billion as of the end of 2015). Chinese scholar, Zheng Da, attributes the discrepancy to the MIDA's inclusion of those projects with only letters of investment intent in its calculation method, whereas the Chinese data included only those with actual signed contracts.[24]

Another manifestation of China's economic presence in Malaysia consists of construction projects by Chinese companies. China's Ministry of Commerce has provided the data on such projects in Malaysia. Table 7 lists the value of these projects. The contract value refers to the value of the undersigned projects; the turnover value refers to the value of the actual completed projects.

Who are the Chinese Investors/Enterprises?

While the data in Table 7 shows the value of China's economic presence in Malaysia, it does not identify the Chinese companies investing and operating in Malaysia. For a list of major Chinese companies investing and/or operating in Malaysia, please see the China Enterprises Association in Malaysia website. Table 8 is a rough classification of the 80 member companies according to their sectoral concentration and form of ownership.

The MIDA data shows a higher concentration of investments in basic metal products and electrical and electronic products by Chinese companies. On the other hand, the data from the China Enterprises Association of Malaysia shows that construction companies are by far the most numerous of the Chinese companies operating in Malaysia, with steel, real estate, and information and communications technology (ICT) companies not far behind.

Table 8 Sectoral Concentration and Form of Ownership of the 80 Chinese Companies of the China Enterprises Association of Malaysia[25]

Sector	Banking and Finance	3
	Shipping and Logistics	5
	Harbor Construction and Management	3
	Aviation	4
	Information and Communications Technology	5
	Construction (Unspecified)	12
	Construction (Railway and Road)	3
	Steel and Other Metals	5
	Food Services	3
	Traditional Chinese Medicine	2
	Textiles	3
	Power and Water Supply	4
	Pharmaceutical	2
	Machinery	3
	Mining	2
	Fiber and Plastics	3
	Property and Residences	4
	Others	12
	Unclear	2
Form of Enterprises	State-Owned (including collectives)	37
	Private	30
	Unclear	13

Note: This information is based on a review of these companies' websites.

China's Economic Footprint: Recent Developments

China and Malaysia have set up the so-called dual industrial parks—the Malaysia-China Kuantan Industrial Park (MCKIP) and the China-Malaysia Qinzhou Industrial Park (CMQIP)—as the showcase projects of strengthening mutual investment and Malaysia-China friendship. (The MCKIP has indeed been an important aspect of China's investment in Malaysia in recent years, but it will be discussed in more detail in a later section.) The following section discusses other developments related to China's economic presence in Malaysia.

With the announcement of Chinese President Xi Jinping's proposed Belt and Road Initiative (Silk Road Economic Belt and 21st-Century Maritime Silk Road) in late 2013, there was a strong push for China's infrastructure companies to "go out." Even before this initiative,

China's infrastructure companies had been increasing their presence in Malaysia. For instance, China Harbour Engineering Company (CHEC) is a major partner in the construction of a 24-kilometer "Second Bridge" linking the island state of Penang with Peninsular Malaysia. The project was partly financed by a 20-year soft loan from Beijing amounting to about RMB3.3 billion. There has been further development in China's participation in Penang's infrastructure. In early October 2013, the Penang state government signed an initial agreement with Consortium Zenith BUCG, a consortium set up by Zenith Construction and the Beijing Urban Construction Group, to undertake mega infrastructure projects in the state of Penang, with the ambitious undersea tunnel project chiefly in mind. In turn, the Consortium signed an agreement with the China Railway Construction Corporation (CRCC), for design, procurement and execution plans. The whole deal amounted to about MYR6.3 billion.[26]

It is also significant to note that during Xi Jinping's 2013 visit to Malaysia, he expressed China's interest in the 330-kilometer high-speed railway (HSR) project linking Kuala Lumpur and Singapore. This project triggered an "HSR diplomatic battle" between China and Japan, which had also been aggressively bidding for railway projects throughout Southeast Asia. However, China seemed to be getting ahead after its state-owned enterprises (SOEs) played a major role in helping the troubled Malaysian government-owned firm, 1Malaysia Development Berhad (1MDB) in late 2015. From November to December 2015, a series of moves saw China's SOEs commit to pumping funds amounting to MYR12.79 billion into 1MDB, including the purchase by China General Nuclear Group of 1MDB's power plant assets, and the purchase by China Railway Engineering Corporation (CREC), in partnership with a local firm, of stakes in the Bandar Malaysia project, a huge urban redevelopment project in Kuala Lumpur.[27] These moves were widely seen as China bailing out 1MDB, which is also closely linked to Malaysian Prime Minister Najib Razak. As a result, it is generally believed that in return, a Chinese company will likely be awarded the HSR project.[28]

In addition, the China Railway and Rolling Stock Corporation, an entity created in 2015 as a result of the merger of two leading railway car manufacturers in China—the China South Locomotive & Rolling Stock Corporation and the the China North Locomotive and Rolling Stock Corporation (CNR)—invested MYR400 million to establish a manufacturing and maintenance center in Malaysia.²⁹ The aim was to turn this center into a hub for the ASEAN market. For its part, the CNR Changchun Railway Vehicles (a subsidiary of the CNR before the merger) entered the Malaysian market in 2014 through its partnership with the Kuala Lumpur International Airport (KLIA), to support the expansion of the high-speed railways operated by KLIA.³⁰

In addition to railway infrastructure, China's infrastructure activities in Malaysia also target port facilities. The MCKIP in part is related to the Port of Kuantan. Besides Kuantan, another important port that has received major investment from China is the Malacca Gateway project, which is located in the strategic Strait of Malacca. During Chinese Premier Li Keqiang's visit to Malaysia in December 2015, he paid a visit to the state of Malacca, underscoring the strategic importance of Malacca in the 21st-Century Maritime Silk Road initiative. The state government of Malacca has so far been highly receptive to China's increasing economic presence in the state. Reportedly, China has committed US$10 billion for projects relating to the expansion of the port, land reclamation and property development.³¹

In addition to the presence of these construction companies, another sector that shows China's increasing economic presence is the property sector. Table 9 provides a general picture of China's growing investment in this sector, most of which is concentrated in Iskandar, a special development region in southern Malaysia and within the state of Johor. Country Garden, a well-known Chinese developer, is one of the most important investors in Iskandar. It formed a joint venture with a local company that is closely linked with the development arm of the Johor state government and the royal house of Johor, in a so-called "Forest City" project that involves "the development of 335 hectares of existing land along the Strait of Johor, close to the Second Link to Singapore, and the Port of Tanjung Pelapis. It also entails the reclamation of another 1,620 hectares of land."³²

Malaysia-China Kuantan Industrial Park

In 2011, Malaysia and China decided to develop and establish two joint industrial parks. The China-Malaysia Qinzhou Industrial Park (CMQIP) was first proposed by then Premier Wen Jiabao during his visit to Malaysia in 2011, and it was accepted by his Malaysian counterpart Najib Razak. The official agreement was signed in Nanning

Table 9 China's Property Developers in Malaysia

Developer	Date	Area	Land Bank (hectares)	Development Plans
Qingdao Zhouyuan Investment Holdings/ Zhouyuan Iskandar	July 2012	Medini (Iskandar)	7.2	2,600 condominium units with US$800 million
Country Garden	December 2012	Danga Bay (Iskandar)	23	US$5.5 billion integrated mixed development, 2,000 hectares land reclamation project
Hao Yuan Investment	November 2013	Danga Bay (Iskandar)	15	US$2.5 billion integrated mixed development
Guangzhou R & F	November 2013	Tanjung Puteri (Iskandar)	46.9	US$1.4 billion integrated mixed development
Macrolink	January 2014	Medini (Iskandar)		Reported deal of US$40 million to develop resort house
Agile Group	January 2014	Petaling Jaya, Kuala Lumpur		US$200 million project in the KL-PJ area
Greenland Group	April 2014	Danga Bay (Iskandar)	5.6	US$3.25 billion integrated mixed development

Source: Elaine Tan, "Chinese Eye Malaysia Real Estate," *China Daily Asia*, May 9, 2014, <http://www.chinadailyasia.com/asiaweekly/2014-05/09/content_15134294.html>; *Real Estate Malaysia*, August 2014, 18.

in October 2011 and the CMQIP was officially launched in April 2012. It was during this launch that both prime ministers agreed to set up a sister industrial park—the Malaysia-China Kuantan Industrial Park (MCKIP).

The CMQIP is the third government-to-government industrial park to be established in China. (The first two industrial parks were the Suzhou Industrial Park and Tianjian Eco-city projects, both jointly sponsored by the Chinese and Singaporean governments.) Qinzhou is a mid-level city in Guangxi, but it occupies a strategic position facing the Beibu Gulf region. With the provincial government of Guangxi gearing up for the Beibu Gulf Economic Region (an ambitious regional developmental plan that features more economic cooperation between Guangxi and Southeast Asia), the importance of Qinzhou City has increased significantly. The CMQIP has a total planned area of 5,499 hectares. It will be developed by a Sino-Malaysian joint venture, Qinzhou Development (Malaysia) Consortium Sdn Bhd and Qinzhou Jingwu Investment Co, Ltd. The Malaysian consortium holds 49 percent of the shares in the joint venture, with the Chinese party holding the rest. The consortium was formed by two Malaysian enterprises—S P Setia and Rimbunan Hijau. The director of the board of this Sino-Malaysian joint venture is the former deputy mayor of the Qinzhou city government, while the CEO is a former official of the Malaysian Minister of International Trade and Industry, underscoring the serious involvement of both governments in the management and operation of the CMQIP. In December 2013, it was reported that five projects, worth a total of MYR4.4 billion, had already entered the park, while an additional 15 projects with a total value of MYR9.6 billion had committed to it.[33]

MCKIP on the other hand, occupies about 607 hectares (1,500 acres). It is located in the East Coast Economic Region (ECER), a planning region that comprises the poorer east coast states in Malaysia. However, it has been reported that a further 324 hectares (800 acres) of land will be given and eventually combined into the MCKIP.[34] The estimated cost for building the MCKIP is US$806 million, from which it hopes to draw in investments of US$24 billion (Khor 2013: 2).[35] Kuantan is a port city facing the South China Sea and is the capital of the state of Pahang (where Prime Minister Najib comes from). It has been identified as the strategic integrated industrial and logistics hub for the ECER. The MCKIP, however, was not officially launched until February 2013 because it took some time for China and Malaysia to sort out the ownership stakes of the joint venture company that will act as the master developer of the MCKIP. A Chinese conglomerate comprising firms affiliated with the Guangxi provincial government and the Qinzhou city government holds 49 percent of the shares of the joint venture, while a Malaysian consortium, Kuantan Pahang Holdings Sdn Bhd, which consists of S P Setia, Rimbunan Hijau, the Pahang state government, and Pahang's own investment arm, has the remaining shares. However, by early 2014 both S P Setia and Rimbunan Hijau had withdrawn from the MCKIP project (although they remain committed to the CMQIP) and sold their stakes in the consortium to IJM, a Malaysian construction company and owner of the Kuantan port,[36] and Sime Darby, a Malaysian GLC heavily involved in palm oil plantations and export.

The government of Malaysia has high hopes that the MCKIP will boost Malaysia-China trade and China's investments in Malaysia. According to the government's plan, the MCKIP will be an integral part of the ECER, and the qualified foreign investments will enjoy preferential treatment, including a ten-year tax exemption period. The industries that were identified as focal industries for the MCKIP include oil, electrical products, plastic and metal, automobile components, steel plates, and renewable energy.[37] Thirty percent of the MCKIP site will feature industries in the service sector, and commercial and residential development. Kuantan's status as the major eastern coastal port of Malaysia also holds a special attraction for the Chinese, who are generally interested in investing in port facilities and management. The development of the MCKIP, therefore, is in tandem with China's investment in the development of Kuantan Port.

According to a recent press statement from the ECER, by March 2016 the MCKIP had attracted a total of MYR13.5 billion in investment, with a further MYR2.48 billion intended investments, mostly coming from Chinese investors.[38] In addition, the Guangxi Beibu International Port Group (owned by the Guangxi government) bought 40 percent ownership of the Kuantan Port (the other 60 percent is owned by IJM), and pledged to invest in and upgrade the port facilities of Kuantan.[39] The total value of investment needed to fully expand the port is about MYR4 billion. The expansion will play a key role in enlarging the shipping businesses of the port.[40] Malaysia also hopes that the transformation of the Kuantan Port will turn it into a logistics hub in the Asia-Pacific region and drive the development of the ECER.[41]

Overseeing the activities and progress of both industrial parks is the Joint Council of the Parks, which consists of delegates from the provincial government of Guangxi, the state government of Pahang, the Ministry of Commerce of China and the Ministry of International Trade and Industry of Malaysia.[42] Malaysia also appointed a special envoy, Ong Ka Ting, a former president of the Malaysian Chinese Association, which is one of the main component parties of the then ruling Barisan Nasional government in Malaysia, to help oversee the construction and operations of the industrial parks. Ong is also the chairman of the Malaysia-China Business Council (MCBC), a quasi-non-government organization that links business circles to the industrial parks, the members of which come almost exclusively from the Chinese business elite and selected retired politicians from the ruling parties. In the coming years, the MCBC will be principally tasked with facilitating investments in the MCKIP and other important projects showcasing Malaysia-China friendship, such as the establishment of the overseas campus of Xiamen University in Malaysia.[43]

It is clear that both governments have invested much in terms of developing the industrial parks as showcase projects of the Malaysia-China friendship. The Malaysian government actively seeks to increase China's economic presence in the country. The following section focuses on some of the political factors that have influenced China's investment in Malaysia.

Politics of China's Economic Presence in Malaysia

Khor (2013) has alluded to some of the factors that have driven the increase in Chinese investment in Malaysia, including China's geopolitical considerations and Malaysia's electoral landscape. Accordingly, Malaysia is keen to seek China's foreign direct investment for the purposes of economic development and industrial and technological upgrading, and the Chinese government has been very supportive of meeting Malaysia's demands. Thus, the number of China's state-owned enterprises investing and operating in Malaysia has increased. Given the recent geopolitical tensions surrounding the East and South China Seas, China is keen to maintain stable relations with Malaysia, and encouraging more investment there is seen as a foreign policy tool. From the Malaysian perspective, maintaining good ties with the Chinese government can also be seen as helping to increase the ethnic Chinese voters' support for the ruling coalition in Malaysia, which suffered significant decline in ethnic Chinese electoral support in the last two general elections (2008 and 2013). As mentioned earlier, Lim has provided an analysis of how the investment environment in Malaysia has been shaped by Malaysia's policy for the GLCs and how this in turn contributes to the selection behavior of China's investing companies.

Khor and Lim have laid out the political push-and-pull factors of China's investment in Malaysia and the policy environment that shapes the behavior of Chinese firms. Here, the analysis focuses on examining the political dimensions influencing the process leading to the implementation and outcome of investment projects in Malaysia.[44] In this section I draw attention to two political dimensions: central-local relations and political-business collusion.

Central-Local Relations

Malaysia is a federal system in which the state governments enjoy a high degree of autonomy, notwithstanding the centralizing trend of the federal government over the years. The central-local (state) dynamics can be seen most clearly in the case of the MCKIP. Originally the Chinese government preferred to locate the MCKIP in the abovementioned Iskandar region. Perhaps it made more business sense in the eyes of the Chinese government given the proximity of the region to prosperous Singapore. However, it was Prime Minister Najib who personally selected Kuantan as the site for the MCKIP. Kuantan is located in Najib's home state of Pahang, a relatively underdeveloped part of Malaysia.[45] Since then, the federal government under Najib has been enthusiastically promoting the MCKIP as the future of China's investment in Malaysia, a building platform to transform the relatively poorer eastern coast of Malaysia, and the symbol of Malaysia-China friendship.

Given such emphasis, one would have expected the MCKIP to progress rapidly. However, as the above discussion of the MCKIP shows, while it has progressed somewhat, it lags significantly behind the CMQIP, its counterpart in China. It has also failed to fulfill the expectations of both the Malaysian and Chinese governments. Information gathered from interviews with insiders reveals that while the federal government is enthusiastic about the project, the Pahang state government's attitude is lackluster. While Najib played a role in the decision to locate the industrial park in Kuantan, it was the state government of Pahang that decided which particular area of Kuantan would house the industrial park. Reportedly, not only was the size of the MCKIP dwarfed by the CMQIP, thus creating a significant disparity between the two, the soil at the site selected for the MCKIP was substandard. The site was originally marshland and in need of embankment, which increased the cost of the investment and deterred prospective investors. In early May 2014, two years after the launch of the MCKIP, the Chinese Ambassador to Malaysia paid a visit to the park and it was reported that all he could see was yellow mud.[46] Pheng Yin Huah, an influential ethnic Chinese business and civic leader in Pahang, implicitly blamed the state government when he urged the state and central governments to work closely in developing the park, particularly in resolving the land issue.[47]

Although investments have picked up since then, the MCKIP's progress is still punishingly slow. The government has announced that investments have been made (as mentioned earlier); however, such investments probably remain at the stage of "letter of investment intent" because reportedly no substantial work has begun at the site. Furthermore, the MCKIP master developer, which is a Sino-Malaysian joint venture, has not yet actually started operations. Its board of directors and CEO positions remain vacant. Whatever infrastructure and investment projects have been undertaken within the MCKIP have been the result of the work of the ECER and Guangxi authorities. The inability of the state and central government bureaucracies to figure out a way of developing the MCKIP has been the principal reason it has failed to achieve most expectations, despite the earnest support given to it by the Malaysian and Chinese governments.

Political-business Collusion

Another dimension of the political aspect of China's economic presence in Malaysia is the complex web of political-business collusion that sometimes involves China's enterprises.

An example is the Gemas–Johor Bahru electrified double-track railway project (EDTP). Unlike the high-speed railway (HSR) project, the EDTP connects Johor Bahru, the southern tip of Peninsular Malaysia, to its northern part. It is divided into different stretches. Some stretches of the railway project were awarded to MMC-Gamuda and Ircon International. The last remaining stretch of about 200 kilometers (the Gemas–Johor Bahru stretch) was finally awarded to a Chinese consortium in 2015. This stretch is reportedly worth MYR8 billion.

The EDTP project has a complicated history. In 2002, the China Railway Engineering Corporation (CREC) was issued a letter of intent by the Malaysian government for this project. However, in 2003 the letter was withdrawn by then Prime Minister Mahathir, who awarded it instead to a local consortium, MMC Gamuda. In 2003, the succeeding prime minister, Abdullah Badawi, scrapped the deal altogether. However, it was revived in 2007, and the CREC resubmitted its bid, this time for the Gemas–Johor Bahru stretch. However, two other Chinese companies also emerged to contend for this project—China Railway Construction Corporation (CRCC) and China Communications Construction Company (CCCC).[48] The CREC and the CRCC are two of the largest construction companies in the world. The CCCC was formed through the merging of China Harbour Engineering Corporation (CHEC), the contracted builder for the Penang Second Bridge, and China Road and Bridge Construction (CRBC) in 2005, but both remain subsidiaries of the parent CCCC. As required by the Malaysian government, all of these companies had to have a local partner to win the project, which apparently complicated the issue as all the local partners were backed by different political and business elites.

During Najib's visit to China in 2009, he personally promised Hu Jintao, China's then president and general secretary of the Communist Party of China, that the Gemas–Johor Bahru project would be awarded to a Chinese company. However, the identity of the company was not decided. Reportedly, the CREC was the frontrunner, and it was working closely with a prominent Malaysian Chinese businessman in the bid for this project. However, in December 2011, the CRBC, now a subsidiary of CCCC, emerged as the likely contractor, "because of some last minute lobbying" in Putrajaya (Malaysia's administrative capital).[49] Prime Minister Najib is alleged to have preferred the CCCC, thanks to the brokering of an ethnic Chinese golfing friend, George Kent, who also happened to be the owner of a construction firm that had won a number of government projects.[50] In the meantime, the participation of the CRCC (which was also involved in the Penang undersea tunnel project) was allegedly facilitated by Daim Zainuddin,[51] the aforementioned former minister and influential insider, and supported by the Sultan of Johor and another prominent Chinese Malaysian businessman. The CRCC's local partner was first reported to be Gamuda. The company is partly owned by the Perak royal family and is a partner in the MMC Gamuda consortium that is building another stretch of the EDTP. In August 2015, the Malaysian media reported that the CRCC would likely be the eventual winner.[52] However, there were conflicting reports with others suggesting that the CREC was the winner. In actual fact, the three rivals (CRCC, CREC and CCCC) have teamed up to form a consortium, which will be led by the CRCC. The identity of the main local partner remains unknown.

Table 10 Competition over the Gemas–Johor Bahru Double-Track Railway Project

Chinese Construction Company	Local Partner	Local Political Support	Notes
China Railway Engineering Corporation (CREC)	Malton	Najib?	The CREC teamed up with Iskandar Waterfront Holdings (IWH) and won the bid to buy stakes in the Bandar Malaysia redevelopment project, likely contender for HSR.
China Communications Construction Company (CCCC)	George Kent	Najib?	Parent company of China Harbour Engineering Corporation (CHEC) and China Road and Bridge Construction (CRBC). The CHEC was earlier involved in the building of the Penang Second Bridge.
China Railway Construction Corporation (CRCC)	Gamuda	Sultan of Johor?	Involved also in the Penang undersea tunnel project.

Given the involvement of so many important political figures, it is not surprising that the whole project has dragged on unnecessarily. Table 10 summarizes the different players involved in the competition for this project.

The Gemas–Johor Bahru EDTP is clearly a case of Chinese investors being entangled in the complex lobbying by different private interests (ethnic Chinese tycoons, royal figures, local construction firms) allied with different actors in the political establishment.

Conclusion

This chapter examines China's economic footprint in Malaysia, which is grounded in a strong bilateral economic relationship. The Malaysian government is determined to attract more investment from China because it is viewed as crucial to the economic development of

Malaysia. China has responded positively, as can be seen in the growing size of China's economic presence in Malaysia, especially in recent years. Furthermore, such growing investment from China can be regarded as a manifestation of China's confidence in and endorsement of the government headed by Prime Minister Najib and his Barisan Nasional coalition, which has been facing strong political opposition in recent years. The MCKIP is also a key strategy for realizing the goal of increasing Chinese investment in Malaysia and it has received committed support from both governments. It symbolizes Malaysia-China friendship and is the brainchild of two heads of government—Malaysia's Najib and China's Wen Jiabao. In this sense, China's growing economic presence in Malaysia is also very much a process driven by elites (political and commercial) and perhaps augmented by personal or guanxi ties. Because of these elite links, it can be seen that most of the economic players from China appear to be big companies; only a small number of SMEs have invested in Malaysia.

China's growing economic soft footprint in Malaysia is thus a result of Malaysia's active courtship of Chinese investment and China's positive responses to such courtship. The elite-driven nature of such investment, however, means that beyond purely economic considerations, domestic political factors can also have easily shaped China's economic influence in Malaysia. This chapter has used an analytical perspective that is focused particularly on the domestic Malaysian bureaucratic and political factors, namely central-local relations and political-business collusions, to explain the slow progress of the MCKIP and the protracted process of awarding a stretch of railway project to competing Chinese companies, which found themselves aligned with different sets of political-business ties in Malaysia.

Notes

1. Mahathir Mohamad, *A New Deal for Asia* (Subang Jaya, Selangor: Pelanduk Publications, 1999), 82.
2. Khor Yu Leng, "The Significance of China-Malaysia Industrial Parks," *ISEAS Perspective* 37 (June 17, 2013).
3. Guanie Lim, "The Internationalisation of Mainland Chinese Firms into Malaysia: From Obligated Embeddedness to Active Embeddedness," *Journal of Current Southeast Asian Affairs* 33, no. 2 (2014): 59–90; Guanie Lim, "China's Investments in Malaysia: Choosing the 'Right' Partners," *International Journal of China Studies* 6, no. 1 (2015): 1–30.

4. Andrew Mertha, *Brothers in Arms: Chinese Aid to the Khmer Rouge, 1975-1979* (Ithaca, NY: Cornell University Press, 2014).
5. Lee Poh Ping and Lee Kam Hing, "Malaysia-China Relations: A Review," in *Malaysia, Southeast Asia, and the Emerging China: Political, Economic and Cultural Perspectives*, ed. Hou Kok Chung and Yeoh Kok-Kheng, 3-28 (Kuala Lumpur: Institute of China Studies, University of Malaya, 2003), 13.
6. Ho Khai Leong, "Recent Developments in the Political Economy of China-Malaysia Relations," in *Southeast Asian Chinese and China: The Politico-Economic Dimension*, ed. Leo Suryadinata, 230-48 (Singapore: Times Academic Press, 1995), 230.
7. Kwek Kian-Teng and Tham Siew-Yean, "Trade between Malaysia and China: Opportunities and Challenges for Growh," in *Emerging Trading Nation in an Integrating World: Global Impacts and Domestic Challenges of China's Economic Reform*, ed. Emile Kok-Kheng Yeoh and Evelyn Devadason, 123-37 (Kuala Lumpur: Institute of China Studies, University of Malaya, 2007).
8. Evelyn Devadason, "Malaysia-China Trade Patterns in Manufactures: How Big is Production Sharing?" in *Emerging Trading Nation in an Integrating World: Global Impacts and Domestic Challenges of China's Economic Reform*, ed. Emile Kok-Kheng Yeoh and Evelyn Devadason, 138-52 (Kuala Lumpur: Institute of China Studies, University of Malaya, 2007).
9. Liao Shaolian, "Sino-Malaysian Economic Relations: Retrospect and Prospects," in *Malaysia and Sino-Malaysian Relations in a Changing World*, ed. Liao Shaolian, 187-97 (Xiamen: Xiamen University Press, 2008), 195; Mustafa Rujhan and Rugayah Mohamed, "The Impact of the Rise of China and Regional Economic Integration: A Malaysian Perspective," in *Malaysia and Sino-Malaysian Relations in a Changing World*, ed. Liao Shaolian, 283-306 (Xiamen: Xiamen University Press, 2008), 301.
10. *Nanyang Business Daily*, A19, December 27, 2010.
11. *Oriental Daily News*, A1-A3, November 24, 2015.
12. *Nanyang Business Daily*, A1, February 23, 2010.
13. *Oriental Daily News*, B4, November 19, 2013.
14. *Sinchew Daily*, A1, November 11, 2014.
15. *Nanyang Business Daily*, A5, January 6, 2015.
16. *Sinchew Daily*, A13, August 8, 2015; *Sinchew Daily*, A19, August 29, 2015.
17. *Nanyang Business Daily*, A2, August 17, 2013.
18. *Sinchew Daily*, A7, February 2, 2016.
19. See Lin Youshun, "Zhonogguo youke Dama mianqian quexu fufei" [Chinese Tourists' Visa Waived, Yet Required to Pay Processing Fees], *Yazhou Zhoukan* 30, no. 2 (March 27, 2016): 18.
20. Zheng Da, "On Malaysian Chinese Businessmen's Invesments on Mainland China, 1984-2010" (PhD diss., Xiamen University, 2011), 66.

21. Edmund Terence Gomez, "Chinese Network and Enterprise Development: Malaysian Investments in China," *Journal of Contemporary Asia* 36, no. 3 (2006): 350–63.
22. Lee Kam Hing, "Malaysia-China Economic Relations: 2000–2010," in *China and East Asia: After the Wall Street Crisis*, ed. Lam Peng Er, Qin Yaqing, and Yang Mu, 241–76 (Singapore: World Scientific, 2013), 258–9.
23. *Nanyang Business Daily*, A1, March 4, 2015.
24. Zheng Da, "On Malaysian Chinese Businessmen's Invesments on Mainland China, 1984–2010", 68.
25. Two Hong Kong companies in the list are excluded.
26. *Oriental Daily News*, A13, October 7, 2013.
27. *The Starbiz*, January 1, 2016, 1, 3; *The Starbiz*, January 2, 2016, 13.
28. *The Star*, April 3, 2016, 20–1.
29. Jiang Xun, "Zhongguo gaotie waijiao kangheng Riben zai Dongnanya shili" [China's Railway Diplomacy Resisting Japan's Influence in Southeast Asia], *Yazhou Zhoukan* 27, no. 41 (October 20, 2013): 22–29.
30. *Nanyang Business Daily*, A4, November 26, 2014.
31. *The Star*, November 8, 2015, 4.
32. *The Edge Financial Daily*, January 15, 2015, 5; see also *The Star*, March 23, 2016, 16.
33. *Nanyang Business Daily*, A3, December 4, 2013.
34. *Nanyang Business Daily*, A3, July 16, 2013.
35. Khor Yu Leng, "The Significance of China-Malaysia Industrial Parks," *ISEAS Perspective* 37 (June 17, 2013).
36. *Oriental Daily News*, A8, February 11, 2014.
37. *Nanyang Business Daily*, A3, June 18, 2012.
38. *Sinchew Daily*, A14, March 29, 2016.
39. *New Straits Times*, B3, October 5, 2013.
40. *New Straits Times*, B3, April 6, 2016.
41. *Nanyang Business Daily*, A3, September 8, 2013.
42. Interview with an official of the Malaysia-China Business Council, October 1, 2013.
43. Malaysia-China Business Council, *Report of Activities 2012–2013*, n.d.
44. Andrew Mertha, *Brothers in Arms: Chinese Aid to the Khmer Rouge, 1975–1979* (Ithaca, NY: Cornell University Press, 2014).
45. *Nanyang Business Daily*, A9, December 3, 2013.
46. *Nanyang Business Daily*, A4, May 28, 2014.
47. *Nanyang Business Daily*, A5, December 8, 2014.
48. *South China Morning Post*, Business Section 4, January 16, 2012.
49. Jahabar Sadiq, "Putrajaya Contracts Gemas-JB Double Track to Chinese Firm," *The Malaysian Insider*, December 27, 2011, <http://www.themalaysianinsider.com/malaysia/article/putrajaya-contracts-gemas-jb-double-track-to-chinese-firm> (accessed April 15, 2014).

50. Jose Barrock, "Warlords Battling for RM8 bil Gemas-JB Rail Job," *Kinibiz*, March 11, 2013, <http://www.kinibiz.com/story/corporate/8124/%E2%80%98warlords%E2%80%99-battling-for-rm8-bil-gemas-jb-rail-job.html> (accessed April 15, 2014).
51. *South China Morning Post*, Business Section 4, January 16, 2012.
52. The national press agency Bernama first erroneously reported the winner to be China Railway, the national rail operator in China, an altogether different company from the CRCC.

References

Devadason, Evelyn. "Malaysia-China Trade Patterns in Manufactures: How Big is Production Sharing?" In *Emerging Trading Nation in an Integrating World: Global Impacts and Domestic Challenges of China's Economic Reform*, edited by Emile Kok-Kheng Yeoh and Evelyn Devadason, 138-52. Kuala Lumpur: Institute of China Studies, University of Malaya, 2007.

Gomez, Edmund Terence. "Chinese Network and Enterprise Development: Malaysian Investments in China." *Journal of Contemporary Asia* 36, no. 3 (2006): 350-63.

Ho, Khai Leong. "Recent Developments in the Political Economy of China-Malaysia Relations." In *Southeast Asian Chinese and China: The Politico-Economic Dimension*, edited by Leo Suryadinata, 230-48. Singapore: Times Academic Press, 1995.

Jiang, Xun. "Zhongguo gaotie waijiao kangheng Riben zai Dongnanya shili" [China's Railway Diplomacy Resisting Japan's Influence in Southeast Asia]. *Yazhou Zhoukan* 27, no. 41 (October 20, 2013): 22-9.

Khor, Yu Leng. "The Significance of China-Malaysia Industrial Parks." *ISEAS Perspective* 37 (June 17, 2013).

Lee Kam Hing. "Malaysia-China Economic Relations: 2000-2010." In *China and East Asia: After the Wall Street Crisis*, edited by Lam Peng Er, Qin Yaqing, and Yang Mu, 241-76. Singapore: World Scientific, 2013.

Lee Poh Ping and Lee Kam Hing. "Malaysia-China Relations: A Review." In *Malaysia, Southeast Asia, and the Emerging China: Political, Economic and Cultural Perspectives*, edited by Hou Kok Chung and Yeoh Kok-Kheng, 3-28. Kuala Lumpur: Institute of China Studies, University of Malaya, 2003.

Liao, Shaolian. "Sino-Malaysian Economic Relations: Retrospect and Prospects." In *Malaysia and Sino-Malaysian Relations in a Changing World*, edited by Liao Shaolian, 187-97. Xiamen: Xiamen University Press, 2008.

Lim, Guanie. "The Internationalisation of Mainland Chinese Firms into Malaysia: From Obligated Embeddedness to Active Embeddedness." *Journal of Current Southeast Asian Affairs* 33, no. 2 (2014): 59-90.

⸻. "China's Investments in Malaysia: Choosing the 'Right' Partners." *International Journal of China Studies* 6, no. 1 (2015): 1-30.

Lin, Youshun. "Zhonogguo youke Dama mianqian quexu fufei" [Chinese Tourists' Visa Waived, Yet Required to Pay Processing Fees]. *Yazhou Zhoukan* 30, no. 2 (March 27, 2016): 18.

Mahathir, Mohamad. *A New Deal for Asia*. Subang Jaya, Selangor: Pelanduk Publications, 1999.

Mertha, Andrew. *Brothers in Arms: Chinese Aid to the Khmer Rouge, 1975–1979*. Ithaca, NY: Cornell University Press, 2014.

Mustafa, Rujhan and Rugayah Mohamed. "The Impact of the Rise of China and Regional Economic Integration: A Malaysian Perspective." In *Malaysia and Sino-Malaysian Relations in a Changing World*, edited by Liao Shaolian, 283–306. Xiamen: Xiamen University Press, 2008.

Zheng, Da. "On Malaysian Chinese Businessmen's Invesments on Mainland China, 1984–2010." PhD diss., Xiamen University, 2011.

CHAPTER 5

Producing Power: China-Indonesia Cooperation in the Fast Track Program I

Natalia Soebagjo

Introduction

China's current interest in funding and participating in overseas projects can be traced back to 2000, when the Chinese government initiated its "Going Out" strategy in response to a call from the 5th Plenary Session of the 15th Congress of the Communist Party of China (CPC) to increase the country's economic growth. This strategy involved a two-pronged approach that encouraged:

- Chinese state-owned enterprises (SOEs) to become involved in overseas infrastructure projects and projects for the extraction, processing and trading of natural resources; and
- Chinese banks to invest in overseas projects, especially those involving Chinese companies.

By 2010, outward investment flows from China (excluding Hong Kong) reached US$69 billion, making the country the world's fourth-largest outward investor. China's outward foreign direct investment (FDI) stock amounted to US$298 billion invested in more than 34,000 foreign affiliates and controlled by about 12,000 Chinese parent companies.[1]

Although Chinese investments in ASEAN constituted only 6.5 percent of its FDI between 2011 and 2013, China has become Indonesia's eighth-largest foreign investor in response to Indonesia's calls for overseas companies and investments to develop its infrastructure. China's realized investments, however, only reached US$800 million for 501 projects in 2014.[2] Despite China being a significant potential investor in Indonesia, there have been no systematic studies made of Chinese FDI in Indonesia except Gammeltoft and Tarmidi's 2013 research which focuses on the manufacturing sector, primarily the automotive and motorcycle industries, the sectors most attractive to the Chinese in 2008 when the authors carried out their research.[3] The study notes that besides manufacturing, Indonesian companies and their Chinese investment partners are becoming increasingly involved in construction and engineering projects that are crucial to Indonesia's economic growth. The authors caution that for this reason it is necessary to understand Chinese companies' investment motives, operational strategies and ability to cooperate with Indonesian partners in order to evaluate these companies' potential to contribute positively to the success of important development projects.[4]

How seriously should Indonesian project planners and managers take Gammeltoft and Tarmidi's caution? This chapter suggests that planners and managers should take this caution very seriously, based on its analysis of the planning and implementation of the Fast Track Program Phase I (FTP-I), a project intended to increase power plant capacity to meet the growing electricity needs of Indonesian households, industries and businesses. The chapter argues that the FTP-I project suffered procurement issues, financing problems and delays for two reasons:

- Indonesian government officials and project managers failed to develop a tendering process that would ensure that only companies with the experience and capacity to complete their parts in the FTP-I would be chosen to bid; and
- they were slow to develop an oversight process for identifying and resolving logistical problems in order to avoid costly delays.

The paper argues that proposals put forward by FTP-I planners for developing a more robust oversight process are likely to be ineffective unless:

- they have sufficient understanding of the economic, political and social milieu underlying the practices of Chinese construction companies and banks; and
- they clearly articulate the practices Indonesia expects from overseas and local companies participating in crucial development projects.

Building an oversight process from these two conditions will allow project initiators and planners to develop criteria for ascertaining which companies have the experience and capacity to complete a project successfully and to develop courses of action to respond to financing and logistical problems before they lead to serious consequences.

However, how important are robust oversight processes? This chapter suggests that they are absolutely vital because they avoid situations like the following. A decade after negotiations for the FTP-I began in 2005, the project is still only 90 percent complete and running at only 35 to 50 percent capacity. During his visit to China in March 2015, President Joko Widodo conveyed the Indonesian government's disappointment with the FTP-I to the Chinese government, which prompted a review of the project implementation. The Chinese government has acknowledged the project's low quality and is assuming responsibility for it by offering to buy back the power plants and make the necessary repairs. After the buy-back, the state-owned power company, PT Perusahaan Listrik Negara (PT PLN) would then lease the plants from the Chinese.[5] This gesture of goodwill, however, was ultimately not taken up.

Planning the FTP-I: Rationale, Goals and Organization of the Project

In 2005, Indonesia faced an energy crisis. The country's total electricity supply was about 25,000 megawatts (MW), 78 percent of which was concentrated in Java and Bali. About 30 percent of the supply was produced using petroleum, which had become increasingly expensive. That year, for instance, the government spent IDR50.3 trillion for fuel alone. A solution was needed to meet the demand for electricity and deal with the rising cost of fuel without increasing the consumer price for electricity. Coal-fired plants were an alternative as they could produce electricity cheaply at only IDR132/kilowatt-hour (kWh) compared to IDR611/kWh by oil-fired plants. Consequently, the government decided to implement FTP-I, a crash program to produce an additional 10,000 MW of electricity using coal.

In March 2006, Indonesian Vice President Jusuf Kalla called for a meeting at the head office of PT PLN. At the two-hour meeting, Jusuf Kalla discussed with management the energy crisis and the challenges faced by the government. PT PLN was running a deficit of IDR27 trillion,[6] but even with a government subsidy of IDR17 trillion there was a shortfall of IDR10 trillion. Several options were put forward involving the government increasing the subsidy or raising the price of electricity. However, Jusuf Kalla suggested that the company improve its efficiency by reducing the use of fuel through the adoption of other alternatives such as gas and coal.[7]

A month later, between April 18 and 22, 2006, Jusuf Kalla visited Shanghai, Shenzhen and Haikou. His high-level entourage included the Minister of Energy and Mineral Resources, the Minister of Transportation, the Minister of State-Owned Enterprises, the head of the Investment Coordinating Board, the chair of the Indonesian Chamber of Commerce and Industry, and legislators chairing Commission VII in charge of energy and natural resources and Commission VI in charge of trade, investments and SOEs. Besides cabinet ministers and legislators, governors from three key provinces —Jakarta, West Java and Central Java—were included. CEOs of the following state-owned companies were present: PT Jasa Marga (a toll road operator); PT Wijaya Karya (a construction company); PT Garuda Airlines (the national airline); and PT Perusahaan Listrik Negara (the power company). The only private company included was Bank Mega, which was represented by its CEO, Chairul Tanjung. Despite the high caliber of the delegation, Beijing was not on the itinerary and no meetings were held with senior Chinese government officials.[8]

During the visit, PT PLN signed memorandums of understanding with four consortia led by major Chinese SOEs administered by the State-Owned Assets Supervision and Administration Commission of the State Council (SASAC): China National Machinery Import and Export Corporation (CMC); China National Technical Import and Export Corporation (CNTIC); China National Machinery and Equipment Import and Export Corporation (CMEC); and China Huadian Corporation (CHD).

PT PLN is Indonesia's biggest SOE in terms of asset size, and it is wholly owned by the government. It provides all the public electricity and electricity infrastructure in Indonesia, including power generation, transmission, distribution, construction of power plants and retail sales. It controls 83 percent of Indonesia's total generating capacity, owns and operates 1,546 power plants across the country, and is the main buyer of electricity produced by independent power producers. It is also the sole distributor of electricity to approximately 52 million customers. To provide electricity to the people, the government subsidizes PT PLN to cover the shortfall between the price charged for the electricity and the cost of producing it.

In May 2006, a follow-up meeting was held in the vice president's office, attended by Indonesia's Ambassador to China, the Coordinating Minister for Economic Affairs, the Minister for Energy and Natural Resources, the Minister for SOEs, and the senior management of PT PLN. It was reported that out of the four consortia, only CNTIC submitted a preliminary proposal to build a plant with an 8,000-MW capacity at the lower than the normal rate of US$1 million/MW. Participating in the consortium were Dongfang Electric Corporation, Harbin Power Equipment Co. Ltd., and Shanghai Electric Corporation Ltd.[9]

In July 2006, President Susilo Bambang Yudhoyono issued Presidential Regulation No. 71/2006, which gave PT PLN the mandate to build coal-fired plants. A total of 40 projects were identified, 10 of which were located in Java, for a total of 80 plants (a power plant can have several units). The capacity of the 20 units in Java ranged from 300 MW to 700 MW, while those outside Java were smaller, ranging from 5 MW to 150 MW. The aggregate capacity of the ten locations in Java and Bali would be 6,900 MW while those outside Java and Bali would be 1,852 MW, or a total of 8,752 MW. The presidential regulation specified that all the plants and transmission systems had to be operational by December 2009. Projects financed with unconditional funds would be tendered through open bidding while those with conditional funds would be awarded through direct appointment. Environmental impact assessments and land procurement had to be done within 120 days based on the principles of efficiency, effectiveness, transparency, fairness and accountability. Wherever possible, Indonesian-produced materials were to be used on the condition that they met quality standards and competitive pricing. PT PLN would submit monthly reports to the Minister of SOEs, Minister of Finance, and the Minister of Energy and Natural Resources. The Minister of SOEs would be responsible for oversight. A Tim Koordinasi Percepatan Pembangunan Pembangkit Tenaga Listrik

(Coordinating Team for the Acceleration of Power Plant Construction) was formed and given the responsibility of resolving inter-ministerial bottlenecks and setting new timetables to adjust for delays. The chair of this team was the Coordinating Minister of Economic Affairs and the team members were the ministers of Finance, Energy and Mineral Resources, SOEs, and the National Development Planning Agency.[10]

When it became clear towards the end of 2009 that PT PLN and the contractors could not meet the December 2009 deadline, a new Presidential Regulation No. 59/2009 was issued extending the deadline to December 31, 2014 for the plants outside Java and Bali. Two more projects were added to build four 100-MW plants in Riau Province and four 100-MW plants in East Kalimantan. In July 2011, the regulation was again revised stating that the transmission systems also had to be developed. The Coordinating Team was disbanded and its responsibilities were passed directly to the implementing ministers without involving the Coordinating Minister of Economic Affairs.[11]

In the end, 36 engineering, procurement and contract (EPC) agreements were signed to build plants in ten locations in Java and Bali that would produce a combined total of 7,500 KW of electrical energy, and plants in 22 locations in Sumatra and Eastern Indonesia that would produce a combined total of 2,400 KW. All the tenders to build the plants in Java, except for a two-unit plant in Rembang in Central Java, were awarded to Chinese companies in partnership with local companies. The majority of the tenders for smaller plants outside Java were also awarded to Chinese companies, while contracts for four small capacity units in Riau were terminated and the contract for Timika, Papua was not finalized until 2013.

Total funding for the FTP-I was estimated at US$5.8 billion and IDR32.4 trillion, of which 15 percent would be covered by global bonds issued in 2006 and 2007 while the rest would be covered by domestic and international loans.[12]

The first batch of contracts with Chinese companies was signed on March 12, 2007 for seven power plants to be commercially operational by either July 2009 or January 2010. In the following month (April 2007), construction began on the two 315-MW units of the power plants in Labuan, Banten, West Java. The project was a sizable one. Valued at IDR1.25 trillion, its construction required a workforce of 1,700 people, and 300 to 400 people would be needed to operate it once it was completed. At the groundbreaking ceremony, the Minister of SOEs, Sugiharto, pointed out that, "The success of the project will make this the role model for the construction of other power plants in the Fast Track 10,000-MW project."[13]

Providing Power

The implementation of the FTP-I faced several obstacles, which led to delays in the delivery of fully operational electric plants. Lip service was given to the principles of good governance. Transparency and accountability had to be implemented in the procurement process, especially since the management of PT PLN was under scrutiny for alleged corruption. Technical standards had to be met, and, most importantly, financing had to be in place. However in the end, the urgency of meeting the rising demand for electricity caused good preparation and planning to be put aside in favor of speedily implementing the FTP-I.

The Procurement Process

The procurement process was an open, two-step tendering procedure. The first step required companies to fulfill certain technical and administrative criteria before submitting bids, while the second step required companies to bid against each other to ensure that Indonesia got the lowest price for the satisfactory completion of the FTP-I. However, from the onset the procurement process was flawed in three ways.

First as previously discussed, Chinese companies were the Indonesian government's preferred builders of the FTP-I power plants before the procurement process started because of these companies' proven abilities to meet China's much higher demand for power (up to 100,000 MW per year) as opposed to Indonesia's lower demand for electricity which was growing at an average of 3,000 MW per year. The Indonesian government's preference for Chinese companies was clearly stated by Fahmi Mochtar, the president director of PT PLN at the time. During the 42nd Annual Asian Development Bank Meeting in Bali, he said that 10,000-MW power plants are commonly found in China and Chinese companies could easily construct power plants capable of generating 15,000 MW, implying that the FTP-I project in Indonesia would not be too difficult for them to execute.[14]

Second, the integrity of the tendering process was questionable given the terms and conditions in the government's criteria, which were seemingly formulated to be unattractive to established power plant builders outside China. In evaluating the bids, the government focused on competitive pricing, the competency to build, the speed of construction, and the financing scheme offered. As a result, when the tender procedure for the plants in Java and Bali began, there were only a few interested parties.

In August 2006, the Coordinating Team for the Acceleration of Power Plant Construction noted that out of the 24 companies that submitted pre-qualification tender documents for building 300- to 400-MW plants, 17 were Chinese companies. Of the 19 companies that qualified to build 600- to 700-MW power plants, 10 were Chinese.[15] The Chinese companies responded to the concerns of the Indonesian government by agreeing to:

- undertake the projects according to the terms set by the government;
- build the power plants at the indicative price of US$700,000/MW, which was about 30 percent lower than the normal rate; and
- complete the 300-MW plants within 30 months and the 600-MW plants within 36 months.[16]

Moreover, the Chinese government was willing to provide export credits at competitive rates.[17] The low cost and the tight schedule to which the Chinese companies committed precluded other companies from participating.[18] Besides the price, those who withdrew also cited the lack of clarity regarding the extent of government support, the availability of funding and clear procedures for land acquisition. Government support entailed not only providing a clear subsidy mechanism and the timely and adequate payment of subsidies, but also better coordination between ministries, particularly in licensing and land acquisition. The companies also raised the fact that 36 months was too short a time to construct 600-MW plants given the condition of the locations. At least 40 months would be needed.[19]

The third way in which the procurement process was flawed involved the bidding procedure. By October 2006, the 19 companies that had expressed an interest in building 700-MW power plants in Java and the 24 companies that had expressed interest in building 300- to 400-MW plants, were ready to begin the tendering process. The Indonesian government required each proposed plant to have at least three bids; otherwise it would have to be retendered. Table 1 shows the number of bids for each proposed plant.

Table 1 Number of Bids Submitted for the Java Projects

	Plant	Plant Size	Number of Bids
1	PLTU Suralaya Banten, West Java	625 MW	4
2	PLTU Paiton East Java	660 MW	6
3	PLTU Labuan Banten	600 MW	5
4	PLTU Indramayu West Java	990 MW	4
5	PLTU Rembang Central Java	630 MW	4
6	PLTU Tanjung Awar-awar Tuban, East Java	700 MW	4
7	PLTU Adipala Tanjung Jati Central Java	660 MW	2
8	PLTU Pelabuhan Ratu West Java	1050 MW	2
9	PLTU Lontar Teluk Naga Banten, West Java	945 MW	2
10	PLTU Pacitan East Java	630 MW	2

Plants that had less than three bids had to re-do the tender process. Companies were allowed to re-submit their bids if they had passed the pre-qualification stage. This delayed the tendering process.

Other delays arose from alleged irregularities in the bidding process. For example, the Coordinating Team for the Acceleration of Power Plant Construction had asked the Attorney General's Office to look into the bidding process for the 300- to 400-MW plants and provide a legal opinion verifying that the process was in order and in accordance with the Presidential Regulation No. 8/2006 on Procurement of Public Goods and Services. The Coordinating Team was concerned because of the several consortia participating in each project that had passed the administrative and technical screening process, only one consortium per project had gone on to the next stage of posting a bid bond.[20] This meant that there was no competitive bidding process. In the end, the contracts were still awarded to these consortia, with only one contract won by a non-Chinese consortium.[21] The Chinese EPC contractors who were awarded the projects in Java included some of China's biggest electrical engineering equipment manufacturers. However, there was little information about the capacity and credibility of their local partners and subcontractors. The exception is PT Truba Alam Manunggal Engineering Tbk, which is a publicly listed company on the Indonesian Stock Exchange whose affiliates are involved in several plants, including Labuan and Pelabuhan Ratu. Table 2 outlines the results of the procurement process.

Table 2 Contracts Awarded for the Java Projects

	Plant	EPC Contractors	Plant Size	Estimated/Realized Commercial Operational Dates
1	PLTU Suralaya	CNTIC consortium (China Nat'l Technical I&E Corp, China Nat'l. Machinery I&E Corp, Zhejiang Electric Power Design Institute) & PT Rekayasa Industri	625 MW	August 22, 2011
2	PLTU Paiton	Harbin Power Engineering Co. Ltd consortium & PT Mitra Selaras	660 MW	June 25, 2012
3	PLTU Labuan	Chengda Engineering Corp of China consortium and PT Truba Jurong Engineering	600 MW	Unit 1: October 29, 2009 Unit 2: April 15, 2010
4	PLTU Indramayu	Joint operation of Sinomach, CNEEC & PT Penta Adi Samudra	990 MW	Unit 1: January 29, 2011 Unit 2: March 23, 2011 Unit 3: September 15, 2011
5	PLTU Rembang	Zelan Holding Sdn Bhd, Tronoh Consolidated Malaysia and PT Priamanaya	630 MW	December 10, 2011
6	PLTU Tanjung Awar-awar	Joint operation of Sinomach, CNEEC & PT Penta Adi Samudra	700 MW	Unit 1: January 24, 2014 Unit 2: August 1, 2014
7	PLTU Adipala Tanjung Jati	CNTIC, Shanghai Electric, PT Cahaya Mulia & PT Bajradaya Sentranusa	660 MW	October 2015
8	PLTU Pelabuhan Ratu	Shanghai Electric & PT Maxima (subsidiary of PT Truba Alam Manunggal Engineering Tbk)	700 MW	Unit 1: August 26, 2013 Unit 2: January 27, 2014 Unit 3: January 21, 2014
9	PLTU Lontar Teluk Naga	Dongfang Electric Corp & PT Dalle Energy Batam	945 MW	Unit 1: December 28, 2011 Unit 2: February 29, 2012 Unit 3: April 10, 2012
10	PLTU Pacitan	Dongfang Electric Corp & PT Dalle Energy Batam	630 MW	Unit 1: August 2012 Unit 2: December 2012

Source: 2013 PT PLN Annual Report.

At the end of 2013, the construction of these coal-fired plants under the FTP-I was only 64 percent complete, and it appears that the target of 10,000MW was not fully achieved. In late 2016, for instance, President Joko Widodo himself noted that there were 34 power plants built under Yudhoyono's FTP-I which were idle and thus placed under review.[22] There was also some talk about the Komisi Pemberantasan Korupsi (KPK, Anti-Corruption Agency) opening an investigation of these projects, pending reports from the state Audit Board.[23]

The Problem of Financing

After Presidential Regulation No. 71/2006 was signed, Vice President Jusuf Kalla requested a letter of acknowledgement from Indonesian Finance Minister Sri Mulyani Indrawati to guarantee PT PLN's loan. At the time, the Export-Import Bank of China (Exim Bank) and China Development Bank had agreed to provide a loan of US$4 billion to finance PT PLN's initial investment of US$5.7 billion for the FTP-I on condition that Chinese contractors would be used. Without the guarantee, the Chinese banks would not provide the loans. It was reported that Sri Mulyani as well as Boediono, the Coordinating Minister for Economic Affairs, were reluctant to issue the letter as it was against Presidential Decree No. 59/1972, which prohibits the government from guaranteeing loans secured by corporations, regardless of whether they are privately or state-owned. The finance minister would only issue such a letter if authorized to do so by the president. In October 2006, the president issued Presidential Regulation No. 86/2006, which guaranteed the export credits provided by Chinese banks specifically for the FTP-I, stating that it was an exception to Presidential Decree No. 59/1972.

The first time China financed a PT PLN project was in 2003 when, according to PT PLN's head of corporate finance, the Chinese government provided soft loans in the amount of IDR1.5 trillion (US$166 million) for the 230-MW Labuhan Angin power plant in North Sumatra. The loan was small in comparison to the total loans secured by PT PLN at the time. However by 2008, PT PLN had increased its exposure to China significantly when the Exim Bank, the Bank of China, and China Development Bank agreed to provide IDR40.58 trillion, which constituted approximately 45 percent of the total IDR89.91 trillion investment required for the FTP-I.[24]

At the time, the world was suffering from the global financial crisis of 2008 and PT PLN suffered foreign exchange losses due to the fall in the IDR-to-USD exchange rate. Its revenues were in Indonesian rupiah while its operational costs were mostly in US dollars. Additionally, PT PLN's creditors were slow in processing and disbursing loans, forcing the company to use its cash reserves, which were meant to cover its operational costs. As a result, it had to rearrange its priorities and evaluate its investment plans. In 2008, PT PLN was able to secure credit facilities from several banks to finance 85 percent of the EPC contracts. Exim Bank agreed to provide a maximum loan facility of US$284.3 million, a 15-year loan for PLTU 1 Suralaya in Banten, and a US$330.8 million for PLTU 2 Paiton, East Java at the rate of 0.84% + LIBOR semi-annually. The loans had credit terms that included a credit availability period of 36 months and were fully guaranteed by the Indonesian government, with PT PLN having to fulfill certain general covenants.[25]

However, problems began to surface. In January 2009, China Development Bank pulled out of financing a power plant in South Sulawesi sponsored by PT Bosowa Corp, the major business group owned by the brother-in-law of Vice President Jusuf Kalla. In the following month, the disbursement of most of the loans for the FTP-I were postponed, and it was reported that the financing deal between the Chinese banks and PT PLN could be cancelled. The stakes were high because if the financing were delayed or cancelled, Indonesia's power supply could drop between 20 to 30 percent.[26]

Despite the previously signed contracts, the Chinese banks asked for an increase in the interest rates, citing liquidity problems as the reason. This was, however, not the only reason for the delay. Sometime in February, a dispute between the Indonesian state-owned PT Merpati Nusantara Airlines and Xi'an Aircraft Industry came to a head. Two years earlier, Merpati had signed a purchase order for 15 Xinzhou-60 aircraft at US$15 million each, financed by a concessional loan from the Exim Bank. After delivery of only two aircraft, financial problems forced Merpati to seek a new deal. At most they could afford eight aircraft at a re-negotiated price. Xi'an threatened to take Merpati to court. In a hearing at the House of Representatives, the Minister of Energy and Natural Resources reported that the governments of Indonesia and China were holding each other hostage. Unless the dispute between Merpati and Xi'an was settled, the Chinese banks would not go ahead with the financing for the FTP-I.[27]

Acting Coordinating Minister for Economic Affairs Sri Mulyani flew to China at the end of March, bringing with her a letter from President Yudhoyono to President Hu Jintao in order to resolve the impasse.[28] By May 2009, it was reported that the dispute with Merpati had been resolved and that the Exim Bank was providing an additional 15-year maturity loan of US$606 million for power plants in Pelabuhan Ratu and Aceh with a three-year grace period, while the Bank of China was providing a 13-year maturity loan of US$455 million for the plants in Teluk Naga.[29] Sri Mulyani also asked PT PLN to consider using RMB-denominated loans instead of US dollar-denominated loans in the procurement of goods from China, considering that the countries had signed a bilateral currency swap agreement.

In June, another issue arose which caught PT PLN off guard. *Caijing*, a well-respected Chinese financial magazine, reported that Shanghai Electric was going to sue PT PLN for allegedly not honoring a contract signed in 2007 for the construction of a US$100 million power plant in West Java.[30] Although the article did not name the plant, and officials from both PT PLN and Shanghai Electric would not elaborate on the matter, the news report reflected the problems that Chinese and Indonesian companies faced in doing business together.

Although PT PLN had difficulties with the Chinese banks in securing and drawing down the loans, between 1997 and 2009 China became an important source of funding. During those years, PT PLN's total financing commitments amounted to IDR183,288 trillion, in the form of bonds, both foreign and domestic. Approximately 23 percent of the total was funded by the Chinese, making Chinese banks PT PLN's biggest lenders.[31]

Technical Aspects, Logistical Problems and Mismatched Expectations

The FTP-I was a high-stakes project given its scope and PT PLN's dependence on Chinese companies. The FTP-I was expected to meet almost 25 percent (10,000 MW) of Indonesian's total national power generation (44,000 MW). However, when negotiations began, the FTP-I initiators and planners gave little thought to the technical aspects of the FTP-I projects. They were primarily concerned with choosing contractors who could meet the Indonesian government's terms and conditions, which focused on price and speed of construction. The choice of Chinese contractors proved unfortunate for several reasons.

First, PT PLN had considerable experience with Japanese and European technology but very limited experience with Chinese technology. PT PLN and its Chinese partners were also unfamiliar with each other's way of working.

Second, PT PLN assumed its Chinese partners understood and would honor the obligations of entering into engineering, procurement and construction (EPC) contracts. These contracts are standard for turnkey projects the size of the FTP-I. They obligate contractors to deliver a complete facility at a guaranteed price, by a guaranteed date, operating at an agreed-upon level of performance. However, the majority of the Chinese EPC contractors were unable to meet these contractual expectations.

There were constant problems with meeting agreed-to deadlines during the construction of the power plants. Indonesian project managers ascribed these problems to the Chinese EPC contractors' lack of professionalism, that is, a "trader's mentality" with little concern for prudent project management and for after-construction service and support. For example, these contractors were seen as keen to deliver equipment long before it was needed and to be immediately paid for it. The equipment would then be placed in storage. However, by the time the project had reached the stage when the stored equipment was needed, the condition of the equipment had deteriorated. When there were construction delays, contractors did not inform PT PLN personnel. The level of irritation on the Indonesian side can be gauged by a suggestion from a Ministry of Energy and Mineral Resources official during a hearing with the parliament that Chinese contractors learn how to manage their projects from the Japanese.[32]

There were also constant problems with service and technical support after the plants were finished. For example, PT PLN found it difficult to source replacement parts from its contractors. PT PLN would order replacement parts, only to find that even though the part number they gave was correct, the part itself was not that which was needed. This led to delays in keeping power plants on the line while PT PLN searched for local Indonesian suppliers who could supply the right components. Repair manuals were only in Chinese and contractors did not supply translations in languages that local technicians could understand as they attempted to repair broken or worn-out equipment.

Finding Solutions

The delays in delivering fully operational power plants and poor after-construction service and support did not go unnoticed. Because the Indonesian government's guarantees for FTP-I loans were irrevocable and unconditional, the Ministry of Finance paid close attention to the implementation of the project. In January 2012, Finance Minister Agus Martowardojo asked the Minister for Planning and National Development to review the FTP-I project when it was found that two Chinese contractors were unable to build the power plants in Takalar, North Sulawesi and Pangkalan Susu, North Sumatra. These companies were subsequently barred from future projects financed by the state budget. He also advised that technical ministries be more prudent in the selection of contractors for large-scale projects, taking into consideration the principles of good governance.[33] A director of PT PLN gave the analogy of Chinese motorbikes, which were once very popular in Indonesia because they were cheap and financing was readily available. When buying a motorbike on credit, the customer could easily replace the bike even though it still had not been paid for in full. Unlike the Chinese motorbikes, however, when buying turnkey projects PT PLN could not replace the under-performing plants, and still had to continue paying installments.[34]

Current PT PLN officials are caught between Indonesian officials who are angry at being saddled with as-yet unfinished power plants and finished plants that are inoperable, as well as Chinese contractors who are not keen to complete the unfinished plants and repair those that are not working. PT PLN officials tasked with overhauling the FTP-I's weak planning and implementation describe the situation as very difficult and traumatic.

PT PLN's assessment of the FTP-I program identified multiple layers of administrative, financial and construction problems arising from the contractors' incompetence, delays in the construction of the plants and higher interest rates due to unforeseen loan extensions. In addition, a lack of coordination between the lead contractors and subcontractors was made more difficult by the communication barriers between Chinese and local contractors. Delays were also caused by land acquisition disputes and customs clearance procedures.

However, PT PLN has taken some steps to accelerate the completion and repair of the FTP-I power plants and to reduce the technical, communication and human resources problems that have contributed to the delays in completing and repairing the FTP-I plants. These steps include:

1. terminating poorly performing or incompetent subcontractors and site managers;
2. imposing maximum penalties on contractors building plants in Rembang, Suralaya, Paiton, Indramayu and Bima;
3. banning contractors involved in the construction of plants in Lombok, Bima and Gorontalo from participating in power plant construction for the next five years;
4. conducting a study and formulating guidelines for plant construction;
5. increasing the number of specialized workers (welders, fitters, commissioning experts etc.), specialized working tools and work shifts;
6. prioritizing the completion of the main works for plant operation;
7. consulting legal firms and independent bodies for contract dispute resolution;
8. optimizing project design for contractors to execute without altering specifications and performance guarantees;
9. asking certification agencies to provide coaching and help to contractors who have difficulties in testing and commissioning projects;
10. reinforcing human resources personnel and project organization in PT PLN;
11. holding workshops on coal-fired power plants to improve supervisors' competence.[35]

However, such measures are likely to be ineffective unless their implementation is based on a sufficient understanding of the economic, political and social milieu underlying the practices of Chinese construction companies and banks, and there is a clear articulation of the practices Indonesia expects from overseas and local companies participating in crucial development projects.

The Milieu Underlying the Practices of Chinese Construction Companies and Banks

It would help Indonesian project initiators and planners to create a robust oversight process if they are aware that Chinese companies going global are mainly SOEs rather than private companies accountable to their shareholders. Moreover, Chinese SOEs, particularly the large ones, are structurally tied to the Chinese state as instruments for achieving its political and economic goals.

Pearson depicts Chinese SOEs as having three tiers according to the ways the government regulates them, with each tier having its own regulatory characteristics. SOEs in the top tier are those operating in economically and politically strategic sectors such as mining, telecommunications, manufacturing, aerospace and aviation, technology, steel, shipping and transport, financial services, and energy. Although these SOEs have been restructured as joint-stock operations or limited liability companies, the state still has a majority ownership and maintains control to ensure profitability. The CPC also has substantial authority over these top-tier SOEs as they are considered to be strategic "lifeline" or "commanding heights" industries. The second-tier SOEs are companies considered important by the state. They are governed by explicit industrial policies in some instances but there is less state intervention in how they are run. The third tier consists of the majority of China's private and collective firms and many of the 90,000 smaller SOEs, some of which the state has sold to private or foreign investors. These companies are small and medium manufacturers, offer personal services, or are in retail. As such they are subject to regulations related to business scope and operations, consumer protection and standards rather than strategic industria policies.[36]

Oversight and control of companies in the top two tiers are carried out by supra-regulatory institutions, namely the State-Owned Assets Supervision and Administration Commission (SASAC), the National Development and Reform Commission (NDRC) and the CPC. SASAC, which is overseen by the State Council, exerts authority over assets, privatization, sales, acquisitions and the appointment of senior management of over 100,000 central, provincial, municipal and subsidiary entities. The NDRC determines industrial policy and approves major investments and industry decisions, while the CPC appoints top executives to major SOEs and places Party members on the boards of companies.[37]

Because the Chinese state regards first- and second-tier SOEs as central to its economic and political goals, the state supports these SOEs with soft budget constraints and indirect subsidies through favorable bank credits with preferential payback terms and interest rates that support their profitability and help them to modernize. This support is designed to increase these companies' chances of successfully competing against companies from other countries in the global market that, in turn, increases China's presence as a political and economic actor, which the rest of the world must accommodate. Trinidad (in this volume) notes that Chinese SOEs play a central role in China's aid programs. They assist potential aid recipient countries in preparing aid requests, conduct preliminary project assessments, implement contracted projects, and provide advice on policy to China's aid officials.

This is not to say that Chinese SOEs are uninterested in making profits. Many of the EPC contractors in the FTP-I are companies that fall under the first and second tiers. With the support of the NDRC and in line with the government's "Going Out" policy, they are entering the Indonesian power sector in a major way. Indonesia is a big market offering export opportunities for Chinese technology and manufactured goods, and Chinese companies want to take advantage of these opportunities. However, they need to build their brand and their credibility. The NDRC has encouraged Chinese companies to invest not just in Indonesian electrical power plants but also in coal, oil and gas as resource-rich Indonesia is considered to be a "gold rush" destination by China.[38]

All of this suggests that Chinese SOEs are primarily driven to serve the political and economic goals of the Chinese state and to show a profit rather than serve development outcomes of foreign states. This is something of which Indonesian development initiators and planners need to be aware.

Chinese banks, such as the Exim Bank and the China Development Bank Corporation, provide concessional loans that are tied to conditions whereby Chinese companies must participate in projects as lead contractors. In other words, these loans are conditional loans.

The Bank of Finland has identified four hypothetical types of conditionality: political conditionality, embedded conditionality, cross-conditionality and emergent conditionality. All but the first are imposed in the various business activities conducted by Chinese state-linked lenders and enterprises in developing countries.[39] In the case of Indonesia's FTP-I, the disagreement mentioned earlier between Merpati and Xi'an is an example of cross-conditionality by which the Chinese government used the FTP-I loans its bank provided as leverage to demand a settlement of the dispute.

Conclusion

While China-Indonesia cooperation in the FTP-I seemed to be rational and mutually beneficial, hasty planning and implementation led to problems that have nearly derailed the project, which was the first collaboration of this size and importance between Chinese contractors and PT PLN. Both parties were unfamiliar with each other's business practices and the partners and subcontractors with which they were dealing. Indonesian officials clearly did not consider the political, economic and operational assumptions of the Chinese SOEs and banks that they invited into the project. As a result, only 64 percent (6,377 MW) out of the 9,900 MW that the FTP-I was supposed to provide had been produced by June 2014. The target of 100 percent was not expected to be achieved until the end of 2015, or six years behind the original schedule,[40] but it appears that the target has not been achieved.

For the Chinese EPC contractors, the FTP-I was a golden opportunity for Chinese power plant equipment manufacturers to export their equipment as well as acquire name recognition in the Indonesian market. Financially, there was no risk because the loans made by the Chinese policy banks were backed by the Government of Indonesia. However, to compensate for the Indonesian government's tight budget, the Chinese EPC contractors sourced low-cost, poor-quality equipment and parts, which led to the construction of unreliable power plants. In the end, this has hurt the reputation of the Chinese electrical power industry.

If there is a takeaway lesson from this situation, it is that the success of China's economic footprint does not hinge alone on the magnitude of its investments and the willingness of both parties to engage in what they see as a mutually beneficial partnership. Rather, China's footprint will steadily and visibly remain if on-the-ground considerations in planning and implementation, such as those discussed in this chapter, are also considered.

Notes

1. Karl P. Sauvant, "Chinese investment: New kid on the block learning the rules," *East Asia Forum*, August 29, 2012, <http://www.eastasiaforum.org/2012/08/29/chinese-investment-new-kid-on-the-block-learning-the-rules/> (accessed July 25, 2013).

2. Galih Gumelar, "BKPM: Indonesia Siap Tampung Relokasi Investasi dari China," CNN Indonesia, July 10, 2015, <https://www.cnnindonesia.com/ekonomi/20150710143107-92-65720/bkpm-indonesia-siap-tampung-relokasi-investasi-dari-china> (accessed September 16, 2015).
3. P. Gammeltoft and Lepi T. Tarmidi, "Chinese Foreign Direct Investment in Indonesia: Trends, Drivers and Impacts," *International Journal of Technological Learning, Innovation and Development* 6, nos. 1/2 (2013).
4. Ibid.
5. Safrezi Fitra, "Kualitas Pembangkit Listrik Buruk, Cina Siap Tanggung Jawab," April 24, 2015, <https://katadata.co.id/berita/2015/04/24/kualitas-pembangkit-listrik-buruk-cina-siap-tanggung-jawab> (accessed September 16, 2015).
6. Approximately US$2.7 billion based on the middle rate quoted by the Bank of Indonesia on June 30, 2006 of US$1 = IDR9,300.
7. "Wapres Rapat di PLN Bahas Pembangkit Listrik Murah," March 17, 2006, <https://www.antaranews.com/berita/30087/wapres-rapat-di-pln-bahas-pembangkit-listrik-murah> (accessed January 27, 2014).
8. This was conveyed to the author in an interview with Sudrajat, Indonesia's former Ambassador to China, 2005–9.
9. "Konsorsium China Ajukan Proposal Bangun Pembangkit Listrik Batubara," May 18, 2006, <https://www.antaranews.com/berita/33988/konsorsium-china-ajukan-proposal-bangun-pembangkit-listrik-batubara> (accessed August 12, 2015).
10. Presidential Regulation No. 72, "Regulation of the President of the Republic of Indonesia Concerning Coordination Team to Accelerate the Development of Electric Power Generation," July 5, 2006.
11. Presidential Regulation No. 46/2011 disbanding the Coordinating Team for the Acceleration of Power Plant Construction, July 27, 2011.
12. PT PLN (Persero) Annual Report 2008.
13. "Program 10 Ribu MW Dimulai," April 28, 2007, <https://www.esdm.go.id/id/media-center/arsip-berita/program-10-ribu-mw-dimulai> (accessed September 20, 2015).
14. "Di Cina, Bangun Pembangkit 10 Ribu Megawatt Hal Biasa," May 5, 2009, <https://bisnis.tempo.co/read/174455/di-cina-bangun-pembangkit-10-ribu-megawatt-hal-biasa> (accessed September 20, 2015).
15. "China Dominasi Tender PLTU 10.000 MW," July 31, 2006, <https://www.antaranews.com/berita/39122/china-dominasi-tender-pltu-10000-mw> (accessed August 12, 2015).
16. China Huadian Corporation claimed it could complete the 300-MW and 600-MW plants within 18 and 25 months, respectively.
17. Lin Chewei and Reza B Zahar, "Mencari Listrik Murah ke China," *Kompas*, May 1, 2006.

18. Among these non-Chinese companies were Alstom Power Centrales (France), Hyundai Engineering Construction Co Ltd (South Korea), AES Transpower Pte Ltd (Singapore), Bharat Heavy Electrical Limited (India), and Japanese companies Mitsubishi Corporation, Itochu, and Marubeni.
19. "Sepi Peminat, Empat Proyek PLTU 10.000 MW Ditender Ulang," October 4, 2006, <https://www.antaranews.com/berita/43700/sepi-peminat-empat-proyek-pltu-10000-mw-ditender-ulang> (accessed August 12, 2015).
20. "Tender Listrik dikaji Kejagung" [Power project tenders under review by the Attorney General's Office], *Kompas*, October 17, 2006.
21. Zelan Holding Sdn Bhd and Tronoh Consolidated Malaysia are Malaysian companies.
22. Michael Agustinus, "Jokowi Sebut Ada 34 Proyek Pembangkit Listrik Mangkrak, Ini Daftarnya," *Detik Finance*, November 23, 2016, <https://finance.detik.com/energi/d-3352544/jokowi-sebut-ada-34-proyek-pembangkit-listrik-mangkrak-ini-daftarnya> (accessed January 3, 2017).
23. Abba Gabrillin, "Usut Proyek Listrik Mangkrak Era SBY, KPK Tunggu Laporan BPKP," February 10, 2017, <https://nasional.kompas.com/read/2017/02/10/15101041/usut.proyek.listrik.mangkrak.era.sby.kpk.tunggu.laporan.bpkp> (accessed March 3, 2017).
24. "Chinese banks pledge to finance more power projects," *The Jakarta Post*, April 12, 2010, <http://www.thejakartapost.com/news/2010/04/12/chinese-banks-pledge-finance-more-power-projects.html> (accessed December 10, 2013).
25. PT PLN (Persero) Annual Report 2008.
26. *The Jakarta Post*, April 12, 2010.
27. "Kasus Merpati Hambat Dana Program 10 Ribu MW," February 23, 2009, <https://bisnis.tempo.co/read/161621/kasus-merpati-hambat-dana-program-10-ribu-mw> (accessed December 29, 2013).
28. Erwida Maulia and Aditya Suharmoko, "RI resolves rifts with China, mends ties," *The Jakarta Post*, March 24, 2009, <http://www.thejakartapost.com/news/2009/03/24/ri-resolves-rifts-with-china-mends-ties.html> (accessed January 10, 2014).
29. Aditya Suharmoko, "PLN secures Chinese loans for power plants program after Merpati spat solved," *The Jakarta Post*, May 5, 2009, <http://www.thejakartapost.com/news/2009/05/05/pln-secures-chinese-loans-power-plants-program-after-merpati-spat-solved.html> (accessed December 28, 2013).
30. "Shanghai Electric Likely to Sue Indonesia State Power Company PLN," June 4, 2009, <http://english.caijing.com.cn/2009-06-04/110177962.html> (accessed December 29, 2013); "PLN May Face $100M Suit from China Firm," *The Jakarta Globe*, June 12, 2009, <http://jakartaglobe.id/archive/pln-may-face-100m-suit-from-china-firm/> (accessed December 29, 2013).

31. *The Jakarta Post*, April 12, 2010.
32. "Garap PLTU, Kontraktor Cina Diminta Tiru Jepang," May 30, 2012, <https://bisnis.tempo.co/read/407130/garap-pltu-kontraktor-cina-diminta-tiru-jepang> (accessed July 25, 2013).
33. "Menkeu minta pemilihan kontraktor proyek lebih selektif," January 15, 2012, <http://nasional.kontan.co.id/news/menkeu-minta-pemilihan-kontraktor-proyek-lebih-selektif> (accessed July 25, 2013).
34. Interview with the author on July 2, 2013.
35. PT PLN (Persero) Annual Report 2013.
36. Margaret M. Pearson, "Variety Within & Without: The Political Economy of Chinese Regulation," in *Beyond the Middle Kingdom: Comparative Perspectives on China's Capitalist Transformation*, ed. Scott Kennedy, 25–43 (Palo Alto, CA: Stanford University Press, 2011).
37. Ibid.
38. "Indonesian 'gold rush'," *China Daily*, November 15, 2010.
39. Mikael Mattlin and Matti Nojonen, *Conditionality in Chinese Bilateral Lending* (Helsinki: Bank of Finland, Institute for Economies in Transition, BOFIT Discussion Paper 14/2011, June 15, 2011), <http://dx.doi.org/10.2139/ssrn.1868792> (accessed June 30, 2014).
40. Reported by the Finance Director of PT PLN at a public dialogue on the future of electricity organized by the Institute of Essential Services Reform (IESR) in Jakarta on July 4, 2014.

References

Agustinus, Michael. "Jokowi Sebut Ada 34 Proyek Pembangkit Listrik Mangkrak, Ini Daftarnya." *Detik Finance*, November 23, 2016. <https://finance.detik.com/energi/d-3352544/jokowi-sebut-ada-34-proyek-pembangkit-listrik-mangkrak-ini-daftarnya> (accessed January 3, 2017).

"China Dominasi Tender PLTU 10.000 MW," July 31, 2006. <https://www.antaranews.com/berita/39122/china-dominasi-tender-pltu-10000-mw> (accessed August 12, 2015).

"Chinese banks pledge to finance more power projects," *The Jakarta Post*, April 12, 2010. <http://www.thejakartapost.com/news/2010/04/12/chinese-banks-pledge-finance-more-power-projects.html> (accessed December 10, 2013).

"Di Cina, Bangun Pembangkit 10 Ribu Megawatt Hal Biasa," May 5, 2009. <https://bisnis.tempo.co/read/174455/di-cina-bangun-pembangkit-10-ribu-megawatt-hal-biasa> (accessed September 20, 2015).

Fitra, Safrezi. "Kualitas Pembangkit Listrik Buruk, Cina Siap Tanggung Jawab," April 24, 2015. <https://katadata.co.id/berita/2015/04/24/kualitas-pembangkit-listrik-buruk-cina-siap-tanggung-jawab> (accessed September 16, 2015).

Gabrillin, Abba. "Usut Proyek Listrik Mangkrak Era SBY, KPK Tunggu Laporan BPKP," February 10, 2017. <https://nasional.kompas.com/read/2017/02/10/15101041/usut.proyek.listrik.mangkrak.era.sby.kpk.tunggu.laporan.bpkp> (accessed March 3, 2017).

Gammeltoft, Peter and Lepi T. Tarmidi. "Chinese Foreign Direct Investment in Indonesia: Trends, Drivers and Impacts." *International Journal of Technological Learning, Innovation and Development* 6, nos. 1/2 (January 2013): 136–60.

"Garap PLTU, Kontraktor Cina Diminta Tiru Jepang," May 30, 2012. <https://bisnis.tempo.co/read/407130/garap-pltu-kontraktor-cina-diminta-tiru-jepang> (accessed July 25, 2013).

Gumelar, Galih. "BKPM: Indonesia Siap Tampung Relokasi Investasi dari China," CNN Indonesia, July 10, 2015. <https://www.cnnindonesia.com/ekonomi/20150710143107-92-65720/bkpm-indonesia-siap-tampung-relokasi-investasi-dari-china> (accessed September 16, 2015).

"Kasus Merpati Hambat Dana Program 10 Ribu MW," February 23, 2009. <https://bisnis.tempo.co/read/161621/kasus-merpati-hambat-dana-program-10-ribu-mw> (accessed December 29, 2013).

"Konsorsium China Ajukan Proposal Bangun Pembangkit Listrik Batubara," May 18, 2006. <https://www.antaranews.com/berita/33988/konsorsium-china-ajukan-proposal-bangun-pembangkit-listrik-batubara> (accessed August 12, 2015).

Mattlin, Mikael and Matti Nojonen. *Conditionality in Chinese Bilateral Lending*. BOFIT Discussion Paper 14/2011. Helsinki: Bank of Finland, Institute for Economies in Transition (BOFIT), June 15, 2011. <http://dx.doi.org/10.2139/ssrn.1868792> (accessed on June 30, 2014).

Maulia, Erwida and Aditya Suharmoko. "RI resolves rifts with China, mends ties," *The Jakarta Post*, March 24, 2009. <http://www.thejakartapost.com/news/2009/03/24/ri-resolves-rifts-with-china-mends-ties.html> (accessed January 10, 2014).

"Menkeu minta pemilihan kontraktor proyek lebih selektif," January 15, 2012. <http://nasional.kontan.co.id/news/menkeu-minta-pemilihan-kontraktor-proyek-lebih-selektif> (accessed July 25, 2013).

Pearson, Margaret M. "Variety Within and Without: The Political Economy of Chinese Regulation." In *Beyond the Middle Kingdom: Comparative Perspectives on China's Capitalist Transformation*, edited by Scott Kennedy, 25–43. Palo Alto, CA: Stanford University Press, 2011.

Presidential Regulation No. 46/2011. "Peraturan Presiden Republik Indonesia Nomor 46 tahun 2011 tentang Pembubaran Tim Koordinasi Percepatan Pembangunan Pembangkit Tenaga Listrik" (Termination of the Coordinating Team for the Acceleration of the Construction of Power Plants), July 27, 2011.

Presidential Regulation No. 72/2006. "Peraturan Presiden Republik Indonesia Nomor 72 tahun 2006 tentang Tim Koordinasi Percepatan Pembangunan Pembangkit Tenaga Listrik" (Regulation of the President of the Republic of Indonesia Concerning Coordination Team to Accelerate the Development of Electric Power Generation), July 5, 2006.

"Program 10 Ribu MW Dimulai," April 28, 2007. <https://www.esdm.go.id/id/media-center/arsip-berita/program-10-ribu-mw-dimulai> (accessed September 20, 2015).

PT PLN. Laporan Tahunan 2010 PT PLN (Persero): Dedikasi untuk Melayani dan Menerangi Seluruh Negeri (Annual Report 2010: Dedicated to Serve and Liven Up the Whole Country), 2010.

———. Annual Report 2008: Light for a Greener Future, 2008.

———. Laporan Tahunan 2013: Peningkatan Kualitas Tata Kelola dan Inovasi Operasional (Annual Report 2013: Improvement of Governance and Operational Innovation), 2013.

Sauvant, Karl P. "Chinese investment: New kid on the block learning the rules." *East Asia Forum*, August 29, 2012. <http://www.eastasiaforum.org/2012/08/29/chinese-investment-new-kid-on-the-block-learning-the-rules/> (accessed July 25, 2013).

"Sepi Peminat, Empat Proyek PLTU 10.000 MW Ditender Ulang," October 4, 2006. <https://www.antaranews.com/berita/43700/sepi-peminat-empat-proyek-pltu-10000-mw-ditender-ulang> (accessed August 12, 2015).

Suharmoko, Aditya. "PLN secures Chinese loans for power plants program after Merpati spat solved," *The Jakarta Post*, May 5, 2009. <http://www.thejakartapost.com/news/2009/05/05/pln-secures-chinese-loans-power-plants-program-after-merpati-spat-solved.html> (accessed December 28, 2013).

"Wapres Rapat di PLN Bahas Pembangkit Listrik Murah," March 17, 2006. <https://www.antaranews.com/berita/30087/wapres-rapat-di-pln-bahas-pembangkit-listrik-murah> (accessed January 27, 2014).

CHAPTER 6

Limits of China's Aid Diplomacy: Lessons from the Philippines

Dennis D. Trinidad

Introduction

The nexus of economics and security in the conduct of foreign affairs in East Asia has become more evident since the onset of the new millennium. The People's Republic of China (hereafter China) has employed a combination of soft-power tools such as aid, trade and investment policies in order to pursue its national goals. China's economic rise has created perceptions of threat and opportunity among its neighboring countries and elsewhere. In part, Chinese diplomacy in the new millennium was intended to counter that perception and to project its rise to power as peaceful. Given the long history of animosity between China and the Philippines caused by communist ideology and the more recent territorial dispute over the South China Sea, it is unsurprising that China has utilized foreign aid as part of its diplomacy with the Philippines. Indeed, the Chinese government has tapped a mix of soft-power instruments to improve its bilateral relations with the country. China has built three Confucius Institutes in the Philippines since 2007, signed memoranda of understanding and framework agreements on economic cooperation with the Philippine government, promoted cultural exchanges, and pledged huge amounts of highly concessional loans and grants in the 2000s.

One of the tools of diplomacy that China has increasingly employed since the onset of the new millennium is foreign aid.

However, while China's aid diplomacy has succeeded in co-opting recipient countries like Cambodia and several others in sub-Saharan Africa to embrace its aid modality and practice, it has been much less successful in the Philippines. To increase its allure, the Chinese government has stressed the values that are attractive to borrowing states in its aid-giving, including the principles of no-conditionality and "win-win." In spite of this, there was a pervasive perception that Chinese aid was prone to corruption during the term of President Gloria Macapagal-Arroyo (2001–10). The purpose of this chapter is to examine why this is the case.

The chapter explores the limits in the use of soft-power tools such as foreign aid in co-opted recipient countries. The limitations of Chinese aid diplomacy, seen here as China's tangible footprint in the region, are due primarily to the very nature of China's aid system. Compared to Western counterparts, Chinese aid institutions are still in a formative stage.[1] Because these aid institutions have developed outside the Development Assistance Committee of the Organisation for Economic Co-operation and Development club (DAC/OECD hereafter, DAC), many observers view China's practices and modality of administering aid as not conforming to the DAC-based international aid regime. The Chinese government tends to define aid to include both official development assistance (ODA) and other official flows (OOFs) like export credits, whereas DAC aid donors define aid more narrowly to include only ODA. Moreover, the trend among DAC donor countries is to untie their aid and not to limit procurement only to firms from donor countries. China-funded projects, on the other hand, are often tied to Chinese businesses. In 2007, the average percentage of DAC aid to less developed countries that was untied was 86 percent.[2] Aid tying is generally not favored because it "prevents recipient countries from receiving good value for money for services, goods, or works"[3] and may "result in welfare losses for recipient economies compared with the alternative of unrestricted aid transfers made in the form of foreign exchange."[4]

As an aid recipient country, the Philippines is more dependent on DAC donors to provide ODA. The ensuing aid relations that have been formed by the Philippines' interactions with DAC donors over the years have gradually led to the formation of aid institutions that conform to the DAC-based aid regime. To encourage aid contributions for development, the Philippines has closely followed the latest aid-effectiveness paradigms such as the Paris and Busan declarations. The Philippines has adopted a definition of aid consistent with DAC's definition, availed of untied rather than tied aid, and made its procurement system competitive.

Since the Corazon Aquino administration, aid management in the Philippines has gradually evolved into a more transparent and participatory system that is based on DAC standards. Both the Philippine president and Congress are involved in the aid processes. The Official Development Assistance Act of 1996, which is also known as Republic Act (RA) 8182, officially adopts DAC's definition of ODA.[5] Other legislation and rules have also been passed to further strengthen inter-ministerial checks and balances.[6] Legal institutions in the Philippines do not just define the scope of ODA activities. They also describe the entire aid process at various levels: project identification, aid negotiation and implementation. These legal rules also specify the veto powers of actors as well as the constraints in contracting and using bilateral loans.

The Philippine aid management system also explicitly sets the limitations on bidding and procurement. Section 11 of the Official Development Assistance Act of 1996 provides that:

- consultants for the feasibility and design aspects of a project are forbidden from participating directly or indirectly in any subsequent phase of project implementation;
- project execution can only be delegated by the implementing agency when it does not have the capacity to implement a project;
- Filipinos are given preference when hiring consultants, contractors, architects, engineers and other professionals necessary for a project's implementation;
- as amended by RA 8555, preference is also given to Filipino suppliers and manufacturers in the purchase of supplies and materials, although the president can waive this restriction when contracting loans if necessary; and
- project implementation is carried out by any department, bureau, office, commission, authority or agency of the national government, including government-owned or controlled corporations (GOCCs) that are authorized to do so by law or their respective charters, or local government units (LGUs) that are authorized by law to undertake development projects, except in some cases where the implementing agencies are not competent to undertake a task.

Moreover, Section 8 of said Act assigns oversight functions of ODA-funded projects to the following three agencies:

- National Economic and Development Authority (NEDA), which conducts an annual review of all ongoing development projects and reports their status to Congress not later than June 30 of each year;
- Commission on Audit (COA), which reviews all ongoing and completed projects and submits a report to Congress not later than June 30 of each year; and
- Congressional Oversight Committee on ODA Law.

The evolution of China's aid practices and modality outside DAC and the adoption of DAC-conforming aid practices in the Philippines have restricted the effectiveness of China's aid diplomacy for the following reasons. When aid institutions and practices of a non-DAC aid donor such as China are applied in a recipient country whose aid management is based on DAC standards, legal and political controversies may arise due to the mismatch of these practices. The foreign aid in question subsequently becomes entrenched in domestic politics and thereby creates bad public relations. As a result, foreign aid as a soft-power resource fails to achieve its objective of attraction and co-optation. As will be shown later, this was compellingly manifested in legal and political controversies in the 2000s that arose from the incompatible, and often conflicting, aid institutions of China and the Philippines.

Limits of Foreign Aid as a Tool of Soft Power: The Case of China's Aid

Soft power is the ability to affect others in order to obtain the outcomes one wants through attraction rather than coercion or payment.[7] It is the use of attraction to make others want what you want using resources of culture, values and policies.[8] Soft power is attractive power; it is co-optation rather than coercion.[9] Nye stresses the crucial role of public diplomacy in the delivery of resources that produce soft power.[10] Among the many potential resources of attraction, foreign aid is one of the most common tools employed by governments and its footprint can be the result of hard or soft power or both. Foreign aid is hard (coercive) when it is used to sanction or alter specific external or internal policies of the target state through significantly reducing allotments or suspending aid allocations. For example, this is what

China's Western donors did after the Chinese government cracked down on pro-democracy protesters in Tiananmen Square in 1989. On the other hand, foreign aid policy becomes an effective soft-power resource when it reflects values and practices that are desirable or acceptable to recipient governments. This can contribute to changing recipients' perceptions of the giver/donor from less attractive to more attractive. In this sense, aid relations create bonds between aid givers and receivers. To do this, aid donors must provide a continuous stream of assistance and produce developmental results to cultivate this kind of relationship.

Nonetheless, the effective use of soft-power resources depends on several factors. D'Hooghe points out China's lack of credibility as an obstacle to its public diplomacy in Europe.[11] Because the state is the main messenger of soft power, she argues, the non-democratic nature of China's government and its opaque political decision-making raises questions about the legitimacy of the Chinese government to speak for its own people.[12] The compatibility of political values is another aspect of projecting soft power successfully. Paradise points out that China's image is more favorable in developing countries that share its political values.[13] Moreover, "institutions can enhance a country's soft power."[14] In foreign aid relations, it is important that the practices and modality of aid giving are acceptable to both donors and recipients. In this respect, opinion setters like the media, local government units, implementing agencies and civil society groups play an important role in the efficacy of soft power.[15]

The Chinese government has consciously used foreign aid along with its culture and language—the latter two promoted through overseas Confucius Institutes—as tools of soft power to enhance China's appeal internationally. Blanchard and Lu note that, for many Chinese, the idea of realizing one's ends through attraction is not new but rather deeply embedded in Chinese theory and praxis.[16] The Chinese concept of soft-power resources also neatly falls within Nye's framework of culture, political values and foreign policies that are attractive to recipient countries. Zhang claims that even though China's hard-power assets have significantly increased in the past few decades, Beijing continues to use soft-power tools in its pursuit of "reinventing the nation and restoring it to its historical place in the world."[17]

To enhance the allure of China's foreign aid, the Chinese government has employed a strategy of creating a distinctive type of aid that is different from mainstream DAC aid. For instance, the Chinese government labels its aid under a South-South cooperation modality in comparison to the North-South aid relations that typically define DAC donors and recipients. South-South cooperation is rooted in the Afro-Asian solidarity movement of the 1950s and represents a symbolic regime that distinguishes non-DAC aid from DAC aid.[18] This framework is more appealing to governments of developing countries because recipients are treated as equal partners instead of just receivers of assistance. More importantly, China claims that its aid does not have political strings or impose conditions. The Chinese government also emphasizes mutual benefit, equality, win-win, self-reliance and respect for sovereignty as the core values of its aid policy. Finally, as pointed out in one study, Chinese aid is provided more swiftly and often allotted to infrastructure development, which DAC donor-countries have neglected or ignored[19] because their aid is allotted more to the social sector. This is true of nearly all recipients of Chinese aid in sub-Saharan Africa, Asia and elsewhere. Yet, despite its attractive attributes, China's aid has failed to impress its footprints on the Philippines during the period under study (2001-10).

The Chinese government capitalized on distinctive features of China's foreign aid to increase its attraction in the Philippines. Chinese aid does not come with strings or conditions; it adheres to the principles of mutual benefit, win-win and self-reliance; and it follows the South-South cooperation framework. However, the evolution of China's aid institutions and practices outside the DAC has posed challenges to the Philippines' aid institutions, which are based on the DAC aid regime. The next two sections discuss the broad foreign policy objectives of China's aid diplomacy and how they relate to China's aid relations with Southeast Asia and the Philippines.

China's Aid Diplomacy: Continuity and Changes

China's role as an aid donor began in 1950 with North Vietnam and North Korea as its first recipients. In terms of aid giving, China is, therefore, as old as traditional Western aid donors. However, China's relative isolation during the Cold War caused it to have little impact on shaping the discourse of development assistance that became dominated by the West. This is the reason why some scholars currently tend to distinguish between traditional and emerging, or non-DAC, aid donors. However, like most Western donors, non-DAC aid donors strategically employ aid as an instrument of diplomacy. Likewise, the strategic purposes of China's aid have been shaped by its foreign and commercial policy goals.

From the 1950s to the 1960s, these goals were the pursuit of international recognition and the expulsion of Taiwan (Republic of China) as the representative of the Chinese nation from the United Nations (UN). China's early aid to countries in Africa, Latin America and elsewhere was intended to achieve these objectives. Indeed in 1971, 26 African countries voted for China's accession to the UN[20] while 31 of the 34 recipients of Chinese aid voted for the expulsion of Taiwan from the UN General Assembly.[21] China also provided assistance for nation-building and national movements,[22] which included material support to local communist revolutionaries in countries like the Philippines and Indonesia.

Western dominance of the developmental aid discourse began when the DAC/OECD was established as an exclusive club of mainly Western industrialized donor countries in 1961. Three years later, then Chinese Premier Zhou Enlai declared China's "Eight Principles for Economic Aid and Technical Assistance to Other Countries," which became the core principles of China's foreign aid policy.[23] The adoption of these principles has symbolic and political significance. For one thing, the declaration contains values such as respect for sovereignty (no conditions) and mutual benefit that many developing countries deemed important for ensuring aid effectiveness. It also symbolizes China's close affinity with Third World countries because the declaration embodies the core philosophies that were adopted in the 1955 Afro-Asian Conference in Bandung, Indonesia. Today, these principles have become the distinguishing feature of China's foreign aid.

After assuming its seat in the UN in 1971, one of China's major foreign policy objectives was to internationally isolate Taiwan. Between 1972 and 1978, foreign aid played a crucial role in enticing developing countries to establish diplomatic ties with Beijing.[24] China also implemented ambitious infrastructure projects in Africa such as the Tan-Zam railway project, which connected Tanzania and Zambia. The period between 1978 and 1992 marked China's transition to a socialist market economy. This was the era of China's great "Reform and Opening Up" which was launched at the 3rd Plenum of the Central Committee of Communist Party in 1978. Also in this period, China's foreign aid allotments were reduced significantly, and the country became a major recipient of Japanese ODA.[25]

By the 1990s, China was experiencing rapid economic growth and modernization. The 14th National Congress of the Communist Party of China in 1992 declared that China's goal was to establish a socialist market economy. The major concrete goals of its foreign and economic policies were (1) reintegration into the global economy; (2) the creation of a peaceful environment to sustain China's economic growth; and (3) the mitigation of the "China-as-a-threat" perception. To dispel fears of China's rising power, the "Good Neighbor Policy," which aimed to build friendly relationships and partnerships, was adopted in 1997 by then President Jiang Zemin. Premier Zhu Rongji pledged to increase assistance to Southeast Asia during the 4th China-ASEAN Summit meeting. In 1999, China's "Going Out" policy was launched. This policy encouraged Chinese manufacturing firms to increase their global competitiveness and brand recognition by establishing production bases overseas "where they could integrate into new markets and acquire Western technology, management skills and foreign currency."[26] The Going Out policy also tied China's foreign aid to Chinese firms as a result of the Chinese government's commitment to provide export tax rebates and financial assistance to firms that utilized materials, parts and machinery from China.

This decade also witnessed an attempt by the Chinese government to further reorganize its foreign aid institutions in terms of funding sources, aid management and financing schemes.[27] The state-owned Export-Import Bank of China (Exim Bank) was established in 1994 in order to provide medium- to long-term low-interest loans to developing countries. The Chinese government worked to improve mechanisms for inter-agency coordination in administering aid in the 2000s.[28] In response to the international aid community's growing interest and lack of information about Chinese assistance, the Information Office of the State Council of China released two white papers on China's Foreign Aid in 2011 and 2014. Both papers

- reiterated adherence to the 1964 eight principles of foreign aid;
- mapped out the geographical distribution of Chinese aid which showed African and Asian countries as China's major recipients;
- highlighted China's contribution to the Millennium Development Goals (MDGs)—climate change mitigation and debt relief efforts for least developed countries; and
- noted the sectoral distribution of Chinese aid which showed that China apparently gave priority to infrastructure development in its foreign aid programs.

Estimates of China's annual foreign aid volume vary considerably.[29] The 2011 White Paper mentioned that by 2009 China had provided an aggregate total of RMB256.59 billion, of which RMB106.2 billion was in the form of grants, while RMB76.54 billion was given as interest-free loans and RMB73.55 billion was given as concessional loans.[30] The 2014 White Paper, on the other hand, reported that China provided a total of RMB89.34 billion (or US$14.41 billion) for a period of three years from 2010 to 2012. Of this, 36.2 percent was in the form of grants, 8.1 percent in interest-free loans, and 55.7 percent in the form of concessional loans.[31]

At present, China has yet to establish a single aid agency to manage its aid system. The Ministry of Commerce (MOFCOM) serves as the main administrative agency authorized by China's State Council to oversee foreign aid. MOFCOM is in charge of the "formulation of foreign aid policies, regulations, overall and annual plans, examination and approval of foreign aid projects and management of the project execution."[32] The Executive Bureau of International Economic Cooperation, the China International Center for Economic and Technical Exchanges, and the Academy of International Business Officials are entrusted with the tasks of managing the implementation of complete and technical cooperation projects, material aid projects, and training programs.[33] China's Exim Bank is the main source of concessional loans. It conducts project assessments and receives loan repayments. MOFCOM works closely with the Foreign Affairs and Finance ministries as well as with the Exim Bank in drafting the aid programs for each recipient country. Moreover, Chinese embassies play a liaising role in the early stage of the aid process. Lancaster notes that "Chinese ambassadors come together periodically to propose aid levels for their countries, and that individual project proposals are vetted by country desk officers of the Ministry of Foreign Affairs"[34] while high-cost projects must also be vetted by the Ministry of Finance. Other government ministries participate in the implementation of relevant technical cooperation projects.

Following the adoption of the Going Out policy, China's state-owned enterprises (SOEs), particularly those in the construction, information and technology, and mining sectors, have increasingly become influential in shaping China's foreign aid process. The Going Out policy was a call for expansion in which "enterprises were encouraged to develop overseas processing and assembly operations" which would enable Chinese businesses "to extend manufacturing beyond their safe bases in China."[35] To do so, the central government provides SOEs with incentives such as preferential taxes, low-interest bank loans and foreign exchange access.[36] This has enabled Chinese businesses to venture into international trade by securing overseas contracts using offers of concessional loans from the Exim Bank. In pursuing their goal of securing contracts in other countries, SOEs have become involved in three different stages of China's foreign aid process: (1) assisting potential recipient countries in preparing aid requests; (2) conducting preliminary project assessments; and (3) implementing contracted projects.[37]

Situating the Philippines in China's Foreign Aid Diplomacy in Southeast Asia

Understanding China's post-Cold War relations with ASEAN provides a helpful guide in thinking about China's aid diplomacy in Southeast Asia. Lu divides post-Cold War China-ASEAN relations into three phases: (1) the era of putting in place a comprehensive dialogue framework (1991–6); (2) the era of increased regional cooperation and trust (1997–2002); and (3) the era of consolidation and development of strategic partnerships (2003 to the present).[38] Following Chinese presence on the Philippine-claimed Mischief Reef in 1994–5, the Chinese government intensified its use of soft-power resources to improve relations with the Philippines and other claimant states in the South China Sea. During the third phase, China signed several cultural, political, security, trade and investment cooperation agreements with ASEAN-member countries, including the "Joint Declaration on Strategic Partnership and Prosperity" during the 7th ASEAN-China Summit in October 2003 and the Treaty of Amity and Cooperation (TAC). Bui summarizes China's rationale in seeking proactive engagement with the ASEAN as follows: [39]

- facilitate a more peaceful regional security environment critical to China's continued economic rise;
- reduce risks from globalization after accession to World Trade Organization;
- allay the China threat perception;
- assist in implementing China's Western Development Strategy; and
- demonstrate China's regional leadership ability.

By virtue of their historical and cultural affinity with China and their importance in materializing the Western Development Strategy,[40] the mainland countries of Southeast Asia—particularly Cambodia, Laos, Myanmar and Vietnam—have received a stream of continuous financial support from China. In contrast, China's relations with the maritime countries of Indonesia and the Philippines have long been characterized by animosity. Both countries have accused the communist regime in Beijing of supporting local communist insurgencies in the 1950s and 1960s. Moreover, the Philippines is also one of the parties in the South China Sea dispute, its claim affirmed by the Hague tribunal in 2016. The Going Out strategy and the need to address the animosity that has beleaguered China-Philippines relations were the main reasons for China's aid diplomacy in the Philippines in the new millennium.

Since the onset of the 2000s, China has provided concessional loans and grants to the Philippines. Chinese concessional loan pledges have been very large and meant for infrastructure developments such as the North Luzon Railway (Northrail) and Philippine National Broadband Network (NBN) projects. The National Economic and Development Authority (NEDA) reports that between 2003 and 2013, China's financing pledges reached a total of USD1.26 billion.[41] However, as Table 1 shows, there were only three recorded grants and instances of humanitarian assistance provided by the Chinese government to the Philippines between 2003 and 2013. It also indicates that only a small fraction of that pledge was actually utilized. Moreover, after the completion of the Angat Water Utilization and Aqueduct Improvement project in May 2014, the Philippine government suspended accepting new loans from China. The low utilization of loan pledges from China by the Philippine government is a clear indication that attraction through the use of foreign aid has failed.

DAC-Conforming Aid Recipient Meets Non-DAC Aid Donor: Challenges to Sino-Philippines Aid Relations

Because China does not have strategic country planning or country-specific aid programs,[42] framework agreements, memoranda of understanding (MOUs) and other similar official agreements have served as the main basis of loan assistance from China. Some NEDA staff interviewed by the author commented that Chinese aid is just business. This seems to be the case as well for other Chinese aid

Table 1 Completed China-Assisted Loans and Grants in the Philippines (2003–13)

Concessional Loans

Project Title	Implementing Agency	Net Commitment (USD millions unless otherwise indicated)	Date of Signing	Date of Completion
Angat Water Utilization and Aqueduct Improvement Project	Metropolitan Waterworks and Sewerage System (MWSS)	116	January 7, 2010	May 7, 2014
Agno River Integrated Irrigation Project	National Irrigation Administration (NIA)	89.15	November 9, 2009	December 31, 2013
Northrail Project Phase 1 Section 1	North Luzon Railway Corporation (NLRC)	180.79	February 26, 2004	September 13, 2009
Banaoang Pump Irrigation Project	NIA	35	October 31, 2001	June 27, 2008
General Santos Fishing Port Complex Expansion/Improvement Project	Department of Agriculture (DA)	24.99	December 20, 2002	March 15, 2009
Northrail Project Phase 1 Section 2	NLRC	0	January 15, 2007	Declared not effective

Grants and Humanitarian Assistance

Philippine-Sino Center for Agricultural Technology (PhilSCAT)	DA	7 (for phase 1)	2003	2008
Mobile clinics (motor vehicles with diagnostic and treatment facilities)	Department of Health (DOH)	PHP85 million	2010	
Assistance to victims of typhoon Haiyan		100,000 and 3.08 million worth of construction materials*	2013	

Sources: For concessional loans: NEDA Monitoring and Evaluation Staff, 2014.
For grants and humanitarian assistance: http://philscat.orgfree.com/about_project.php; http://ph.china-embassy.org/eng/sgdt/t780167.htm.
*Provided to the author by a staff member from Embassy of the People's Republic of China to the Philippines.

recipients such as Cambodia.[43] These framework agreements and MOUs commit China to provide technical cooperation or concessional financial assistance, or both. In the Philippines, many of the framework agreements and MOUs with China were signed under the administration of then President Gloria Macapagal-Arroyo. A total of 30 economic and technical agreements were signed during Wen Jiabao's 2007 Manila visit alone.[44] Table 2 provides a partial list of the signed framework agreements and MOUs between the Philippines and China in the 2000s.

Table 2 Selected China-Philippines Framework Agreements and MOUs

Agreements and MOU	Year Signed	Coverage
1. Agreement on Strengthening Cooperation in Agriculture and Related Fields	1999	Technical cooperation
2. Credit Facility Agreement	2000	US$100 million export credit
3. MOU on Cooperation in Constructing the Northern Luzon Railway Project	2003	Concessional loans
4. MOU on Fisheries Cooperation	2004	Technical cooperation
5. MOU on Cooperation in the Field of Infrastructure	2005	Concessional loans
6. MOU on Broadening and Deepening Agriculture and Fisheries Cooperation	2007	US$1.9 million in technical cooperation and concessional loans
7. A framework agreement, covering the next ten years, on expanding and deepening bilateral economic and trade cooperation	2007	Trade cooperation
8. A framework agreement for the provision of a concessional loan to the Philippines for a Non-Intrusive Container Inspection System		Concessional loan
9. A US$300 million preferential buyer's credit from the Exim Bank to finance rural development programs in the Philippines		Export credit

continued next page

154 Dennis D. Trinidad

Table 2 *continued*

Agreements and MOU	Year Signed	Coverage
10. An engineering procurement and construction contract for the rehabilitation and upgrading of the Philippine mainline South Railway Project Phase 1		Concessional loan
11. MOU allowing the Chinese Fuhua Group Ltd. to invest US$3.8 billion to develop 1 million hectares for higher yielding corn, rice and sorghum		Investment in agriculture
12. MOU on Philippine-China Five-Year Development Program for Trade and Economic Cooperation (2012–6)	2011	Cooperation in the sectors of agriculture and fishery, infrastructure and public works, mining, energy, information and communications technology (ICT), processing and manufacturing, tourism, engineering services and forestry; with US$2 billion to 7 billion in investments

Sources: http://ph.china-embassy.org/eng/zfgx/zzgx/t180703.htm; http://www.gov.ph/2011/09/01/joint-statement-of-the-philippines-and-the-peoples-republic-of-china-september-1-2011/; and http://wikileaks.org/plusd/cables/07MANILA212_a.html.

The content of the above framework agreements and MOUs shows that Chinese aid to the Philippines generally follows its observed pattern of aid giving, which features the following:

- Signed MOUs include support for Chinese SOEs and an overwhelming focus on infrastructure development. At least two MOUs pertained to two infrastructure projects—the North Luzon Railway (Northrail) and South Railway projects.
- Chinese assistance is a mix of what DAC donors refer to as ODA and OOF. At least two signed agreements contain provisions for preferential buyers' credit, which is considered a type of OOF.
- Finally, one MOU straightforwardly shows the tied nature of China's assistance (Item 11 in Table 2). This MOU, in particular, allows a Chinese firm, Fuhua Group Ltd, to invest US$3.8 billion

to develop 1 million hectares of land for high-yielding corn, rice, and sorghum in the Philippines. Moreover, it was confirmed by NEDA staff members that China's aid did not come with strings or conditions and that the Chinese aid process (from project identification to negotiation, approval and actual disbursement) was relatively quicker than DAC aid.

Why was China's aid strikingly underutilized in the 2000s by the Philippines in spite of its attractive conditions? There are two factors that plausibly explain this. First, in the 2000s the public perceived Chinese aid to be prone to corruption and legal irregularities. This was a direct result of two controversial China-assisted projects that were cancelled and terminated due to legal and constitutional violations—the Northrail and NBN projects. At the time of its initial implementation, Chinese Embassy Deputy Chief of Mission Xiao Qian described the Northrail project as the "largest Chinese project in Southeast Asia."[45] It was also hailed as a great milestone in China-Philippine relations by some observers and a manifestation of a growing "partnership in its golden age."[46]

The Northrail project originally consisted of four phases. Phase 1 would involve rehabilitating 32 kilometers of existing track (Section 1) and building an additional 32-kilometer railway through the various municipalities and towns of Bulacan Province to the Clark Freeport Zone in Pampanga Province (Section 2). The completion of Phase 1 would link Caloocan City, north of Metro Manila, and Clark in central Luzon and it was expected to ferry about 150,000 passengers daily.[47] Phase 2 would involve the construction of a branch line to the Subic Bay Freeport Zone in the province of Zambales. Phase 3 would extend the railway from Caloocan City to Bonifacio Global City in Taguig, Metro Manila, while Phase 4 was an extension from Pampanga to San Fernando in La Union Province.[48] The plan was finalized under the Arroyo government with North Luzon Railway Corporation (NLRC) acting as the lead implementing agency to undertake the project. Originally, it was proposed to the Japanese government for funding. However, the Japan Bank for International Cooperation (JBIC) that was supposed to provide the funding backed out[48] due to complicated relocation issues in the implementation of Phase 1.[50]

JBIC's refusal to allot funding gave an opportunity for Chinese financial assistance. The Chinese were less concerned about the relocation issues. Thus, financial assistance for the project was quickly secured, signed in 2003, and released in 2004 in the amount of US$400 million to cover the cost of the project's first phase. With a 3 percent annual interest rate, five-year grace period, and 20-year maturity, Chinese financing was highly concessional and very attractive.[51] A Chinese company, China National Machinery and Equipment Corporation Group (CNMEG, which later changed its name to Sinomach), was chosen as the main contractor. Three years later, the Exim Bank pledged an additional US$500 million funding to Phase 1, Section 2 of the project. However, instead of enhancing bilateral ties, the Northrail project soon became a source of embarrassment for both countries.

The controversy started in August 2005 when an opinion of the University of the Philippines (UP) Law Center on the legal, economic, financial and technical aspects of the deal was submitted to the Philippine Senate. This was followed in February 2006 by a legal suit filed by a group headed by Attorney Harry Roque who questioned the legality of the supply deal between CNMEG and Northrail. Roque's group called for the immediate annulment of the deal because it violated the Philippine law on government procurement (RA 9184). During the 2006 trial, CNMEG claimed that it was immune from such a suit because it represented the People's Republic of China and that the deal was an executive agreement (this was eventually denied by the court). In 2009, CNMEG filed a petition in the Supreme Court to stop the proceedings in the lower court, arguing that the project was an executive agreement and, therefore, the lower court did not have the jurisdiction to hear the case.[52] In February 2012, the Supreme Court denied CNMEG's petition. On top of the legal controversies, the project was also delayed by communication problems between the Northrail and CNMEG engineers, and allegations of kickbacks and corruption.[53] The government's poor handling of the relocation issues regarding the affected families along the tracks also created bad public relations for the project.

While the case for annulling the contract against CNMEG was being tried, the Arroyo government signed the US$329 million ZTE Corp-National Broadband Network (NBN) deal with China in February 2007. This project supposedly aimed to link government offices throughout the country via a nationwide telecommunications network. The implementing agency was the Department of Transportation and Communication (DOTC) while the contract was awarded to China's ZTE. Before the project started, allegations of kickbacks and corruption surfaced five months after the deal was signed and threatened at one point to embroil the country in a political crisis. Because of the involvement of several prominent political figures in the project, the Senate blue ribbon committee called for an investigation, which eventually led to the project's cancellation and the resignation of Benjamin Abalos, who purportedly brokered the NBN deal, from the Commission on Elections (COMELEC).

As the 2010 presidential election approached, the controversies involving Chinese financing became enmeshed in political bickering between former President Arroyo and her successor, President Benigno "Noynoy" Aquino III. Because the Northrail and NBN projects were signed during Arroyo's term, they were associated with her allegedly corrupt administration.[54] Aquino campaigned under the slogan *daang matuwid* (straight path), which was intended to rectify the irregularities of his predecessor. After winning the presidency, Aquino made reference to his "corrupt" predecessor in a speech before the delegates and participants to the Philippine-Eastern China Business Forum during his visit to China in 2011, saying

> ensuring a level playing field today requires undoing the mistakes of the past ... this means reviewing contracts entered into without particular care for due process ... holding accountable errant public officials who encouraged anomalous business deals ... "*Kung walang corrupt, walang mahirap.*" [If no one is corrupt, there will be no poor people.] An end to corruption means an end to poverty.[55]

The eventual suspension of the Northrail project and cancellation of the NBN project have tarnished Chinese aid-funded projects in the Philippines. As Figure 1 shows, the legal and political controversies that arose from Chinese-assisted loan projects were the result of conflicting aid systems and processes between a non-DAC aid donor (China) and a DAC-conforming aid recipient (the Philippines). The institutional mismatch is evident at two levels of the aid process: project identification and project implemetation.

In the case of China, the Going Out policy has created incentives for Chinese businesses, particularly SOEs, to initiate project proposals in recipient countries. Moreover, the request-based Chinese aid system, in which loans or grants are provided based on official requests of the recipient government submitted through diplomatic channels, enables Chinese companies to typically initiate the process.[56] Chinese SOEs in the Philippines approach implementing agencies and introduce

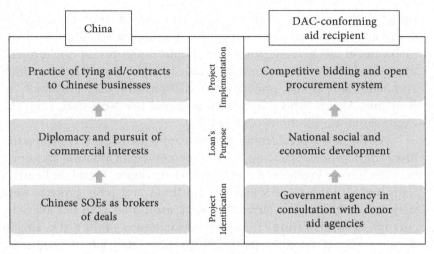

Figure 1 Mismatch of Chinese Aid Institutions and DAC-conforming Aid Recipient

proposals with supply contracts and financing support from the Exim Bank.[57] If the agency accepts the proposal, an application for foreign aid funding is channeled through NEDA, which reviews the proposal to ascertain whether the details are consistent with the Philippine Development Plan and then evaluates the technical and financial viability of the project. After this, the proposal is submitted to the Investment Coordination Committee (ICC) for further evaluation.[58] Once approved, it is elevated to the NEDA Board which is typically composed of the president as chair, the secretary of Socio-Economic Planning and NEDA director-general as vice chairs, and secretaries from eight departments as members. When the Board approves the project, NEDA endorses it to development partners/donors for funding. If China is the prospective partner, the proposal is submitted to an official diplomatic channel (such as the Chinese Embassy in Manila) through the Department of Foreign Affairs, and since Chinese loans are usually tied, NEDA also notifies the Exim Bank to coordinate payments for Chinese firms that receive the contract. The Department of Finance (DOF) signs the loan agreement.

The absence of a central aid agency in China and the growing role of Chinese SOEs as project identifiers provide strong incentives for Chinese firms with an interest in aid financing to maintain close contacts with recipient government agencies and officials who have direct or indirect links to aid implementing agencies in the Philippines. The practice of Chinese SOEs in initiating projects to be financed by Chinese loans invites corruption through kickbacks and commissions. Corruption is lessened, if not eradicated, in the case of traditional donors like Japan by allowing only the official aid agency such as the Japan International Cooperation Agency (JICA) to engage its counterpart in a series of transparent policy dialogues.

As for project implementation, the Going Out policy has enabled Chinese firms to have access to concessional financing from the Exim Bank by tying and awarding to them China's aid projects. The tied nature of the agreement has indeed put China's aid diplomacy in the Philippines in a bad light. In the trial for the annulment of the Northrail deal, CNMEG insisted that it was immune from legal suit because it represented the People's Republic of China and that the supply deal with Northrail was an executive agreement; hence, the tied procurement system mentioned in the agreement was valid. Indeed, Philippine law allows aid tying when it is part of the executive agreement to implement an aid-funded project. The bone of contention in the high-profile Northrail case that was submitted before the Philippine Supreme Court was "whether CNMEG is entitled to immunity, precluding it from being sued before a local court and whether the contract is an executive agreement, such that it cannot be questioned by or before a local court."[59]

On the other hand, as an aid recipient the Philippines is more accustomed to dealing with official aid agencies of DAC countries. As part of the project identification process, DAC and their counterparts in recipient countries conduct a series of transparent, formal and informal policy dialogues. As shown in the preceding sections, the Philippine government has developed a competitive and open bidding system of procurement for implementing national infrastructure projects. After the Northrail trial, the Investment Coordination Committee (ICC) circulated a memorandum to all implementing agencies on February 18, 2013, which stipulates that the potential financing source of a project must be separate from project appraisals. The appraisal of an agency's project proposal should be based on technical and economic merit and financial viability rather than the source of financing.[60] The memorandum evidently intended to address the problem of some firms from donor countries (such as Chinese SOEs) approaching national government agencies in order to introduce project proposals.

Conclusion

Foreign aid policy is an important resource for both hard and soft power. It can be used to sanction or to attract; to make a country want what another country wants through attraction and co-optation. China employed foreign aid strategically in the 1950s to achieve its national goals of international recognition in the UN and the diplomatic isolation of Taiwan. In the 1970s, the Chinese government used aid as a reward to countries that established diplomatic relations with China. In the new millennium, China's use of foreign aid has shifted to enhance its international and regional image and to sustain its economic development and modernization. China has also used foreign aid to pursue its Good Neighbor and Going Out policies, as well as to respond to the China-as-a-threat perception that has spread as China has risen to prominence. The foundation of China's foreign aid policy ever since it started has been its broad foreign policy goals.

China's aid is still in a formative stage and continues to evolve in terms of management style and modality. The features of Chinese aid, which differ considerably from DAC standards are outcomes of a long and gradual evolution of China's aid diplomacy, rather than direct responses to Western aid donors' dominance over the development of international aid architecture. The core of China's aid principles is not new but is based on Zhou Enlai's 1964 declaration. China's South-South cooperation label of its foreign aid goes back to the 1955 Afro-Asian Conference in Bandung, Indonesia. In the 2000s the same principles and values—respect for sovereignty, no conditionality, win-win, and self-reliance—have been stressed to enhance the allure of China's aid. Compared to Western aid, Chinese aid is often allotted to sectors that are neglected or ignored by DAC donors, particularly infrastructure.

China's aid to Southeast Asia in general and the Philippines in particular has been allotted for historical, cultural, economic and political reasons. China has provided a stream of financial assistance to mainland countries of Southeast Asia with which it shares long historical, ideological and cultural affinities. The mainland countries of Cambodia, Laos, Myanmar and Vietnam are crucial in realizing the development of China's western region, which has lagged behind the coastal and eastern regions ever since the country opened up. Meanwhile, aid relations with maritime countries like Indonesia and the Philippines are intended to overcome the animosity and distrust brought about by ideological differences and territorial disputes in the South China Sea. China's foreign aid to the Philippines affirms the existence of aid practices and institutions that do not conform to DAC rules. The case of Chinese aid to the Philippines during the 2000s is one in which aid institutions and practices of a non-DAC aid donor were applied to a recipient country that has adopted DAC-based practices and institutions in its aid management system. This explains why the soft footprint in the case of the Philippines became controversial: a mismatch on at least two levels of the aid process—project identification and project implementation—was at work. In terms of project identification, Chinese aid is not managed by a single agency, and other forms of official flows such as preferential buyers' credit are not reported separately from its foreign aid. China also ties its aid to procurement from its own SOEs. As the above case of the Philippines illustrates, Chinese SOEs initiate the first move in project identification. As a foreign aid recipient, which closely follows the DAC practices in project identification, the Philippines is more used to dealing directly with DAC aid agencies.

In terms of project implementation, applying China's style of awarding project contracts and tying supplies to Chinese firms in a country that tries to adopt an open and competitive system of bidding and procurement has proved to be a disaster for China's aid diplomacy. The awarding of supply contracts to CNMEG by Northrail led to legal and political controversies, which created bad public relations for Chinese aid in the Philippines during the administration of President Gloria Macapagal-Arroyo. This bad image was amplified by Chinese aid's entanglement in domestic politics. President Noynoy Aquino campaigned under the slogan *daang matuwid* (straight path), which highlighted the involvement of then President Macapagal-Arroyo in questionable projects funded by Chinese aid. As this study has suggested, soft-power resources such as foreign aid are more effective in countries that share the political values of their donor state. This is a plausible reason why Chinese aid is more acceptable and popular in countries that lack DAC-based aid institutions such as sub-Saharan African countries, Cambodia and elsewhere.

Notes

1. Naohiro Kitano, "China's Foreign Aid at a Transitional Stage," *Asian Economic Policy Review* 9, no. 2 (2014): 301–317 <http://ssrn.com/

abstract=2464358> or <http://dx.doi.org/10.1111/aepr.12074> (accessed March 7, 2016); Carol Lancaster, "The Chinese Aid System," Center for Global Development, June 2007: 5, <https://www.cgdev.org/files/13953_file_Chinese_aid.pdf> (accessed May 27, 2014).

2. Edward J. Clay, Matthew Geddes, and Luisa Natali, *Untying Aid: Is It Working? An Evaluation of the Implementation of the Paris Declaration and of the 2001 DAC Recommendation of Untying ODA to the LDCs* (Copenhagen: Danish Institute for International Studies, 2009), 12.

3. OECD, "Untying aid: The right to choose," <http://www.oecd.org/dac/financing-sustainable-development/development-finance-standards/untyingaidtherighttochoose.htm> (accessed on March 30, 2016).

4. Edward J. Clay, Matthew Geddes, Luisa Natali, and Dirk Willem te Velde, *The Developmental Effectiveness of Untied Aid: Evaluation of the Implementation of the Paris Declaration and of the 2001 DAC Recommendation on Untying ODA To The LDCs, Phase I Report* (Copenhagen: Ministry of Foreign Affairs of Denmark, 2008), 35.

5. Section 2 of R.A. 8182 states that ODA is a loan or loan and grant which meets the following criteria: (a) it must be administered for the purpose of promoting sustainable social and economic development and national welfare; (b) it must be contracted with governments of foreign countries with whom the Philippines has diplomatic, trade relations, or bilateral agreements or which are members of the United Nations, their agencies, and international or multilateral lending institutions; (c) there are no available comparable financial institutions; and (d) it must contain a grant element of at least 25 percent. The DAC, on the other hand, defines ODA as "grants or loans which are: (a) undertaken by the official sector; (b) with promotion of economic development and welfare as the main objective; and (c) at concessional financial terms (if a loan, having a grant element of at least 25 percent." OECD, "Official development assistance – definition and coverage," <http://www.oecd.org/dac/stats/officialdevelopmentassistancedefinitionandcoverage.htm> (accessed January 28, 2013).

6. These laws include National Economic and Development Authority's (NEDA) Implementing Rules and Regulations (IRR) for R.A. 8182, Foreign Borrowings Act of 1966 (R.A. 4860), and R.A. 8555 which amended some sections of R.A. 8182.

7. Joseph S. Nye, Jr., "Public Diplomacy and Soft Power," *The Annals of the American Academy of Political and Social Science* 616, *Public Diplomacy in a Changing World* (March 2008): 94–109.

8. Ibid.

9. Joseph S. Nye, Jr., *Soft Power: The Means to Success in World Politics* (New York: PublicAffairs, 2004).

10. Nye, "Public Diplomacy and Soft Power."
11. Ingrid d'Hooghe, *The Limits of China's Soft Power in Europe: Beijing's Public Diplomacy Puzzle* (The Hague: Netherlands Institute of International Relations 'Clingendael,' 2010).
12. Ibid., 30.
13. James F. Paradise, "China and International Harmony: The Role of Confucius Institutes in Bolstering Beijing's Soft Power," *Asian Survey* 49, no. 4 (July August 2009): 647–69.
14. Nye, *Soft Power: The Means to Success in World Politics*, 10.
15. Jean-Marc F. Blanchard and Fujia Lu, "Thinking Hard About Soft Power: A Review and Critique of the Literature on China and Soft Power," *Asian Perspective* 36, no. 4 (2012): 580.
16. Ibid.
17. Wanfa Zhang, "Has Beijing Started to Bare Its Teeth? China's Tapping of Soft Power Revisited," *Asian Perspective* 36, no. 4 (2012): 617.
18. Emma Mawdsley, *From Recipients to Donors: Emerging Powers and the Changing Development Landscape* (London: Zed Book, 2012).
19. Thomas Lum, Hannah Fischer, Julissa Gomez-Granger, and Anne Leland, *China's Foreign Aid Activities in Africa, Latin America and Southeast Asia: CRS Report for Congress* (Washington, DC: Congressional Research Service, 2009).
20. Takaaki Kobayashi, "Evolution of China's Aid Policy," JBIC Working Paper No. 27 (Tokyo: Japan Bank for International Cooperation Institute, 2008).
21. Teh-chang Lin, "Beijing's Foreign Aid Policy in the 1990s: Continuity and Change," *Issues and Studies*, 1996: 52.
22. Zhenming Zhu, "China's Foreign Economic Cooperation for CLMV: Contract Engineering for CLMV," in *Economic Relations of China, Japan and Korea with the Mekong River Basin Countries (MBRCs)*, BRC Research Report No. 3, ed. Mitsuhiro Kagami, 69–106 (Thailand: Bangkok Research Center, IDE-JETRO, 2010), 70.
23. The eight principles of China's foreign aid include (1) mutual benefit, equality and win-win, (2) respect for sovereignty, no conditionality, (3) flexible, long-term repayment, (4) self-reliance and independent economic development, (5) low-cost but with quick results, (6) ensure best quality, (7) facilitate technology transfer, and (8) equal treatment of Chinese and local experts.
24. Lin, "Beijing's Foreign Aid Policy in the 1990s," 50.
25. Takaaki Kobayashi and Yasutami Shimomura, "Aid Volume in a Historical Perspective," in *A Study of China's Foreign Aid: An Asian Perspective*, ed. Y. Shimomura and H. Ohashi, 46–57 (Basingstoke: Palgrave MacMillan, 2013), 54–5.

26. Paul Nash, "China's Going Out Strategy," *Diplomatic Courier*, May 10, 2012, <http://www.diplomaticourier.com/china-s-going-out-strategy/> (accessed March 12, 2016).
27. Dennis D. Trinidad, "The Foreign Aid Philosophy of a Rising Asian Power: A Southeast Asian View," in *A Study of China's Foreign Aid: An Asian Perspective*, ed. Y. Shimomura and H. Ohashi, 19–45 (Basingstoke: Palgrave MacMillan, 2013), 32.
28. Shuaihua Cheng, Ting Fang, and Hui-Ting Lien, "China's International Aid Policy and Its Implications for Global Governance," Research Center for Chinese Politics and Business Working Paper No. 29, Indiana University, November 1, 2012.
29. For a more recent estimation of China's annual aid volume, see Kobayashi and Shimomura, "Aid Volume in a Historical Perspective;" Charles Wolf, Jr., Xiao Wang, and Eric Warner, *China's Foreign Aid and Government-Sponsored Investment Activities: Scale, Content, Destinations, and Implications* (Santa Monica, CA: RAND Corporation, 2013); Naohiro Kitano and Yukinori Harada, "Estimating China's Foreign Aid 2001–2013," JICA-Research Institute Working Paper No. 78, 2014.
30. Information Office of the State Council, The People's Republic of China, "China's Foreign Aid," Beijing, April 2011, 5, <http://english.gov.cn/archive/white_paper/2014/09/09/content_281474986284620.htm> (accessed June 10, 2013).
31. Information Office of the State Council, The People's Republic of China, "China's Foreign Aid," Beijing, July 2014, <http://english.gov.cn/archive/white_paper/2014/08/23/content_281474982986592.htm> (accessed on March 12, 2016).
32. "China's Foreign Aid," (2011): 20.
33. Ibid.
34. Lancaster, "The Chinese Aid System."
35. Aravind Yelery, "China's 'Going Out' Policy: Sub-National Economic Trajectories," Analysis No. 24, Institute of Chinese Studies, Delhi, December 2014, <http://www.icsin.org/uploads/2015/04/12/e50f1e532774c4c354b24885fcb327c5.pdf> (accessed March 29, 2016).
36. Linda Jackobson, "China's Diplomacy toward Africa: Drivers and Constraints," *International Relations of the Asia Pacific* 9, no. 3 (2009): 414.
37. Cheng, et al., "China's International Aid Policy and Its Implications for Global Governance," 2012, 8.
38. Jianren Lu, "Evolution of the Relations between China and ASEAN," in *Making New Partnership: A Rising China and Its Neighbors*, ed. Yunling Zhang, Jin Xi-de, and Zheng Yu, 115–35 (Beijing: Paths International Ltd., 2010), 128–30.
39. Truong Giang Bui, "ASEAN and China Relations: Seeking for Economic Cooperation," in *Making New Partnership: A Rising China and Its*

Neighbors, ed. Yunling Zhang, 153–76 (Beijing: Paths International Ltd., 2010), 170.

40. Wang Gungwu, "China and Southeast Asia: The Context of a New Beginning," in *Power Shift: China and Asia's New Dynamics*, ed. David Shambaugh, 187–204 (Berkeley, CA: University of California Press, 2006); Yasuo Onishi, "Chinese Economy in the 21st Century and the Strategy for Developing the Western Region," in *China's Western Development Strategy: Issues and Prospects, Spot Essay No. 22*, ed. Onishi Yasuo (Chiba, Japan: IDE-JETRO, 2001).

41. "CY 2012 ODA Portfolio Review" (Pasig City: National Economic and Development Authority [NEDA], 2013), 11.

42. Lancaster, "The Chinese Aid System;" Interview with NEDA Public Investment Staff, 2014.

43. See for instance the study of Jin Sato, Hiroaki Shiga, Takaaki Kobayashi, and Hisahiro Kondoh, "'Emerging Donors' from a Recipient Perspective: An Institutional Analysis of Foreign Aid in Cambodia," *World Development* 39, no. 12 (2011): 2091–104.

44. "Visit of China Premier Wen Jiabao Highlights Enhanced Engagement," January 18, 2007, <https://wikileaks.org/plusd/cables/07MANILA212_a.html> (accessed June 19, 2014).

45. Quoted in Roel Landingin, "Chinese Foreign Aid Goes Offtrack in the Philippines," in *The Reality of Aid, South-South Cooperation: A Challenge to the Aid System?* ed. The Reality of Aid Management Committee, 87–94 (Philippines: IBON Books, 2010), 87, <http://www.realityofaid.org/wp-content/uploads/2013/02/ROA-SSDC-Special-Report English.pdf> (accessed February 20, 2013).

46. Former Secretary of Foreign Affairs Alberto Romulo, "The Golden Age of Philippine-China Relations," *The Manila Times*, June 23, 2007, p. A5, <https://news.google.com/newspapers?nid=2518&dat=20070523&id=fk1aAAAAIBAJ&sjid=KSgMAAAAIBAJ&pg=1814,11512343&hl=en> (accessed March 30, 2016).

47. Roel Landingin, "Chinese Foreign Aid Goes Offtrack in the Philippines."

48. Northrail Annual Report 2012, p. 2, <http://www.northrail.com.ph/downloads/GCG/43.3%20C%20Annual%20Reports%202012.pdf> (accessed March 30, 2016).

49. Interview with NEDA Public Investment Staff, 2014. In November 2015 Japan granted a loan amounting to JPY241.991 billion (approximately PHP 93.457 billion or about US$2 billion) to refinance the Northrail project. See "Northrail gets a new life from Japan," Philstar Global, November 24, 2015, <http://www.philstar.com/business/2015/11/25/1525529/northrail-gets-new-life-japan> (accessed March 28, 2016).

50. Based on one estimate, there were about 20,000 families that were relocated during the first phase of the project while another 19,500

residents would have to be relocated during the second phase. See Philippine Human Rights Information Center, "The Herculean Task of Relocating 40,000 NorthRail Families," 2010, <http://philrights.org/wp-content/uploads/2010/10/The-Herculean-Task-of-Relocating-40000-NorthRail-Families.pdf> (accessed June 27, 2014).

51. Landingin, "Chinese Foreign Aid Goes Offtrack."
52. "High court asked to stop railroad project case," BusinessWorld Online, February 2, 2009, <http://philippinerealestatenews.blogspot.com/2009/02/high-court-asked-to-stop-railroad.html> (accessed July 5, 2018).
53. Landingin, "Chinese Foreign Aid Goes Offtrack."
54. The Northrail project was cited in a long list of corruption charges against the Arroyo administration. See, for instance, Movement for the Advancement of Student Power, "Scandals under Gloria Macapagal-Arroyo from 2001–2009," July 20, 2009, <https://maspnational.wordpress.com/2009/07/20/scandals-under-gloria-macapagal-arroyo-from-2001-2009/> (accessed March 5, 2016). Both Northrail and ZTE-NBN were also part of the 2008 impeachment complaint charges filed against former President Arroyo. See Neri Javier Colmenares, "Summary of 2008 Impeachment Complaint," October 11, 2008, <http://www.gmanetwork.com/news/story/126477/news/summary-of-2008-impeachment-complaint-vs-arroyo> (accessed March 5, 2016).
55. Speech of President Benigno S. Aquino III at the Philippines-Eastern China Business Forum, September 2, 2011, *Official Gazette of the Republic of the Philippines*, <http://www.gov.ph/2011/09/02/president-aquino-speech-at-the-philippines-eastern-china-business-forum-september-2-2011/> (accessed March 26, 2015).
56. See "'Emerging Donors' from a Recipient Perspective" in the case of Chinese aid in Cambodia.
57. Interview with NEDA Public Investment Staff, 2014.
58. The ICC consists of the Secretary of Finance, as chair; the NEDA Director-General, as co-chair; and the Executive Secretary, the Secretaries of Agriculture, Trade and Industry, Budget and Management, and the Governor of the Central Bank of the Philippines, as members. See NEDA, "ICC Guidelines and Procedures," March 4, 2005, <http://www.neda.gov.ph/wp-content/uploads/2013/10/Revised-ICC-Guidelines-and-Procedures-as-of-4-March-2005.pdf> (accessed July 15, 2018). The ICC evaluation covers six areas: (1) financial evaluation to ascertain financial viability of the project; (2) economic evaluation to ensure its economic and social contribution to the nation as a whole; (3) technical evaluation to determine the project/program's technical feasibility, cost effectiveness, and implications for the environment; (4) social analysis to determine if the proposed program/project is responsive to national objectives of

poverty alleviation, employment generation and income redistribution; (5) institutional evaluation to ensure institutional coordination for efficient program/project implementation; (6) sensitivity analysis to determine whether the program/project will remain feasible if changes in the assumptions used in the calculation/projections were to take place according to the degree in which they are likely to vary from the estimated or projected values; and (6) public consultation to determine the project's socio-political impact.

59. Supreme Court of the Philippines, En banc decision, G.R. No. 185572, China National Machinery & Equipment Corp. (Group) versus Honorable Cesar D. Santamaria et al., <http://sc.judiciary.gov.ph/jurisprudence/2012/february2012/185572.htm> (accessed June 19, 2014).

60. NEDA, "Investment Coordination Committee Memorandum Re: Proposed Revision on ICC Review/Evaluation Procedures and Parameters (Evaluating Proposals Separate from Source of Financing)," February 18, 2013, <http://www.neda.gov.ph/wp-content/uploads/2014/01/New-Financing-Framework.pdf> (accessed May 8, 2014).

References

Aquino, Benigno S. III. Speech at the Philippines-Eastern China Business Forum, September 2, 2011, *Official Gazette of the Republic of the Philippines*. <http://www.gov.ph/2011/09/02/president-aquino-speech-at-the-philippines-eastern-china-business-forum-september-2-2011/> (accessed March 26, 2015).

Blanchard, Jean-Marc F. and Fujia Lu. "Thinking Hard About Soft Power: A Review and Critique of the Literature on China and Soft Power." *Asian Perspective* 36, no. 4 (2012): 565–89.

Brautigam, Deborah. *The Dragon's Gift: The Real Story of China in Africa*. Oxford: Oxford University Press, 2009.

Bui, Truong Giang. "ASEAN and China Relations: Seeking for Economic Cooperation." In *Making New Partnership: A Rising China and Its Neighbors*, edited by Yunling Zhang, 153–76. Beijing: Paths International Ltd., 2010.

Cheng, Shuaihua, Ting Fang, and Hui-Ting Lien. "China's International Aid Policy and Its Implications for Global Governance." Research Center for Chinese Politics and Business Working Paper No. 29, Indiana University, November 1, 2012.

Clay, Edward J., Matthew Geddes, and Luisa Natali. *Untying Aid: Is It Working? An Evaluation of the Implementation of the Paris Declaration and of the 2001 DAC Recommendation of Untying ODA to the LDCs*. Copenhagen: Danish Institute for International Studies, 2009.

Clay, Edward J., Matthew Geddes, Luisa Natali, and Dirk Willem te Velde. *The Developmental Effectiveness of Untied Aid: Evaluation of the Implementation of the Paris Declaration and of the 2001 DAC Recommendation on Untying ODA To The LDCs, Phase I Report*. Copenhagen: Ministry of Foreign Affairs of Denmark, 2008.

Colmenares, Neri Javier. "Summary of 2008 Impeachment Complaint," October 11, 2008. <http://www.gmanetwork.com/news/story/126477/news/summary-of-2008-impeachment-complaint-vs-arroyo> (accessed March 5, 2016).

d'Hooghe, Ingrid. *The Limits of China's Soft Power in Europe: Beijing's Public Diplomacy Puzzle*. The Hague: Netherlands Institute of International Relations 'Clingendael,' 2010.

"High court asked to stop railroad project case," *BusinessWorld Online*, February 2, 2009. <http://philippinerealestatenews.blogspot.com/2009/02/high-court-asked-to-stop-railroad.html> (accessed July 5, 2018).

Information Office of the State Council, The People's Republic of China. "China's Foreign Aid," Beijing, April 2011. <http://english.gov.cn/archive/white_paper/2014/09/09/content_281474986284620.htm> (accessed June 10, 2013).

———. "China's Foreign Aid," Beijing, July 2014. <http://english.gov.cn/archive/white_paper/2014/08/23/content_281474982986592.htm> (accessed on March 12, 2016).

Jackobson, Linda. "China's Diplomacy toward Africa: Drivers and Constraints." *International Relations of the Asia Pacific* 9, no. 3 (2009): 403–33.

Kitano, Naohiro. "China's Foreign Aid at a Transitional Stage." *Asian Economic Policy Review* 9, no. 2 (2014): 301–317. <http://ssrn.com/abstract=2464358> or <http://dx.doi.org/10.1111/aepr.12074> (accessed March 7, 2016).

Kitano, Naohiro and Yukinori Harada. "Estimating China's Foreign Aid 2001–2013." JICA-Research Institute Working Paper No. 78, 2014.

Kobayashi, Takaaki. "Evolution of China's Aid Policy." JBIC Working Paper No. 27. Tokyo: Japan Bank for International Cooperation Institute, 2008.

Kobayashi, Takaaki and Yasutami Shimomura. "Aid Volume in Historical Perspective. In *A Study of China's Aid: An Asian Perspective*, edited by Yasutami Shimomura and Hideo Ohashi, 46–57. Basingstoke: Palgrave Macmillan, 2013.

Lancaster, Carol. "The Chinese Aid System." Center for Global Development, June 2007. <https://www.cgdev.org/files/13953_file_Chinese_aid.pdf> (accessed May 27, 2014).

Landingin, Roel. "Chinese Foreign Aid Goes Offtrack in the Philippines." In *The Reality of Aid, South-South Cooperation: A Challenge to the Aid System?* edited by The Reality of Aid Management Committee, 87–94.

Philippines: IBON Books, 2010. <http://www.realityofaid.org/wp-content/uploads/2013/02/ROA-SSDC-Special-ReportEnglish.pdf> (accessed February 20, 2013).

Lin, Teh-chang. "Beijing's Foreign Aid Policy in the 1990s: Continuity and Change." *Issues and Studies* 32, No. 1 (1996): 32–56.

Lu, Jianren. "Evolution of the Relations between China and ASEAN." In *Making New Partnership: A Rising China and Its Neighbors*, edited by Yunling Zhang, Jin Xi-de, and Zheng Yu, 115–35. Beijing: Paths International Ltd., 2010.

Lum, Thomas, Hannah Fischer, Julissa Gomez-Granger, and Anne Leland. *China's Foreign Aid Activities in Africa, Latin America and Southeast Asia: CRS Report for Congress*. Washington, DC: Congressional Research Service, 2009.

Mawdsley, Emma. *From Recipients to Donors: Emerging Powers and the Changing Development Landscape*. London: Zed Books, 2012.

Movement for the Advancement of Student Power. "Scandals under Gloria Macapagal-Arroyo from 2001–2009," July 20, 2009. <https://maspnational.wordpress.com/2009/07/20/scandals-under-gloria-macapagal-arroyo-from-2001-2009/> (accessed March 5, 2016).

Nash, Paul. "China's Going Out Strategy." *Diplomatic Courier*, May 10, 2012. <http://www.diplomaticourier.com/china-s-going-out-strategy/> (accessed March 12, 2016).

National Economic and Development Authority (NEDA). "ICC Guidelines and Procedures," March 4, 2005. <http://www.neda.gov.ph/wp-content/uploads/2013/10/Revised-ICC-Guidelines-and-Procedures-as-of-4-March-2005.pdf> (accessed July 15, 2018).

———. "Investment Coordination Committee Memorandum Re: Proposed Revision on ICC Review/Evaluation Procedures and Parameters (Evaluating Proposals Separate from Source of Financing)," February 18, 2013. <http://www.neda.gov.ph/wp-content/uploads/2014/01/New-Financing-Framework.pdf> (accessed May 8, 2014).

———. "Implementing Rules and Regulations (IRR) for Republic Act (R.A.) 8182, Otherwise Known as 'The Official Development Assistance (ODA) Act of 1996,'" July 23, 1996.

———. *ODA Loan Performance, List of Ongoing and Completed China-Assisted Loans from 2003 to 2013*. Pasig City: NEDA, 2014.

———. *2012 ODA Portfolio Review*. Pasig City: National Economic and Development Authority, 2013. <http://www.neda.gov.ph/wp-content/uploads/2014/04/CY2012-ODA-Portfolio-Review-Full-Report.pdf> (accessed February 3, 2014).

Northrail Annual Report. 2012. <http://www.northrail.com.ph/images/pdf/43.3%20C%20Annual%20Reports%202012.pdf> (accessed March 30, 2016).

"Northrail gets a new life from Japan," Philstar Global, November 24, 2015. <http://www.philstar.com/business/2015/11/25/1525529/northrail-gets-new-life-japan> (accessed March 28, 2016).

Nye, Joseph S., Jr. "Public Diplomacy and Soft Power." *The Annals of the American Academy of Political and Social Science* 616, Public Diplomacy in a Changing World (March 2008): 94–109.

──────. *Soft Power: The Means to Success in World Politics*. New York: PublicAffairs, 2004.

Onishi, Yasuo. "Chinese Economy in the 21st Century and the Strategy for Developing the Western Region." In *China's Western Development Strategy: Issues and Prospects, Spot Essay No. 22*, edited by Onishi Yasuo, 1–16. Chiba, Japan: Institute of Developing Economies, 2001.

Organization for Economic Co-operation and Development. "Official Development Assistance – Definition and Coverage." <http://www.oecd.org/dac/stats/officialdevelopmentassistancedefinitionandcoverage.htm> (accessed January 28, 2013).

──────. "Untying aid: The right to choose." <http://www.oecd.org/dac/financing-sustainable-development/development-finance-standards/untyingaidtherighttochoose.htm> (accessed on March 30, 2016).

Paradise, James F. "China and International Harmony: The Role of Confucius Institutes in Bolstering Beijing's Soft Power." *Asian Survey* 49, No. 4 (July/August 2009): 647–69.

Philippine Human Rights Information Center. "The Herculean Task of Relocating 40,000 NorthRail Families," 2010. <http://philrights.org/wp-content/uploads/2010/10/The-Herculean-Task-of-Relocating-40000-NorthRail-Families.pdf> (accessed June 27, 2014).

Republic Act No. 4860, "An Act Authorizing the President of the Philippines to Obtain Such Foreign Loans and Credits, or to Incur Such Foreign Indebtedness, as May Be Necessary to Finance Approved Economic Development Purposes or Projects, and to Guarantee, on Behalf of the Republic of the Philippines, Foreign Loans Obtained or Bonds Issued by Corporations Owned or Controlled by the Government of the Philippines for Economic Development Purposes Including Those Incurred for Purposes of Re-lending to the Private Sector, Appropriating the Necessary Funds Therefor and for Other Purposes," August 8, 1966.

Republic Act No. 8182, "An Act Excluding Official Development Assistance (ODA) from the Foreign Debt Limit in Order to Facilitate the Absorption and Optimize the Utilization of ODA Resources, Amending for the Purpose Paragraph 1, Section 2 of Republic Act No. 4860, as Amended," June 11, 1996.

Republic Act No. 8555, "An Act Amending Republic Act No. 8182, and for Other Purposes," February 26, 1998.

Sato, Jin, Hiroaki Shiga, Takaaki Kobayashi, and Hisahiro Kondoh. "'Emerging Donors' from a Recipient Perspective: An Institutional Analysis of Foreign Aid in Cambodia." *World Development* 39, No. 12 (2011): 2091–104.
Supreme Court of the Philippines. En banc decision, G.R. No. 185572: China National Machinery & Equipment Corp. (Group) versus Honorable Cesar D. Santamaria et al. <http://sc.judiciary.gov.ph/jurisprudence/2012/february2012/185572.htm> (accessed June 19, 2014).
"The Golden Age of Philippine-China Relations." *The Manila Times*, June 23, 2007, p. A5. <https://news.google.com/newspapers?nid=2518&dat=20070523&id=fk1aAAAAIBAJ&sjid=KSgMAAAAIBAJ&pg=1814,11512343&hl=en> (accessed March 30, 2016).
Trinidad, Dennis D. "The Foreign Aid Philosophy of a Rising Asian Power: A Southeast Asian View." In *A Study of China's Foreign Aid: An Asian Perspective*, edited by Yasutami Shimomura and Hideo Ohashi, 19–45. Basingstoke: Palgrave Macmillan, 2013.
"Visit of China Premier Wen Jiabao Highlights Enhanced Engagement," January 18, 2007. <https://wikileaks.org/plusd/cables/07MANILA212_a.html> (accessed June 19, 2014).
Wang Gungwu. "China and Southeast Asia: The Context of a New Beginning." In *Power Shift: China and Asia's New Dynamics*, edited by David Shambaugh, 187–204. Berkeley: University of California Press, 2006.
Wolf, Charles, Xiao Wang, and Eric Warner. *China's Foreign Aid and Government-Sponsored Investment Activities: Scale, Content, Destinations, and Implications*. Santa Monica, CA: RAND Corporation, 2013. <http://www.rand.org/pubs/research_reports/RR118.html> (accessed May 27, 2014).
Yelery, Aravind. "China's 'Going Out' Policy: Sub-National Economic Trajectories." Analysis No. 24, Institute of Chinese Studies, Delhi, December 2014. <http://www.icsin.org/uploads/2015/04/12/e50f1e532774c4c354b24885fcb327c5.pdf> (accessed March 29, 2016).
Zhang, Wanfa. "Has Beijing Started to Bare Its Teeth? China's Tapping of Soft Power Revisited." *Asian Perspective* 36, No. 4 (2012): 615–39.
Zhu, Zhenming. "China's Foreign Economic Cooperation for CLMV: Contract Engineering for CLMV." In *Economic Relations of China, Japan and Korea with the Mekong River Basin Countries (MBRCs)*, BRC Research Report No. 3, edited by Mitsuhiro Kagami, 84–120. Thailand: Bangkok Research Center, IDE-JETRO, 2010.

CHAPTER 7

The Re-recognition of Confucianism in Indonesia: An Example of China's Soft Footprint in Southeast Asia[1]

Yumi Kitamura

Introduction

Since the early 2000s, the People's Republic of China (hereafter China) has used soft power in Southeast Asia to achieve its political and economic goals, which has gained the attention of the mass media and governments around the world. The concept of soft power was introduced by Joseph Nye in his book, *Bound to Lead*, during a time when the United States (hereafter the US) was seeking a new position in the post-Cold War world.[2] Nye emphasizes the importance of "cooperative power" or "soft power" based on the attraction of culture, political ideology or values and foreign policy.[3]

The concept of soft power was first introduced to China by scholars in 1993 and eventually adopted as an approach for formulating government policy after 2004.[4] While the cultural asset of the US's soft power is mainly thought of in terms of pop culture, revitalizing the elements of traditional culture became one aim of China's soft power foreign policy, economic development model and external media initiatives.[5] This aim has become a central component of

China's relationships with developing countries in Southeast Asia and Africa.[6] In terms of cultural footprints, the most notable is the promotion of language education through the government-sponsored Confucius Institute language schools.[7]

The cultural and economic aspects of soft power are not separable from each other in state-to-state affairs. Moreover, soft-power actors not only include state agencies and government policymakers but also other parties from civil society.[8] In the case of Southeast Asia, overseas Chinese populations are sometimes themselves creators of China's soft footprints. This chapter argues that during the time when China was expanding its soft power in Indonesia, Chinese Indonesians used the Indonesian government's openness to China to facilitate negotiation and recognition of their own cultural practices within the state of Indonesia. Their success came about after 30 years of an assimilation policy designed to suppress the public expression of Chinese culture in Indonesia.

Historical Background

The relationship between China and Indonesia resembles the relationships between China and other Southeast Asian countries in terms of a long history of trade and a large presence of Chinese migrants in major cities. After Indonesian independence in 1949, this relationship took on a new political significance when Indonesia became the fourth non-socialist country following India, the United Kingdom and Vietnam to recognize and establish diplomatic ties with China in 1950. The relationship between the two countries grew during the 1945–67 presidency of Sukarno.

Liu points out that China influenced the political thinking of some Indonesian intellectuals and government officials during the Sukarno period.[9] Though the relationship between the two nations was not always smooth, China was an important non-Western country to the newly independent Indonesia.[10] China's ascendancy came about in part because Sukarno wanted to dissolve the power of Muslim groups in political affairs after the Islamic rebellions in Sumatra and Sulawesi.[11] In 1959, Sukarno instituted Guided Democracy, which enforced the president's political power by reinstalling the 1945 Constitution. This shift was an attempt to create a balance of power between the Indonesian Communist Party or Partai Komunis Indonesia (PKI) and the army.[12] However, the balance of power eventually shifted to the PKI as Sukarno tried to isolate Indonesia from Western influence in the 1960s. Consequently, the China-Indonesia relationship became closer.[13] However, this relationship ended after the 30 September Movement in 1965 (G30S), an alleged coup by the PKI to seize control of the government. The coup attempt was immediately quelled by Suharto, an army officer, and his fellows. Sukarno's suppression of Muslim political groups and his support for the PKI eventually led the Muslim groups, including Nahdlatul Ulama, the largest Muslim group in 1965, to cooperate with the military in carrying out the nationwide massacre of communists and suspected communists that occurred after the G30S incident.[14]

Though the truth behind the G30S is still unclear, the official history of the Suharto period justifies Suharto's suppression of the G30S, and the mass killings that followed as a necessary response to the attempted coup by the PKI.[15] Whatever the case, Suharto succeeded in taking over the government in 1967. He then suspended diplomatic relations with China, claiming that it was behind the G30S movement.[16] Between 1966 and 1967, the Suharto regime passed several laws to separate Chinese Indonesians from their native culture. There was only one approved Chinese-language newspaper; all public manifestations of Chinese culture, language and religion were banned; Chinese-medium schools were phased out; and Chinese Indonesians were strongly encouraged to change their Chinese names to Indonesian-sounding names. Most Chinese Indonesians complied with these laws.

The assimilation policy and the anti-communist orientation of the state were entwined. In particular, being affiliated with a state-recognized religion became increasingly important to avoid being considered a communist. In response to Presidential Instruction No. 14/1967, which prohibited public displays of Chinese cultural and religious activities,[17] many Chinese Indonesians converted to Christianity, with the Pentecostal-Charismatic movement being one of the choices of Chinese Indonesian entrepreneurs.[18] Christianity came to represent one's alignment with modernity while Confucianism, Buddhism and Tridarma (a local mixture of Confucianism, Buddhism and Taoism) came to represent one's continued adherence to Chinese traditions.

Muslim groups hoped to regain political influence under the new regime;[19] however, these hopes were not fulfilled by Suharto. On the contrary, he intensified the depoliticization of religious groups and increased the state's control over religion. Restrictions on the Muslim groups in the political sphere eventually pushed Muslim intellectuals like Nurcholish Madjid, Djohan Effendi and Abdurrahman Wahid to develop a discourse with their interpretation of modern concepts, which supported secularism, liberalism and pluralism.[20] This group of liberal Muslim intellectuals would later help the process of reinstating Confucianism as a state-sanctioned religion.

After Indonesia resumed diplomatic relationships with China in 1990, economic relations developed rapidly between the two nations and grew even faster after the fall of the Suharto regime in 1998. The rapid growth of the Chinese economy in the 21st century coincided with the re-introduction of Chinese culture by the Chinese government and Chinese Indonesians.

Religious Landscape of Chinese Indonesians in the Post-Suharto Era

One major change in the religious practices of Chinese Indonesians was the relisting of Confucianism as one of the officially recognized religions by the state. The re-recognition was the result of a long history of negotiations between the Chinese Indonesians and the government in order to improve their social conditions by mobilizing Chinese soft power in a strategic way. There were also several other religious groups that attracted Chinese Indonesians in the post-Suharto era, such as the Tzu Chi, a Buddhist sect from Taiwan, and the Christian Pentecostal and evangelical churches. The rapid growth of these groups suggests a strong connection to being Chinese. These groups became the gateway of soft power from China and Taiwan into Indonesia.

Confucianism as the Crossroad of Being Chinese and China's Soft Footprint

The history of Confucianism in Indonesia goes back to the 19th-century Dutch East Indies. During this period, a substantial proportion of the Chinese population in Java and Madura was locally born and tended to culturally assimilate into the Muslim majority. Tjoa Djien Ho, a well-educated businessman from an elite Surabaya family, noted that even though Chinese Indonesians read Confucian teachings, their religious practices reflected a fusion of Taoist and Buddhist elements, native practices such as the worship of tombs of Muslim saints, and the celebration of Muslim festivals.[21] Despite the similarity of these syncretistic practices to the mixture of local-god veneration, Confucianism and Taoism found in China, Tjoa saw these practices as non-traditional and non-Chinese, which led him and other elite Chinese Indonesians to conclude that their fellow Chinese Indonesians must be re-Sinicized (reoriented to their cultural roots). They chose Confucianism as the ideological framework for this effort because they regarded Confucian teachings as the only authentic traditional source of Chinese religion and rituals. Such thinking gave rise to a number of initiatives focused on inculcating a sense of being Chinese in the Chinese communities of the Dutch East Indies. Early efforts included the following:

- In 1864, Tjoa, along with other elite Surabaya Chinese, founded the Hokkien Kong Tik Soe, a Chinese social association dedicated to the re-Sinicization of the Chinese in Surabaya.[22]
- In 1899, the Chinese gentry and merchants of Surabaya dedicated to Confucius a temple consecrated to Wen Mian (Boen Bio in Hokkien), the God of Literature.
- Salmon argues that the rise of Confucianism in Surabaya is suggested by two events—the establishment in the 1870s of Nanyang Xunmeng Guang, a Chinese school that followed Confucian principles, and Kang You Wei's movement which sought to establish Confucianism as a state religion in China in 1895, both of which predate similar movements in other parts of Southeast Asia.[23]

However, Chinese Indonesians only began to regard Confucianism as the basis of an organized religion after 1900, when the re-Sinicization movement occurred along with a widespread desire for traditional Chinese education, a growing anti-Chinese movement among the Javanese and the growth of Confucian associations.

The first "modern" Chinese school, Thiong Hua Hui Guan (THHK), was established in Batavia by local Chinese Indonesian elites in 1901.[24] Schools based on the same model as THHK eventually spread to different parts of the Dutch East Indies and gained the attention of the Chinese government, which began to provide THHK schools with textbooks and teachers. When Chinese Indonesians started to involve themselves in China's political affairs,[25] the Dutch colonial officials became concerned. In response, the colonial government changed its education policy towards Chinese Indonesians in

1908, which resulted in the establishment of the Holland-Chinese schools with Dutch as the language of instruction.[26] The influence of THHK schools declined partly because Chinese parents considered it more practical for their children to attend the Holland-Chinese schools. Nevertheless, THHK schools were instrumental in establishing a monotheistic form of Confucianism built around the concepts of *Tien* (Heaven), a single God, and Confucius as a *Nabi* (prophet).[27] This monotheistic notion of a single God later helped Confucianism to be recognized as a legitimate religion by the Indonesian government.

An anti-Chinese movement among the Javanese began to spread with the growth of the re-Sinicization movement. It eventually spurred the formation of Javanese organizations such as Sarekat Islam, which began to spread all over Java,[28] especially after the Chinese revolution in 1911 when Chinese Indonesians were considered "arrogant" and thus treated inimically.[29] The widening gap between the Chinese and non-Chinese contributed to the desire of the Chinese Indonesians for a religion of their own, like the non-Chinese groups had.

In addition to the THHK schools and the anti-Chinese movement, a growing number of associations promoted Confucianism. In 1918, the first general Confucian association, the Khong Kauw Hwee, was established in Solo and gradually spread its network to other cities. In 1923, the Confucian associations held a congress in Yogyakarta and established the Khong Kauw Tjong Hwee as a general headquarters for Confucian organizations. This center existed until the Japanese invasion in 1942. Likewise, the Sam Kauw Hwee, an association committed to promoting Confucianism, Taoism and Buddhism was established in 1934, although it later shifted its attention exclusively to Buddhism.[30]

Confucianism as a Local Indonesian Religion

With the establishment of Indonesia as an independent nation at the end of World War II, the promotion of Confucianism to help Chinese maintain their cultural identity in the Dutch East Indies changed. Newly independent Indonesia sought to integrate its people under Pancasila (the five national principles), and religion became an instrument of the Indonesian nation to create a national identity rather than a means for asserting one's ethnic identity. As a result, Confucianism became a local Indonesian religion despite its obvious connection with being Chinese.[31]

Article 29 of the 1945 Constitution provided that the new republic's foundations would include a belief in the One and Only God. However, it would also guarantee the freedom to worship according to one's own religion or beliefs. These two somewhat conflicting provisions were drafted as a result of negotiations between Muslim and non-Muslim leaders.[32]

A Ministry of Religion was established in 1946 to exercise authority over religion once the war against the Dutch for independence was won. One of its main functions was to draw the line between what constituted religion and what constituted belief. A second main function was to develop a structure in which these issues could be meaningfully addressed. It was within this context that Confucianism also sought to be established as an organized religion under one representative body. However, by 1950 the Ministry of Religion had only recognized Islam, Catholicism and Protestantism as Indonesia's religions, giving each a separate office in the Ministry. The other religious belief systems, including Hinduism and Buddhism, were not given the status that the above religions received.[33]

According to the eldest Confucian leader Haksu Tjhie Tjay Ing,[34] the pre-independence Confucian movement resumed operation shortly after the war, with the general headquarters re-established in 1954 in Solo, supported by contributions from Chinese Indonesians living in Jakarta, Bogor, Cirebon, Malang, Surabaya, Bandung and Tegal. In the following year, the Majelis Tinggi Agama Khonghucu Indonesia (Supreme Council for Confucian Religion in Indonesia) or MATAKIN was established.[35] In 1965, President Sukarno issued a presidential decree, which later became Law No. 5/1969, prohibiting blasphemy and abuse of religions,[36] while embracing Islam, Protestantism, Catholicism, Bali-Hinduism, Buddhism and Confucianism as legitimate Indonesian religions. However, in the same year Suharto ousted Sukarno and took over the government.

The new regime was strongly anti-communist and anti-China. Once Suharto consolidated power, he broke off diplomatic ties with China and initiated his assimilation policy to encourage Chinese Indonesians to abandon the public practice of their culture and to publicly conform to the government's tacitly approved notions of being a good Indonesian citizen. Two of these notions were (1) being non-religious meant one was more likely to be a communist, while being religious meant that one was less likely to be a communist; and (2) being Chinese meant that one was more susceptible to becoming a communist, while being non-Chinese meant that one was less likely to be a communist. In other words, aversion to a religion and adherence to Chinese culture suggested communist tendencies. Followers of Confucianism faced a potentially serious problem. While being religious presented them as less likely to be communists, Confucianism's orientation towards Chinese tradition presented them as more susceptible to becoming communists. Nevertheless, Suharto's regime did not directly seek to abolish Confucianism.

Confucianism and MATAKIN during the Suharto Years

As mentioned earlier, Confucianism emerged as a religion from the ethnic group friction between the Chinese Indonesians and the Javanese. Under the Suharto regime, the issue became a complex mix of antagonism and negotiation between the Chinese Indonesians and the Suharto regime.

Although Presidential Instruction No. 14 prohibited public displays of Chinese religions, beliefs and customs in 1967,[37] it was only in the 1970s that MATAKIN and the followers of Confucianism were prevented from publicly teaching and practicing their religion.[38]

In 1967, MATAKIN held its fourth national meeting in Solo with Suharto sending a welcome letter to the participants of the meeting. The good relationship between Suharto's government and MATAKIN reached its highest point in 1971. In June 1971, MATAKIN was involved in the Golkar Party's (hereafter Golkar) first election campaign, which was held in July 1971. Established in 1964 by the army, Golkar (Golongan Karya) acted as the ruling party throughout the Suharto period. The MATAKIN members supported Golkar in the outer island cities which had high percentages of Chinese Indonesian residents, such as Kisaran (North Sumatra), Manado and Amurang (North Sulawesi), Makassar (South Sulawesi), Sambas and Jawai (West Kalimantan), Pangkal Pinang (then South Sumatera, now Bangka Belitung), and Ternate (North Maluku).[39] Golkar and MATAKIN collaborated partly because Suryo Hutomo, then the head of MATAKIN, was an active member of Golkar. In addition, Suharto's government obviously saw MATAKIN more as a useful connection than as the representative of a harmful Chinese school of thought. In December 1971, MATAKIN held its 8th Congress in Semarang during which the remarks of high-ranking government officials close to Suharto, such as General Abdul Haris Nasution, Ali Moertopo and Sudjono Humardani were read to the members. However, a series of government moves ended this close relationship between Suharto and MATAKIN in the mid to late 1970s. These included:

- the exclusion of Confucianism as a subject in the school curriculum in 1975;[40]
- Law No. 1 in 1974 pertaining to marriage which required couples to marry according to the rites of their stated religion;[41] and
- the delisting of Confucianism as an officially recognized religion in 1978.[42]

In 1979, MATAKIN had to cancel its congress because the government no longer allowed it to function as a religious organization.

There is no clear explanation as to why Confucianism lost its status as a national religion in the 1970s. However, it seems likely that the Suharto regime perceived Confucianism as a symbol of being Chinese, which the overseas and local Chinese opponents of Suharto's Golkar Party could use to undermine the Party's hold on power. The change could also be explained by a shift in the relationship between MATAKIN and the state. Briefly, the state depicted MATAKIN as a dangerous organization to justify its control over religion and ethnicity. It is also possible that other religious groups had pressured the government to abolish Confucianism because they were afraid that MATAKIN had become too close to Golkar. As a result, MATAKIN and its Confucian members were forced to curtail their religious activities from the 1970s until the end of the Suharto regime.[43]

Moving Towards the Re-recognition of Confucianism

On July 23, 1995, Budi Wijaya and Lany Guito, active members of MAKIN, the Surabaya branch of MATAKIN, were married in the Boen Bio Surabaya temple. They subsequently applied for a marriage certificate at the local Civil Records Office on August 7. However, on November 28 their application was denied on the grounds that their stated religion, Confucianism, was not a state-recognized religion. Budi Wijaya and Lany Guito then filed a lawsuit against the Surabaya Civil Records Office of East Java. The case eventually went up to the Supreme Court and it was finally resolved on March 30, 2000, almost two years after the fall of the Suharto regime. Wijaya and Guito won the case and they were able to register their marriage as Confucians.

Why were Wijaya and Guito so committed to going through this hardship even when they had the option of avoiding the administrative requirements by simply choosing another religion? According to Bingky Irawan, former head of the Boen Bio branch of MAKIN in Surabaya, the wedding and the filing of the lawsuit were actually part of a plan to call attention to the state's discrimination against followers of Confucianism, and, by extension, Chinese Indonesians.

Irawan was born to a Chinese father and Javanese mother in the early 1950s. He grew up practicing Kebatinan, a form of Javanese mysticism. However, he joined Boen Bio Surabaya in 1984 after realizing that Confucianism and Kebatinan had much in common.[44] Irawan became the head of the Boen Bio branch of MAKIN in 1990, and he was pressured to stop conducting religious services because the state did not consider MAKIN to be a religious organization. In response, Irawan decided to file a marriage lawsuit, and Wijaya, who was then the vice head of the Boen Bio branch of MAKIN, agreed to take the lead role in this case.[45]

The case became a nationwide sensation as evidenced by the fact that over 300 news articles were published on the issue by the mass media in Java and Bali. It is also noteworthy that the supporters of this movement included prominent Islamic leaders like Abdurrahman Wahid, the longtime president of the Nahdlatul Ulama (Association of Muslim Scholars); Djohan Effendi, who later became the head of the Agency of Research and Development at the Department of Religion between 1998 and 2000; and Nurcholish Madjid, vice president of Ikatan Cendekiawan Muslim Indonesia (Indonesian Association of Muslim Intellectuals). These leaders openly supported the restoration of Confucianism as a national religion.[46]

Under the Suharto regime, the lawsuit was carefully presented as a case involving the civil rights of two followers of Confucianism to avoid complications that might arise from framing the case as an instance of state-instigated discrimination against Chinese Indonesians. Irawan and Trimoelja Darmasetia Soerjahe (the lawyer of Wijaya and Guito) used the wedding case to argue the superiority of Presidential Decree No. 1 (issued in 1965 and became Law No. 5 in 1969) over the Circulation Letter of Ministry of Internal Affairs No. 477 and Instruction of Minister of Religion No. 4 in 1978. Within the range of civil rights discrimination, Irawan also succeeded in bringing up the issue of the national identity card to the attention of the public.[47] After the fall of Suharto's regime, the movement succeeded in obtaining the re-recognition by the state of Confucianism as a religion.

The Fall of Suharto and the Rise of China and Being Chinese

In May 1998, street protests forced Suharto to step down from the presidency. His vice president, Bacharuddin Jusuf Habibie, became president and the Reform Era began. Although the riots were originally a reaction to the killing of students at a protest meeting at Trisakti University in western Jakarta, these riots triggered a widespread outpouring of criticism against the Suharto regime for its handling of the 1997 economic crisis, and against Chinese Indonesians who were seen to have benefited economically under Suharto. Many Chinese Indonesians became the victims of mob violence that included looting, destruction of Chinese homes and businesses, attacks, and rape. The riots aroused international concern, especially from the Chinese government and overseas Chinese, and created feelings of guilt among many non-Chinese Indonesians.

In 1998, President Habibie issued Presidential Instruction No. 26 to all government bodies banning discrimination against ethnic Chinese.[48] Moreover, MATAKIN was allowed to hold a congress in August 1998. However, Confucianism was not recognized as a state-sanctioned religion until Habibie's successor, Abdurrahman Wahid, supported its reinstatement.

There are three major reasons behind Wahid's support for reinstating Confucianism as an officially recognized religion: Wahid's belief in pluralism; his awareness of the growing importance of China as a regional and global power; and his long personal ties with Bingky Irawan.

Wahid's awareness of the rise of China and his domestic policy toward Chinese Indonesians were two sides of the same coin.

Soon after he took office, Wahid announced the implementation of his "looking toward Asia" policy and chose China as the destination of his first official trip outside of Indonesia in December 1999. After returning from China, he allowed MATAKIN to offer the prayer for the Imlek Nasional (Chinese New Year). On January 17, 2000, two weeks prior to the Imlek Nasional, he issued Presidential Decision No. 6[49] repealing Presidential Decision No. 14 of 1967,[50] the law that restricted Chinese cultural, social and religious activities.

On February 7, 2000, Wahid attended the Imlek Nasional, together with his vice president (and successor) Megawati Sukarnoputri, Suryadi Sudirja (Minister of Internal Affairs), Amien Rais (the head of People's Consultative Assembly), and Akbar Tanjung (head of the

People's Representative Council). In his speech Wahid appealed for the contribution to the economic sector by the Chinese Indonesian community.[51] Under the Wahid administration, Confucianism regained its status as a religion. This allowed Chinese government officials to participate in religious and cultural events, which in turn gave rise to the opportunity for the Chinese government to exercise soft power. Thus, the connection of Confucianism with being Chinese benefited both the Chinese Indonesians and the Indonesian government in the post-Suharto era.

In the Megawati administration that followed, Imlek was declared a national holiday like Nyepi, the Hindu New Year, and the Islamic New Year.[52] However, in reality, Imlek is widely celebrated by Chinese Indonesians who are not followers of Confucianism. The same can be said for the Imlek Nasional, a New Year event hosted by MATAKIN. Even though it is a religious ceremony celebrated by MATAKIN, which officially represents Confucianism in Indonesia, all the Indonesian presidents after Wahid have attended the Imlek Nasional. All of them have emphasized the state's efforts to end the discrimination toward Chinese Indonesians and confirmed that they are part of the nation.

Particularly striking was President Susilo Bambang Yudhoyono's reaffirmation on February 4, 2006 of the right of Chinese Indonesians to their cultural identity. In his speech, Yudhoyono stressed that discrimination against Chinese Indonesians was over, thanks mainly to the Reform Era. Chinese Indonesians were now considered members of the Indonesian nation. Yudhoyono also cited the Minister Decision Letter No. 12 of January 24, 2006, which restated that Confucianism was now a state-recognized religion.[53]

Under the Yudhoyono government, Confucianism was added to the school curriculum as an officially recognized subject. In 2009, Yudhoyono promised to build a religious facility promoting Confucianism in a state-run park, the Taman Mini Indonesia Indah, and in 2014, he promised to establish an independent division for Confucianism in the Ministry of Religion.[54]

MATAKIN's lawsuit raised new questions about the official status of religions in Indonesia. Indonesian newspapers and magazines debated the merits of state control over religion. Adherents of the Sikh religion and the followers of Sunda Wiwita and other Javanese religious groups expressed interest in obtaining the same status as Confucianism from the government at some point.[55]

Although MATAKIN successfully negotiated state recognition for Confucianism, there are issues that potentially limit its ability to exert leadership over the development of Confucianism as a religion. First, while the members of MATAKIN regard Confucianism as an organized religion, most Chinese Indonesians outside the organization see Confucianism only as a set of traditional Chinese customs. Second, the number of people who practice Confucianism as a religion is small. The 2010 census reported the number of Confucians as being less than 0.1 percent of the total population.[56] Third, although Confucianism as a religion is expanding, as of August 2014 many of MATAKIN's 134 regional branches were being operated by new members who did not have enough experience in conducting religious rituals—a situation that could lead to a contradiction between people's understanding and practice of the religion.

New Streams of "Chinese" Religion

The long process of negotiation between Chinese Indonesians and the Indonesian government has resulted in frequent changes in the status of Confucianism from a state-recognized religion to a delisted religion and then back to a state-recognized religion. The current re-establishment of Confucianism as a state religion seems partly due to "soft power." In other words, the Indonesian government wants its political reforms to appeal to Chinese Indonesians in order to attract more economic collaboration from them and from the government of China. In post-Suharto Indonesia, soft power from Taiwan and the mainland Chinese provinces has been responsible for introducing other religious groups such as the Taiwan-based Buddhist sect, Tzu Chi, into Indonesia.

In 1966, Tzu Chi was founded by Dharma Master Cheng Yen in Hualien, Taiwan. It is one of the four new major Buddhist sects in Taiwan and has over 350 branches in more than 60 countries. Indonesia's 270 million members make up the second-largest group of Tzu Chi adherents in Southeast Asia, following Malaysia's 400 million members.[57] Tzu Chi Indonesia was first introduced by Liu Su Mei, a Taiwan national, who followed her husband when he relocated to Indonesia to do business there in the 1990s. Tzu Chi became well known in Indonesia for its role in the 2004 Aceh tsunami disaster relief effort. Current members include Chinese Indonesian business leaders such as Eka Tjipta Wijaja and his son, Franky Wijaja, of the

Sinar Mas Group; Sugianto Kusuma of the Agung Sedayu Group and Bank Artha Graha; and Soetjipto Nagaria of Summarecon Agung. These business leaders integrate the teachings of Tzu Chi into their corporate social responsibility practices in order to promote their company's image. Because of its unique organizational structure which is based on volunteers from the middle and upper classes, Tzu Chi seems to attract Chinese Indonesians in post-Suharto Indonesia, indicating support for soft power coming from Taiwan.

A number of Protestant sects have also been attracting a growing number of Chinese Indonesians. For example, a Chinese Indonesian, Stephen Tong, founded the Reformed Evangelical Church of Indonesia in 1989. It now has a megachurch in Jakarta. Many Protestant churches for Chinese Indonesians now have religious services in both Bahasa Indonesia and Mandarin.[58]

Conclusion

This chapter has explored the connection between being Chinese and Chinese soft power by:

- explaining how Confucianism became a cornerstone of a re-Sinicization process initiated by Chinese living in the Dutch East Indies in the late 19th century;
- locating within this process of re-Sinicization an explanation of how Chinese Indonesians negotiated the re-installment of Confucianism as a state-recognized religion following the suppression of public expressions of Chinese culture and identity from the 1970s to the late 1990s; and
- arguing that Chinese Indonesians achieved their objective not only due to the care with which they prepared a persuasive, constitutionally grounded case but also due to China's use of soft power in Indonesia.

To support this argument, the chapter traced how the Chinese government has used a soft power approach to project itself as a non-hostile neighbor willing to engage in economic development with Indonesia (and other Southeast Asian countries). It suggests that the post-Suharto governments' desire for Chinese investment and aid plus the positive image projected by Chinese soft power has encouraged Indonesia to lift its restrictions on Chinese Indonesians' expressions of their culture and identity.

In conclusion, the strategic mobilization of Chinese soft power by Chinese Indonesians has left a soft footprint on Indonesian culture by reconnecting ethnicity and religion.

Notes

1. Part of this chapter is drawn from an earlier paper presented at the *Joint International* Workshop on "Chinese Identities and Inter-Ethnic Coexistence and Cooperation in Southeast Asia. See Yumi Kitamura, "The Question of Identity and Religion in Post-Suharto Era: Successful Negotiations Over the Re-recognition of Confucianism as a 'Religion'," in *Proceedings of the CSEAS-Netherlands Institute of War Documentation Joint International Workshop on "Chinese Identities and Inter-Ethnic Coexistence and Cooperation in Southeast Asia,"* ed. Caroline Hau and Nobuhiro Aizawa, 227–42 (Kyoto: CSEAS, 2009).
2. Joseph Jr. Nye, *Bound to Lead: The Changing Nature of American Power* (New York: Basic Books, 1990).
3. Joseph Jr. Nye, *Soft Power: The Means to Success in the World Politics* (New York: PublicAffairs, 2004).
4. Lai Hong Li, "Introduction: The Soft Power Concept and A Rising China," in *China's Soft Power and International Relations*, ed. Lai Hong Li, 1–20 (London and New York: Routledge, 2012), 11–2.
5. Ibid., 4–12; David Scott, "Soft Language, Soft Imagery and Soft Power in China's Diplomatic Lexicon," in *China's Soft Power and International Relations*, ed. Lai Hong Li, 39–63 (London and New York: Routledge, 2012), 22–3.
6. Joshua Kurlantzick, *Charm Offensive: How China's Soft Power Is Transforming the World* (New Haven and London: Yale University Press, 2007); Ignatius Wibobo, "China's Soft Power and Neo Liberal Agenda in Southeast Asia," in *Soft Power: China's Emerging Strategy in International Politics*, ed. Mingjiang Li, 207–24 (Langham: Lexington Books, 2009); Scott, "Soft Language."
7. Hsin-Huang Michael Hsiao and Alan Hao Yang, "Introduction to the Special Issue," *A Social Science Quarterly on China, Taiwan and East Asian Affairs* 50, no. 4 (2014a): 1–11; Hsiao and Yang, "Differentiating the Politics of Dependency: Confucius Institute in Cambodia and Myanmar," *A Social Science Quarterly on China, Taiwan and East Asian Affairs* 50, no. 4 (2014b): 11–44; Christopher R. Hughes, "Confucius Institute and the University Distinguishing the Political Mission from the Cultural," *A Social Science Quarterly on China, Taiwan and East Asian Affairs* 50, no. 4 (2014): 45–84; Nguyen van Chinh, "Confucius Institutes in the Mekong Region; China's Soft Power or Soft Border,"

A *Social Science Quarterly on China, Taiwan and East Asian Affairs* 50, no. 4 (2014): 85–118.
8. Nye, *Soft Power*.
9. Liu Hong, *China and the Shaping of Indonesia, 1949–1965* (Singapore: NUS Press in association with Kyoto University Press, 2011).
10. Rizal Sukma, *Indonesia and China: The Politics of the Troubled Relationship* (London and New York: Routledge, 1999), 16–32.
11. David Mozingo, *Chinese Policy toward Indonesia, 1949–1967* (Singapore: Equinox Publishing, 2007), 138–46.
12. Sukma, *Indonesia and China*, 27–8.
13. Ibid., 32.
14. Greg Fealy and Katharine McGregor, "East Java and the Role of Nahdlatul Ulama in the 1965–66 Anti-communist Violence," in *The Contours of Mass Violence in Indonesia, 1965–68*, ed. Douglas Kammen and Katharine McGregor, 104–30 (Singapore: NUS Press, 2012).
15. See Roosa's explanation of how the official narrative was created in John Roosa, "The September 30th Movement: The Aporias of the Official Narratives," in *The Contours of Mass Violence in Indonesia, 1965–68*, ed. Douglas Kammen and Katharine McGregor, 25–49 (Singapore: NUS Press, 2012).
16. Sukma, *Indonesia and China*.
17. Instruksi Presiden Republik Indonesia Nomor 14 Tahun 1967 Tentang Agama Kepercayaan Dan Adat Istiadat Cina Kami [Presidential Instruction of the Republic of Indonesia Number 14 of the Year 1967 about Chinese Religion, Beliefs and Traditional Customs], December 6, 1967.
18. Juliette Koning, "Singing Yourself into Existence: Chinese Indonesian Entrepreneurs, Pentecostal-Charismatic Christianity and the Indonesian Nation State," in *Christianity and the State in Asia: Complicity and Conflict*, ed. Julius Bautista and Francis Khek Gee Lim, 115–30 (London and New York: Routledge, 2009).
19. Robert W. Hefner, "Islam, State, and Civil Society: ICMI and the Struggle for the Indonesian Middle Class," *Indonesia*, 56 (1993): 4.
20. Ibid.; Luthfi Assyaukanie, "Muslim Discourse of Liberal Democracy in Indonesia," in Luthfi Assyaukanie, Robert Hefner, and Azyumardi Azra, *Muslim Politics and Democratization in Indonesia* (Victoria: Monash University Press, 2008), 1–31.
21. Claudine Salmon, "Ancestral Halls, Funeral Associations, and Attempts at Resinicization," in *Sojourners and Settlers: Histories of Southeast Asia and Chinese*, ed. Anthony Reid, 183–204 (Honolulu: Allen and Unwin, 1996).
22. Ibid., 184.
23. Claudine Salmon, "Confucianists and Revolutionaries in Surabaya (c1880–c1906)," in *Chinese Indonesians: Remembering, Distorting, Forgetting*, ed. Tim Lindsey and Helen Pausacker, 130–45 (Singapore: ISEAS, 2005).

24. Mona Lohanda, *Growing Pains: The Chinese and the Dutch in Colonial Java, 1890-1942* (Jakarta: Yayasan Cipta Loka Caraka, 2002); Charles Coppel, *Studying Ethnic Chinese in Indonesia* (Singapore: Society of Asian Studies, 2002).
25. Ming Govaars, *Dutch Colonial Education: The Chinese Experience in Indonesia, 1900-1942* (Singapore: Chinese Heritage Center, 2005).
26. Ibid.
27. Leo Suryadinata, "Buddhism and Confucianism in Indonesia," in *Chinese Indonesians: Remembering, Distorting, Forgetting*, 77-94 (ISEAS, 2005), 79.
28. Takashi Shiraishi, "Anti-Sinicism in Java's New Order," in *Essential Outsiders: Chinese and Jews in the Modern Transformation of Southeast Asia and Central Europe*, ed. Daniel Chirot and Anthony Reid, 187-207 (Seattle and London: University of Washington Press, 1997).
29. Ibid.
30. Suryadinata, "Buddhism and Confucianism in Indonesia," 79.
31. For the overview of the history of Confucianism in Indonesia and beginning of its revival after the fall of Suharto, see Andrew J. Abalahin, "A Sixth Religion? Confucianism and the Negotiation of Indonesian-Chinese Identity under the Pancasila State," in *Spirited Politics: Religion and Public Life in Contemporary Southeast Asia*, ed. Andrew C. Willford and Kenneth M. George, 119-42 (Ithaca: Cornell University, 2005).
32. Kenji Tuchiya, *Indonesia Shiso no Keifu* (Tokyo: Keiso Shobo, 1994), 277.
33. Masato Fukushima, *Jawa no Shukyo to Shakai* (Tokyo: Hitsuji Shobo, 2002), 332.
34. *Haksu* is the highest rank of the priesthood in MATAKIN followed by *Bunsu*, and *Kausing*. (Interview with Tjhie Tjay Ing on August 18, 2007.)
35. MATAKIN's Chinese name is the same as Khong Kauw Tjong Hwee.
36. Undang-Undang Republik Indonesia Nomor 5 Tahun 1969 Tentang Pencegahan Penyalahgunaan dan/atau Penodaan Agama [Law No. 5 of the Year 1969 about Preventing the Misuse of Religion and/or Blasphemy], July 5, 1969.
37. Tim Lindsey, "Reconstituting the Ethnic Chinese in Post-Soeharto Indonesia: Law, Racial Discrimination, and Reform," in *Chinese Indonesians: Remembering, Distorting, Forgetting*, 130-45.
38. Jafar Suryomenggolo provides the details on various laws regarding Chinese Indonesians during the Suharto years. See *Hukum Sebagai Alat Kekuasaan: Politik Assimilasi Orde Baru* (Jakarta: Elkasa, 2003).
39. MATAKIN, *Golden Anniversary MATAKIN 16 April 1955-2005: You Jiao Wu Lei-Ada Pendidikan Tiada Perbedaan* (Jakarta: MATAKIN, 2005); Jafar Suryomenggolo, *Hukum Sebagai Alat Kekuasaan*; Interview with Tjhie Tjay Ing.
40. Interview with Xs. Tjhie Tjay Ing.

41. Undang-Undang Republik Indonesia Nomor 1 Tahun 1974 Tentang Perkawinan [Law of the Republic of Indonesia No. 1 of the Year 1974 on Marriage], January 2, 1974.
42. Surat Edaran Mentri Dalam Negeri No. 477/74054/1978 [Circular Letter of the Minister of Internal Affairs No. 477/74054/1978], November 18, 1978.
43. Suryadinata, "Akhirnya Diakui: Agama Khongkucu dan Agama Buddha Pasca-Soeharto," in *Setelah Air Mata Kering: Masyarakat Tionghoa Pasca-Peristiwa Mei 1998*, ed. I. Wibowo dan Thung Ju Lan, 75–104 (Jakarta: Kompas, 2010), 95–99.
44. Information regarding Bingky Irawan is from an interview with him conducted on February 22, 2007. According to him, it was also at a seminar on Kebatinan where he first became acquainted with the future Indonesian president, Abdurrahman Wahid.
45. Interview with Budi Wijaya on August 20, 2007.
46. Opposed to these leaders' position was Tarmizi Taher, the Minister of Religion, who repeatedly argued that Conficianism was not a religion but a philosophy. See, for example, "Mentri Agama: Kong Hu Chu bukan Agama tapi Filsafat," *Media Indonesia*, July 25, 1996.
47. Bambang N. Rahadi, "Nikha bagi umat Khong Hu Cu susah," *Bisnis Indonesia*, August 1, 1996 in *Antara Formalisme Hati Nurani*, ed. Makin and Boen Bio (Surabaya: Makin and Boen Bio, 1996), 40.
48. Instruksi Presiden Republik Indonesia Nomor 26 Tahun 1998 Tentang Menghentikan Penggunaan Istilah Pribumi dan Non Pribumi dalam Semua Perumusan dan Penyelenggaraan Kebijakan, Perencanaan Program, Ataupun Pelaksanaan Kegiatan Penyelenggaraan Pemerintahan [Presidential Instruction of the Republic of Indonesia Number 26 of the Year 1998 about Stopping the Use of Terms such as Indigenous and Non-Indigenous in All Policy Formulation and Implementation, Program Planning, or Implementation of Government Activities], September 16, 1998.
49. Keputusan Presiden Republik Indonesia Nomor 6 Tahun 2000 Tentang Pencabutan Instruksi Presiden Nomor 14 Tahun 1967 Tentang Agama, Kepercayaan, Dan Adat Istiadat Cina [Presidential Decree of the Republic of Indonesia Number 6 of the Year 2000 on the Revocation of Presidential Instruction Number 14 of the Year 1967 on Religion, Belief, and Chinese Customs], January 17, 2000.
50. Instruksi Presiden Nomor 14 Tahun 1967.
51. Abdurrahman Wahid, Speech of the President of Indonesia during the Imlek Nasional of the Year 2551, February 17, 2000.
52. Keputusan Presiden Republik Indonesia Nomor 19 Tahun 2002 Tentang Hari Tahun Baru Imlek [Presidential Decree of the Republic of Indonesia No. 19 Year 2002 on the Chinese New Year], April 9, 2002.

53. Susilo Bambang Yudhoyono, Speech of the President of Indonesia during the Imlek Nasional of the Year 2557, February 4, 2006.
54. Susilo Bambang Yudhoyono, Speech during the Imlek Nasional of the Year 2560, February 3, 2009.
55. "Bebas Lisensi Setengah Hati," *Gatra*, March 4, 2006.
56. Badan Pusat Statistik, *Sensus Penduduk 2010* [Population Census 2010], <https://sirusa.bps.go.id/sirusa/index.php/dasar/view?kd=1&th=2010> (accessed May 14, 2015).
57. Mitsuko Tamaki, "Taiwan no Bukkyo NGO to Taiwankei Kajin," *Center of Overseas Chinese Studies Newsletter* 19 (2013): 3.
58. Kainei Mori, "The Growth of the Overseas Mission by Chinese Churches: From the 19th Century to the 21st Century," *Core Ethics* 6 (2010): 563–60.

References

Abalahin, Andrew J. "A Sixth Religion? Confucianism and the Negotiation of Indonesian-Chinese Identity under the Pancasila State." In *Spirited Politics: Religion and Public Life in Contemporary Southeast Asia*, edited by Andrew C. Willford and Kenneth M. George, 119–42. Ithaca: Cornell University, 2005.

Assyaukanie, Luthfi. "Muslim Discourse of Liberal Democracy in Indonesia." In Luthfi Assyaukanie, Robert Hefner, and Azyumardi Azra, *Muslim Politics and Democratization in Indonesia*, 1–31. Victoria: Monash University Press, 2008.

Badan Pusat Statistik. *Sensus Penduduk 2010* [Population Census 2010]. <https://sirusa.bps.go.id/sirusa/index.php/dasar/view?kd=1&th=2010> (accessed 14 May, 2015).

Coppel, Charles. *Studying Ethnic Chinese in Indonesia*. Singapore: Society of Asian Studies, 2002.

Fealy, Greg and Katharine McGregor. "East Java and the Role of Nahdlatul Ulama in the 1965–66 Anti-communist Violence." In *The Contours of Mass Violence in Indonesia, 1965–68*, edited by Douglas Kammen and Katharine McGregor, 104–30. Singapore: NUS Press, 2012.

Fukushima, Masato. *Jawa no Shukyo to Shakai*. Tokyo: Hitsuji Shobo, 2002.

Govaars, Ming. *Dutch Colonial Education: The Chinese Experience in Indonesia, 1900–1942*. Singapore: Chinese Heritage Center, 2005.

Hefner, Robert W. "Islam, State, and Civil Society: ICMI and the Struggle for the Indonesian Middle Class." *Indonesia*, 56 (1993): 1–35.

Hsiao, Hsin-Huang Michael and Alan Hao Yang. "Introduction to the Special Issue." *A Social Science Quarterly on China, Taiwan and East Asian Affairs* 50, no. 4 (2014a): 1–11.

——— . "Differentiating the Politics of Dependency: Confucius Institute in Cambodia and Myanmar." *A Social Science Quarterly on China, Taiwan and East Asian Affairs* 50, no. 4 (2014b): 11–44.

Hughes, Christopher R. "Confucius Institute and the University Distinguishing the Political Mission from the Cultural." *A Social Science Quarterly on China, Taiwan and East Asian Affairs* 50, no. 4 (2014): 45–84.

Instruksi Presiden Republik Indonesia Nomor 14 Tahun 1967 Tentang Agama Kepercayaan Dan Adat Istiadat Cina Kami [Presidential Instruction of the Republic of Indonesia Number 14 of the Year 1967 about Chinese Religion, Beliefs and Traditional Customs], December 6, 1967.

Instruksi Presiden Republik Indonesia Nomor 26 Tahun 1998 Tentang Menghentikan Penggunaan Istilah Pribumi dan Non Pribumi dalam Semua Perumusan dan Penyelenggaraan Kebijakan, Perencanaan Program, Ataupun Pelaksanaan Kegiatan Penyelenggaraan Pemerintahan [Presidential Instruction of the Republic of Indonesia Number 26 of the Year 1998 about Stopping the Use of Terms such as Indigenous and Non-Indigenous in All Policy Formulation and Implementation, Program Planning, or Implementation of Government Activities], September 16, 1998.

Keputusan Presiden Republik Indonesia Nomor 6 Tahun 2000 Tentang Pencabutan Instruksi Presiden Nomor 14 Tahun 1967 Tentang Agama, Kepercayaan, Dan Adat Istiadat Cina [Presidential Decree of the Republic of Indonesia Number 6 of the Year 2000 on the Revocation of Presidential Instruction Number 14 of the Year 1967 on Religion, Belief, and Chinese Customs], January 17, 2000.

Keputusan Presiden Republik Indonesia Nomor 19 Tahun 2002 Tentang Hari Tahun Baru Imlek [Presidential Decree of the Republic of Indonesia No. 19 Year 2002 on the Chinese New Year], April 9, 2002.

Kitamura, Yumi. "The Question of Identity and Religion in Post-Suharto Era: Successful Negotiations Over the Re-recognition of Confucianism as a 'Religion'." In *Proceedings of the CSEAS-Netherlands Institute of War Documentation Joint International Workshop on "Chinese Identities and Inter-Ethnic Coexistence and Cooperation in Southeast Asia,"* edited by Caroline Hau and Nobuhiro Aizawa, 227–42. Kyoto: CSEAS, 2009.

Koning, Juliette. "Singing Yourself into Existence: Chinese Indonesian Entrepreneurs, Pentecostal-Charismatic Christianity and the Indonesian Nation State." In *Christianity and the State in Asia: Complicity and Conflict*, edited by Julius Bautista and Francis Khek Gee Lim, 115–30. London and NY: Routledge, 2009.

Kurlantzick, Joshua. *Charm Offensive: How China's Soft Power Is Transforming the World*. New Haven and London: Yale University Press, 2007.

———. "China's Soft Power in Africa." In *Soft Power: China's Emerging Strategy in International Politics*, edited by Mingjiang Li, 165–84. Langham: Lexington Books, 2009.

Lai Hong Li. "Introduction: The Soft Power Concept and A Rising China." *China's Soft Power and International Relations*, edited by Lai Hong Li, 1–20. London and New York: Routledge, 2012.

Lai Hongyi and Yiyi Liu. *China's Soft Power and International Relations*. London and New York: Routledge, 2012.
Li, Mingjiang, ed. *Soft Power: China's Emerging Strategy in International Politics*. Langham: Lexington Books, 2009.
Lindsey, Tim. "Reconstituting the Ethnic Chinese in Post-Soeharto Indonesia: Law, Racial Discrimination, and Reform." In *Chinese Indonesians: Remembering, Distorting, Forgetting*, edited by Tim Lindsey and Helen Pausacker, 130–45. Singapore: ISEAS, 2005.
Liu Hong. *China and the Shaping of Indonesia, 1949–1965*. Singapore: NUS Press in association with Kyoto University Press, 2011.
Lohanda, Mona. *Growing Pains: The Chinese and the Dutch in Colonial Java, 1890–1942*. Jakarta: Yayasan Cipta Loka Caraka, 2002.
MATAKIN. *Golden Anniversary MATAKIN 16 April 1955–2005: You Jiao Wu Lei-Ada Pendidikan Tiada Perbedaan*. Jakarta: MATAKIN, 2005.
"Mentri Agama: Kong Hu Chu bukan Agama, tapi Filsafat." *Media Indonesia*, July 25, 1996.
Mori, Kainei. "The Growth of the Overseas Mission by Chinese Churches: From the 19th Century to the 21st Century." *Core Ethics* 6 (2010): 563–70.
Mozingo, David. *Chinese Policy toward Indonesia, 1949–1967*. Singapore: Equinox Publishing, 2007.
Nguyen, Van Chinh. "Confucius Institutes in the Mekong Region: China's Soft Power or Soft Border." *A Social Science Quarterly on China, Taiwan and East Asian Affairs* 50, no. 4 (2014): 85–118.
Nye, Joseph Jr. *Bound to Lead: The Changing Nature of American Power*. New York: Basic Books, 1990.
———. *Soft Power: The Means to Success in the World Politics*. New York: PublicAffairs, 2004.
Rahadi, Bambang N. "Nikha bagi umat Khong Hu Cu susah," *Bisnis Indonesia*, August 1, 1996. In *Antara Formalisme Hati Nurani*, edited by Makin and Boen Bio, 40. Surabaya: Makin and Boen Bio, 1996.
Roosa, John. "The September 30th Movement: The Aporias of the Official Narratives. In *The Contours of Mass Violence in Indonesia, 1965–68*, edited by Douglas Kammen and Katharine McGregor, 25–49. Singapore: NUS Press, 2012.
Salmon, Claudine. "Ancestral Halls, Funeral Associations, and Attempts at Resinicization." In *Sojourners and Settlers: Histories of Southeast Asia and Chinese*, edited by Anthony Reid, 183–204. Australia: Allen and Unwin, 1996.
———. "Confucianists and Revolutionaries in Surabaya (c1880–c1906)." In *Chinese Indonesians: Remembering, Distorting, Forgetting*, edited by Tim Lindsey and Helen Pausacker, 130–45. Singapore: ISEAS, 2005.
Scott, David. "Soft Language, Soft Imagery and Soft Power in China's Diplomatic Lexicon." In *China's Soft Power and International Relations*, edited by Lai Hong Li, 39–63. London and New York: Routledge, 2012.

Shiraishi, Takashi. "Anti-Sinicism in Java's New Order." In *Essential Outsiders: Chinese and Jews in the Modern Transformation of Southeast Asia and Central Europe*, edited by Daniel Chirot and Anthony Reid, 187–207. Seattle and London: University of Washington Press, 1997.

Sukma, Rizal. *Indonesia and China: The Politics of the Troubled Relationship*. London and New York: Routledge, 1999.

Surat Edaran Mentri Dalam Negeri No. 477/74054/1978 [Circular Letter of the Minister of Internal Affairs No. 477/74054/1978], November 18, 1978.

Suryadinata, Leo. "Akhirnya Diakui: Agama Khongkucu dan Agama Buddha Pasca-Soeharto." In *Setelah Air Mata Kering: Masyarakat Tionghoa Pasca-Peristiwa Mei 1998*, edited by I. Wibowo dan Thung Ju Lan, 75–104. Jakarta: Kompas, 2010.

Suryadinata, Leo. "Buddhism and Confucianism in Indonesia." In *Chinese Indonesians: Remembering, Distorting, Forgetting*, edited by Tim Lindsey and Helen Pausacker, 77–94. Singapore: ISEAS, 2005.

Suryomenggolo, Jafar. *Hukum Sebagai Alat Kekuasaan: Politik Assimilasi Orde Baru*. Jakarta: Elkasa, 2003.

Tamaki, Mitsuko. "Taiwan no Bukkyo NGO to Taiwankei Kajin." *Center of Overseas Chinese Studies Newsletter* 19 (2013): 2–4.

Tuchiya, Kenji. *Indonesia Shiso no Keifu*. Tokyo: Keiso Shobo, 1994.

Undang-Undang Republik Indonesia Nomor 1 Tahun 1974 Tentang Perkawinan [Law of the Republic of Indonesia No. 1 of the Year 1974 on Marriage], January 2, 1974.

Undang-Undang Republik Indonesia Nomor 5 Tahun 1969 Tentang Pencegahan Penyalahgunaan dan/atau Penodaan Agama [Law No. 5 of the Year 1969 about Preventing the Misuse of Religion and/or Blasphemy], July 5, 1969.

Wahid, Abdurrahman. Speech of the President of Indonesia during the Imlek Nasional of the Year 2551, February 17, 2000.

Wibobo, Ignatius. "China's Soft Power and Neo Liberal Agenda in Southeast Asia." In *Soft Power: China's Emerging Strategy in International Politics*, edited by Mingjiang Li, 207–24. Langham: Lexington Books, 2009.

Yudhoyono, Susilo Bambang. Speech of the President of Indonesia during the Imlek Nasional of the Year 2557, February 4, 2006.

———. Speech during the Imlek Nasional of the Year 2560, February 3, 2009.

CHAPTER 8

Confucius Institutes in Southeast Asia: Assessing the New Trends in China's Soft Diplomacy

H.H. Michael Hsiao and Alan H. Yang

Introduction

For years China has promoted its soft power to project a new national image to the world.[1] Its soft diplomacy strategies are aimed at rewriting its conservative and negative past and advocating its social and cultural attractiveness.[2] The establishment of Confucius Institutes (CIs) is one of China's flagship projects.[3]

CIs are primarily language institutes, the mandate of which is to provide Chinese language courses and facilitate cultural exchanges between China and other countries. In particular, CIs offer credit/non-credit language courses, promote cultural events and administer Chinese language tests. They collaborate with universities and colleges in the country where they are located. The CI is modeled after Germany's Goethe-Institut and the United Kingdom's British Council.

Since late 2004, there has been much attention on the global proliferation of these Chinese government-sponsored CIs. Liu Yandong, Chairperson of the Council Members of the Confucius Institute Headquarters, Member of the Politburo of the Communist Party of China (CPC), and the Central Committee State Councilor in

China, stated at the opening ceremony of the 6th Confucius Institute Conference held in Beijing in November 2011 that,

> the Chinese government actively supports the cooperation between China and other countries in establishing and running CIs in order to satisfy the pressing desire of the people of all countries to learn Chinese ... now CIs have brought Chinese to all corners of the world ... sowing the seeds of communication, understanding, harmony and friendship in the youths of each country, and yielding positive results.[4]

In her lecture at the 8th Confucius Institute Conference in 2013, Liu once again conveyed that the purpose of establishing CIs is to satisfy "the worldwide desire to learn Chinese" and advance "the friendship and mutual understanding between people in China and elsewhere."[5] CIs have, therefore, become China's most important soft power strategy for re-shaping and improving its image in the world. For example, the largest CI in Chicago contributed US$1.6 million, including teaching materials, to a local high school. This shows how China uses fiscal support to enhance its positive image and increase its sociocultural influence among local students.[6]

Though non-profit public institutions, CIs are tasked by the Confucius Institute Headquarters or Hanban with the specific mission of consolidating and exploring guanxi or networks in the country where they are located.[7]

The spread of CIs is of strategic interest to China. Li Changchun, former head of China's propaganda unit, sees CIs as the core component of China's "Great External Propaganda" (*dawaixuan*).[8] As the CI is "an arm of the Chinese State,"[9] soft diplomacy based on CIs strengthens bilateral relations with the host countries and promotes China's international status from the bottom up.[10] The CIs enjoy strong government support; hence, their purpose and functions are determined by the government and the CPC. They are by no means autonomous. It should be noted that there has been resistance to CIs due to objections to China's authoritarian regime and continuous violation of human rights.

This chapter examines the CI project in Southeast Asia. This project has two components—the CIs themselves and the Confucius Classrooms (CCs), language institutes installed within a high school or a primary school in the host country. References to CIs in this chapter pertain to both CIs and the CCs, unless otherwise specified.

The chapter argues that CIs are more than just language institutes. They are a tool of soft diplomacy and as such, constitute China's soft footprint in Southeast Asia. Their key role is to establish guanxi or networks between China—the CIs themselves, the Chinese embassy in the area, and Chinese political elites—and their Southeast Asian counterparts in order to upgrade bilateral relations.

The chapter begins with a survey of China's CI initiatives followed by an analysis of the current trends in the CI operations. The next section focuses on how the CIs reinforce guanxi with four entities in Southeast Asia where CIs are located—national and local elites, government units, educational institutions, and local overseas Chinese groups, which include overseas Chinese elites and ethnic Chinese associations.[11] Finally, three case studies are presented—Thailand, Singapore and Cambodia.

The CI Project: An Overview

An analysis of the number of CIs and CCs in the different host countries, the CI's budget for major projects, courses taught and activities undertaken, and most importantly, the number of students enrolled in CI courses or in related programs, points to the success of the CI project in terms of the proliferation of China's soft footprints in the world.[12] In particular, this success may be attributed to the fact that the CIs have offered credit and non-credit language courses, cultural events, Chinese language tests and key projects with local stakeholders.

CIs and Host Countries

In November 2004, the first CI was established in Seoul, Korea. Fully supported by the Office of Chinese Language Council International (known as the Hanban or Confucius Institute Headquarters), the global journey of "crossing the river by feeling the stone"[13] was officially launched. As of March 31, 2016 there were 500 CIs and 1,000 CCs in 134 countries.[14] The goal of this soft diplomacy project is to establish more than 1,000 CIs worldwide by the end of 2020.[15]

The number of host countries grew from 49 in 2006 to 134 in 2015, representing an increase of 173.4 percent during the period (see Table 1). In general, there have been significant increases on all

Table 1 Number of Countries by Region that Host CIs and CCs (2006–15)

Year	Asia	Europe	Americas	Africa	Oceania	Total
2006	17 (34.7%)	21 (42.9%)	3 (6.1%)	6 (12.2%)	2 (4.1%)	49 (100%)
2007	21 (31.8%)	25 (37.9%)	7 (10.6%)	11 (16.7%)	2 (3.0%)	66 (100%)
2008	26 (33.3%)	26 (33.3%)	10 (12.8%)	14 (17.9%)	2 (2.7%)	78 (100%)
2009	28 (31.8%)	29 (33.0%)	12 (13.6%)	17 (19.3%)	2 (2.3%)	88 (100%)
2010	31 (32.3%)	31 (32.3%)	13 (13.5%)	19 (19.8%)	2 (2.1%)	96 (100%)
2011	31 (29.5%)	34 (32.4%)	14 (13.3%)	23 (21.9%)	3 (2.9%)	105 (100%)
2012	31 (28.7%)	34 (31.5%)	14 (12.9%)	26 (24.1%)	3 (2.8%)	108 (100%)
2013	32 (26.9%)	37 (31.1%)	16 (13.4%)	31 (26.1%)	3 (2.5%)	119 (100%)
2014	33 (26.2%)	39 (31.0%)	17 (13.4%)	33 (26.2%)	4 (3.2%)	126 (100%)
2015	33 (24.4%)	41 (30.4%)	20 (14.8%)	36 (26.7%)	5 (3.7%)	135 (100%)

Source: Cited from the database of Confucius Institutes Watch, www.ciwatch.net (accessed June 20, 2016).

continents, signifying a global promotion of China's soft diplomacy. In particular, there was a marked increase in the number of CIs and CCs in Europe and Asia from 2004 to 2011. The latter reflects China's intent to prioritize its Asian neighbors since the 1980s. Additionally, in the late 2000s China invested more resources in Africa and the Americas. Consequently, there was a 500 percent increase in the number of host countries in Africa (from 6 in 2006 to 36 in 2015), and a 533 percent increase in the Americas in the same period (from 3 in 2006 to 19 in 2015).

The number of CIs and CCs also increased in the same period, from 125 in 2006 to 1,500 in 2015, or a percentage increase of 1,100 percent (see Table 2). In 2006, both Asia and Europe had more CIs and CCs (45 each) than the Americas (25). However, this situation was markedly reversed in 2009, when the Americas had 292 CIs and

Table 2 Number of CIs and CCs (2006–15)

Year	Asia	Europe	Americas	Africa	Oceania	Total
2006	45	45	25	6	4	125
	(36.0%)	(36.0%)	(20.0%)	(4.8%)	(3.2%)	(100%)
2007	64	81	56	18	7	226
	(28.3%)	(35.8%)	(24.8%)	(8.0%)	(3.1%)	(100%)
2008	90	103	81	21	10	305
	(29.5%)	(33.7%)	(26.6%)	(6.9%)	(3.3%)	(100%)
2009	97	128	292	25	12	554
	(17.5%)	(23.1%)	(52.7%)	(4.5%)	(2.2%)	(100%)
2010	112	187	342	27	23	691
	(16.2%)	(27.1%)	(49.5%)	(3.9%)	(3.3%)	(100%)
2011	123	224	436	30	45	858
	(14.3%)	(26.1%)	(50.8%)	(3.6%)	(5.2%)	(100%)
2012	132	246	470	36	51	935
	(14.1%)	(26.3%)	(50.3%)	(3.8%)	(5.5%)	(100%)
2013	143	302	528	47	66	1,086
	(13.2%)	(27.8%)	(48.6%)	(4.3%)	(6.1%)	(100%)
2014	147	302	528	48	66	1,091
	(13.5%)	(27.7%)	(48.4%)	(4.4%)	(6.0%)	(100%)
2015	201	424	702	69	104	1,500
	(13.4%)	(28.3%)	(46.8%)	(4.6%)	(6.9%)	(100%)

Source: Confucius Institutes Watch, www.ciwatch.net (accessed June 20, 2016).

CCs, compared to Asia's 97 and Europe's 128. The strategic diffusion of China's soft footprints in the US contributed to the impressive rise in the number of CIs and CCs in the Americas from 25 in 2006 to 702 in 2015, or a percentage increase of 2,708 percent. Oceania also manifested a remarkable percentage increase of 2,525 percent within the same period, from 4 in 2006 to 105 in 2015.

Although most of the CIs and CCs are located in the Americas, Asian CIs and CCs are still of strategic importance for two reasons. First, unlike in the US or Europe, there has been minimal local resistance to CIs and CCs in Asia. Second, most of China's Asian neighbors welcome a connection with China as they have enjoyed the benefits of its economic rise. The fact that two out of the five Hanban overseas representative offices are located in Southeast Asia (Singapore and Thailand) is indicative of this positive response.

Interestingly, while the annual growth rate in the number of CIs and CCs was already high (an average of 107.3 institutes per year), there was a spike in this rate in 2015, when the number jumped from 1,091 to 1,500, or 409 new CIs and CCs in 2015. This might have been the result of China's advocacy of a grand strategy, which they called the "Belt and Road Initiative." For example, an increase of 38 CIs and CCs in Oceania in 2015, or 57.5 percent more than the previous year, coincided with China's promotion of the "21st-Century Maritime Silk Route." Additionally, an increase of 197 CIs and CCs in Asia, Africa and Europe (39.6 percent more than in 2014) reflects the strategic importance China placed on the "Silk Road Economic Belt."[16] It seems, therefore, that the CI project became China's social and cultural infrastructure for promoting these new global initiatives.

Fiscal Support from the Chinese Government

China's soft footprints are not naturally shaped but are made by the Chinese government. The cost of running the CI project is massive, and the augmented annual budget sponsored by the Hanban demonstrates China's full support of the project. However, the actual budget of CI projects is unclear.

In the first annual report on the CI project in 2006, the reference to the annual budget was unclear. It simply stated that "various government offices gave the project full support and cooperation

Table 3   Annual Major Expenditures of the CI Project in US dollars (2006–14)

Year	Expenditures (USD)	Growth Rate (%)
2006	44,871,794	–
2007	62,991,780	40.38%
2008	120,476,471	91.26%
2009	180,626,176	49.93%
2010	137,761,000	−23.73%
2011	164,103,000	19.12%
2012	196,330,000	19.64%
2013	278,371,000	41.79%
2014	300,265,000	7.87%
2015	310,854,000	3.53%

Source: Confucius Institutes Watch database, www.ciwatch.net (accessed June 20, 2016).

during its development.... In 2006, the Ministry of Finance allocated RMB350 million."[17] It gave no details on how this amount was spent.

However, since 2007 the annual reports have provided more information by including an accounting for the major CI expenditures. For example, in 2007 the expenditures of the CI project amounted to US$62.9 million, a 40.4 percent increase compared to 2006. In 2008, the budget was US$120.5 million, marking a steep growth of 91.3 percent from the previous year. In 2009, the expenditures reached a record high of US$180.6 million, and in 2014 they reached US$300.3 million.[18]

Despite the above reported expenditures, the actual CI annual budget is still unknown. The expenditures listed in the annual reports from 2007 to 2015 seem to cover only the major projects sponsored by the Hanban. They do not include all the items in the operational budget of the CI project. An analysis of the figures presented in the 2010 annual report only indicates the expenses for major projects of CI operations, while related activities are greater than have been reported. For example, the operation budgets of CIs usually range from US$100,000 to US$200,000. Some CIs, however, receive more, from US$234,000[19] to US$706,000.[20] With regard to CCs, the Hanban provides start-up funds of approximately US$10,000 as well as an annual operating fund of around US$15,000 to US$30,000 per year. If one aggregates the expenditures of 332 CIs and 369 CCs of 2010, the result would be US$1.88 billion, far more than the total expense of all major projects listed in the 2010 annual report.[21]

Beginning in 2012, a new initiative, the Confucius China Studies Program (CCSP), was launched. The initiative seeks to enhance government sponsorship of a number of study programs, including the Joint Research PhD Fellowship, PhD in China Fellowship, Understanding China Fellowship, Young Leaders Fellowship, Publication Grant, and International Conference Grant. Additionally, according to the Confucius Institute Development Plan, the Hanban is planning to establish a training center called the Academy of Confucius Institute Directors to better train CI directors and teachers of China studies.[22] Clearly, these new initiatives will need more funding and support from the government.

This suggests that China's political will and fiscal support are the driving forces for the worldwide operation of CIs and CCs. While the growing number of CIs and host countries, as well as a huge annual budget do not necessarily guarantee the global popularity of CIs, they do help to project a new and benign image of China.

Performance Assessment

CIs seek to promote the internationalization of Chinese culture and China's influence worldwide,[23] framed within China's domestic pursuit of purposeful soft diplomacy[24] that seeks to present the country internationally as "civilized, democratic, open and progressive" (*wenming, minzhu, kaifang yu jinbu de xingxiang*).[25] Largess from the CIs to the host countries is accompanied by propaganda. The goal of these institutes is clear—to provide Chinese language teaching programs combined with comprehensive cultural, social and even diplomatic outreach.

Performance evaluation of the CI project is undertaken by the Hanban. A range of awards such as Pioneers of Confucius Institutes, Confucius Institutes of the Year, Confucius Classrooms of the Year, Confucius Institute Individual Performance Excellence Award of the Year, and Outstanding Confucius Institute Chinese Partners of the Year are all given at the annual Confucius Institute Conference. The criteria for selection and evaluation include innovation in Chinese language teaching, popularity of activities, networking efforts and other unique contributions. In 2013, for example, 28 CIs were selected for the awards. Four of them were in Southeast Asia. The CIs at the Royal Academy of Cambodia (RAC) and Angeles University Foundation (AUF) in the Philippines were chosen for their noteworthy performance in establishing Chinese Teaching Stations (CTSs), promoting the Chinese Proficiency Test (Hanyu Shuiping Kaoshi [HSK] examinations), and providing language programs for local teachers. The RAC established 3 CCs as well as 13 CTSs; the AUF set up 91 teaching stations and trained more than 125 local teachers. The Kongzi Institute for the Teaching of Chinese Language at the University of Malaya in Malaysia and the CI at Bansomdejchaopraya Rajabhat University in Thailand received the same award for the training programs they had designed for government units and local elites.[26]

A common feature of the awardees is their successful management of guanxi in the host countries. The CI project seeks to establish networks with government units and political elites in order to be favorably regarded in their locality. Additionally, only by developing these networks with host institutes and local educational institutions can the CIs' Chinese language programs be recognized as regular credit-bearing courses at local universities. Moreover, the support of local overseas Chinese groups helps to reinforce the popularity and impact of CI-related programs and activities. Therefore, to implement its soft diplomacy, networking with these various segments in the local population is necessary.

CIs as China's Soft Footprints in Southeast Asia

Southeast Asia is a key region where China's recent rise is manifested. It is also a region that enjoys China's economic support despite security tensions and difficulties with Beijing.[27] In order to consolidate the stable relations created by increasing economic interdependence, the Chinese government uses its soft diplomacy to strengthen mutual trust between China and its Southeast Asian neighbors.[28]

China's new leadership wants to project a new national image, that of a peaceful and responsible power. In late 2012, then Vice President Xi Jinping attended the China-ASEAN Expo in Guangxi. There he reiterated China's policy to safeguard sovereignty and territorial integrity through peaceful and friendly negotiation with neighbors. He emphasized that "China will never seek hegemony, nor behave in a hegemonic manner,"[29] in order to gain more strategic trust from neighboring countries. As the country's new president, on July 30, 2013, Xi promoted the building of China's maritime power through mutually beneficial cooperation with other countries. He reiterated that China would use non-violent means and negotiations to settle disputes and that it would strive to safeguard peace and stability.[30]

However, these political statements alone are insufficient in allaying the fears of China's Southeast Asian neighbors. In order to secure its sphere of influence, the Chinese government needs to invest more soft power resources "to soften the hard power projection" in the region. In this regard, CIs and CCs are the soft footprints of China's new "Good Neighbor Diplomacy" (*mulin waijiao*).

Altogether, there are 62 CIs and CCs in Southeast Asia (Table 4). The first CI in the region was established in Singapore in 2005, while at the time of writing, the most recent CI was established in Hanoi in late 2014. By carrying out their mandate as government-funded language institutes—offering credit/non-credit language courses, promoting cultural events, organizing Chinese tests and collaborating with local governments or stakeholders to establish Chinese Teaching Stations—the CIs enhance bilateral relations between China and the host countries.

Table 4 Number of CIs and CCs in Southeast Asia (2015)

Country	CIs	CCs	Total
Thailand	15	18	33
Indonesia	6	2	8
Cambodia	1	3	4
Philippines	4	3	7
Singapore	1	2	3
Myanmar	0	3	3
Malaysia	2	0	2
Laos	1	0	1
Vietnam	1	0	1
Total	31	31	62

Source: Confucius Institutes Watch database, www.ciwatch.net (accessed on June 20, 2016).

By providing a variety of funding programs and scholarships, sponsoring exchange programs, supporting China studies, and cultivating overseas Chinese education, the CI project reinforces China's international cultural and social attractiveness and intensifies the influence of its soft diplomacy at the local level. Additionally, the growing number of staff and teachers trained by CIs and CCs can be regarded as "civilian diplomats" who enhance and improve mutual trust between China and the host countries, echoing the rationale of "for the society."[31]

In summary, this chapter argues that the CIs strategically establish guanxi as both a means and an end to China's soft diplomacy. The CI project in Southeast Asia builds localized networks with national and local elites (for political recognition), government units (for political support), educational institutions (for social impact), and local overseas Chinese groups (ethnic affinity). The interrelationships among these various groups are depicted in Figure 1.

Establishing Guanxi: Thailand, Singapore and Cambodia

Due to the different political, economic and sociocultural structures of the host countries to which CIs need to adjust, there are variations in the way the CIs operate. The following section focuses on how CIs operate in three host countries—Thailand, Singapore and Cambodia.

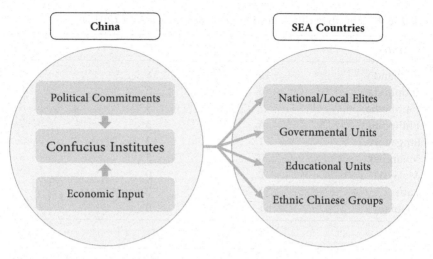

Figure 1　CI Project and Its Guanxi Networks

In particular, it describes how the CIs establish guanxi with the local elites, government units, educational institutions and local overseas Chinese groups in these host countries.

The CI Project in Thailand

Among the countries in Southeast Asia, Thailand has the biggest number of CIs (15) and CCs (18), an indication of its enthusiastic support for China's CI project. Before 1975, the relationship between China and Thailand was tense. However, this tension eased in 1975 when China established diplomatic ties with Thailand. Relations between the two countries improved when China reduced its assistance to the Thai Communist Party. After Deng Xiaoping, then prime minister, visited Thailand, bilateral relations were greatly enhanced.[32] In 2008, during Chinese President Hu Jintao's official visit to Thailand, he commented that "the development of China-Thailand relations is always in the front rank of relations between China and other neighboring nations."[33] In 2011, China's Vice President Xi Jinping stated that "both countries commonly share feelings like those of a family," to describe the intimate Sino-Thai political relationship.[34] In 2016, Chinese Premier Li Keqiang attended the first Lancang-Mekong Cooperation Leaders' Meeting. On this occasion, he had a bilateral meeting with Thai Prime Minister Prayuth Chan-ocha, which resulted in China's support for Thailand as the co-chair for regional cooperation.[35] These examples show the degree of importance that China attaches to Sino-Thai relations.

Guanxi with Thai Elites

Thai national and local elites help to promote Sino-Thai friendship by supporting the CI project in Thailand. Foremost among them is Thai Princess Sirindhorn. Since 1981, Princess Sirindhorn has visited China on several occasions and continued to learn the Chinese language. She has also frequently attended opening ceremonies of the CI projects and supported Chinese cultural events. As the Thai royal family is highly revered by the Thai people, Princess Sirindhorn's cultural appreciation and political support for the CI project is regarded as an extremely significant response from Thailand. China values this support; thus, in 2010, Princess Sirindhorn was declared as one of China's top ten international friends.[36]

Guanxi with Thai Government Units

The most important feature of CIs in Thailand is their working relationship with government units. By promoting Chinese language courses, CIs in Thailand have offered Chinese language training programs to central and local governments. For example, the CI at Chiang Mai University works with the Chiang Mai Immigration Bureau and Education Bureau.[37] The CI at Chulalongkorn University works with the Thai royal family, with the CI director himself teaching the family members conversational Chinese.[38] Moreover, an increasing number of officials from the ministries of Defense, Commerce, Education, and Foreign Affairs, and the Thai Customs (under the Finance Ministry) have been attending CI Chinese language programs.

Since Chinese language teachers are key actors in projecting a positive image of China, the Chinese government places special emphasis on the training of Thai teachers who teach the Chinese language. In connection with this, the Hanban signed a bilateral teaching framework agreement with the Thai Ministry of Education in 2006, which resulted in a training project for Thai Chinese teachers in September 2008.[39] Although examples like these are few and far between, they have already delivered political benefits to China because of the prominent status of government personnel trained under this agreement.

Guanxi with Educational Institutes in Thailand

For its guanxi with Thai educational institutions, China has selected some key Thai universities to jointly establish CIs. Many of these are located in the central districts of main Thai cities. They include Chulalongkorn University in Bangkok and Chiang Mai University in the north. These universities were selected because of their prestigious standing in Thailand. In 2014, the CI at Chiang Mai University was named the Confucius Institute of the Year. In addition, the vice president of Chulalongkorn University and the vice chair of the board of the CI at Chulalongkorn University were both given the Confucius Institute Individual Performance Excellence Award of the Year. Through these universities and CI directors, promising local students are encouraged to study in China through various means, such as offers of scholarships.[40]

Despite this rosy outlook, the 250 Chinese schools in Thailand have some apprehension about the CIs. For example, most of these schools worry that the CIs will compete with them in the local Chinese language education market. To allay these fears, China has allowed local Chinese schools to benefit from its resources, which are disbursed through the CIs. Examples of the local schools that have enjoyed this benefit are the Srinakorn School Confucius Classroom, the Sawang Boriboon Wittaya School Confucius Classroom and the Xingmin Phitsanulok School Confucius Classroom.[41] Courses offered by these joint projects include listening, speaking, reading and writing courses in Chinese; ancient Chinese; business Chinese; and other culture-related programs. Some of these emphasize training of local faculties by jointly promoting cultural activities with local primary and secondary schools. Through these soft footprints, a favorable image of Chinese society and culture is formed.

A number of the CIs have also successfully integrated their courses into the regular curriculum of some local universities. These credit-bearing courses are now offered at the Chulalongkorn University, Khon Kaen University, Mahasarakham University, Suan Dusit Rajabhat University, and Bansomdejchaopraya Rajabhat University.

Guanxi with Local Overseas Chinese in Thailand

Local overseas Chinese groups in Thailand contribute significantly to the operation of the CIs by helping promote Chinese culture, donating funds or teaching materials to the institutes, and sponsoring social or cultural events. In 2006, for instance, the Confucius Institute at Mae Fah Luang University and Xiamen University jointly organized a seminar in Bangkok titled "Embracing the Future with Confucian Optimism and Stability." It focused on the CPC's political ideals. In 2009, CIs in Thailand organized activities and seminars to commemorate the 60th anniversary of the founding of the People's Republic of China (PRC). For example, the CI at Chulalongkorn University conducted a seminar titled "60 Years of the New China: Reform and Development." At its opening ceremony, the CI at Burapha University jointly organized the "60th Anniversary of the People's Republic of China Photo Exhibition" with the Chinese government, which Thai Princess Sirindhorn attended.[42]

Statistics provided by the PRC embassy in Thailand show that there were 54 celebratory activities on the PRC's 60th anniversary.[43] These were jointly conducted in 62 of Thailand's 77 provinces by China, the CIs, and local overseas Chinese groups. About 100,000 people participated.[44] The success of such activities demonstrates the effective use of political mobilization strategies of the CPC as well as the CI's well-established connections with local overseas Chinese.

Thailand's CIs have thus gone beyond the role of mere language institutes, the goal of which is the propagation of Chinese language and culture. Through their classes and programs, these CIs have successfully created a nationwide network for policy interaction, cultural activities, recruitment of students and teachers, social contact with government officials, as well as high-level official visits—all of which help to integrate CIs into Thai society and build a "friendly image" of China.

The CI Project in Singapore

The first CI in Southeast Asia was established in Singapore in 2005. This was because within the region, Singapore has the highest proportion of ethnic Chinese in its population, creating a close affinity with China in terms of language and culture. This ethnic link facilitates bilateral cooperation in the joint CI project.

Singapore also enjoys a close political and economic relationship with China because it views China as a critical support for maintaining its national economic growth. Bilateral trade between the two countries amounted to US$121.5 billion in 2014. With its US$5.8 billion investment in more than 700 projects, Singapore became China's largest foreign investor.[45] These ethnic and economic links drive Singapore to actively seek cooperation with China, thus allowing China's soft diplomacy to permeate Singaporean society and enabling China to use the city state as a setting to enhance its own image.

Guanxi with Singaporean Elites

The positive responses from Singapore's political leaders have facilitated the promotion of the CI project. In his speech at the Speak Mandarin Campaign's 30th Anniversary Launch, Singapore's founding Prime Minister Lee Kuan Yew said that "learning Mandarin for Chinese in Singapore is a must" and that "Mandarin will become our mother tongue."[46] He also commended the contribution of the CIs in promoting the Chinese language and introducing modern China to the world.[47] His son, Prime Minister Lee Hsien Loong, continued to promote the Speak Mandarin Campaign, asserting that most Singaporeans "would like to grow deeper roots and know their culture better," are aware of "the rise and rapid economic development of China,"[48] and also welcome the contribution of CIs in Singapore.

Guanxi with Singapore Government Units

The support from Singapore's leaders has resulted in bilateral government ties in the fields of education and cultural cooperation as manifested in the signing of the Memorandum of Understanding on Cultural Cooperation in 1996[49] and the Agreement on Cultural Cooperation in 2006,[50] both of which provide a solid basis for China's CI project.

Singapore's desire for active cooperation with China paved the way for the establishment of the CI at Nanyang Technological University (NTU), which is the platform for bridging the Singapore and Chinese governments. Its Business Chinese Program is jointly conducted with Singapore's Workforce Development Agency (now Workplace Singapore), attracting young local talents to learn Chinese.[51] Moreover, the CI at NTU has provided numerous executive training courses for middle-rank officials from China's central and local governments, thereby establishing connections with Singapore local government units and enterprises. In 2010, the CI at NTU was recognized with the Confucius Institute of the Year award. Its director, Hock Kiat Koh, was awarded the Confucius Institute Individual Performance Excellence Award of the Year in 2011. Its counterpart in China, Shandong University, was awarded the Outstanding Confucius Institute Chinese Partner of the Year in 2013.[52]

Guanxi with Educational Institutions in Singapore

Singapore's CI focuses on professional business courses. It strongly promotes the "economic value" of learning the Chinese language and offers courses for Singapore business professionals working in China. In particular, the CI at NTU has signed an agreement with Singapore's Ministry of Manpower to be designated as the training institute for business-related Chinese courses for middle-senior management personnel from the government sector, multinational corporations, government-linked corporations and private companies. Upon completion of its business courses, the CI at NTU awards certificates, which include the Diploma in Business Translation and Interpretation Skills. By adopting this strategy, Singapore hopes to integrate its CI courses into the existing local Chinese education market and increase opportunities for offering joint courses with universities in China.[53]

The CI at NTU focuses on nurturing primary and secondary school students as part of China's soft diplomacy towards local overseas Chinese. It believes that the learning of Chinese language and culture is more important for children than for adults. Thus, the design of its courses focuses on primary and secondary students, making the CI at NTU considerably different from other CIs. Additionally, special cultural activities are designed for the young, such as the Young Confucius Cultural Camp. All these programs and activities create cultural awareness and common values, as well as an ethnic identity among Singapore's Chinese community.

In addition to the CI at NTU, a Confucius School was established by the Hanban in Singapore in 2007. This is similar to the Confucius Classroom. The school is managed directly by the Hanban and it is tasked to work "closely with local primary and secondary schools, assisting with Chinese instruction, playing an active role in basic Chinese education in Singapore."[54]

Guanxi with Local Overseas Chinese in Singapore

The CI at NTU also seeks to bind local overseas Chinese in Singapore by organizing various cultural activities. In the words of its former director, Koh Hock Kiat, an important mission of the CI is to play the role of a "cultural gardener" by enhancing the academic interactions between Singapore and China, as well as by making connections with local overseas Chinese around the world.[55] Thus, the CI offers a course titled "Preliminary Study of Contemporary Mainland China." It also established an NTU Confucius Institute Foundation to strengthen the bonds between Singapore and Chinese communities around the world. In 2016, the CI at NTU instituted the Nanyang Chinese Youth Literature Award to encourage Singaporean high school students to practice Chinese writing.

In summary, the Chinese government has taken advantage of the sizeable ethnic Chinese population in Singapore to launch its CI project there. The positive response from the academic and national elites, as well as the ethnic Chinese population, has allowed the CI project to become a policy tool for promoting Chinese language learning in Singaporean society and strengthening the bond between China and Singapore.

The CI Project in Cambodia

The CI project in Cambodia is different from those in Singapore and Thailand. China and Cambodia enjoy a very close political relationship, with frequent mutual high-level visits in recent years. The Chinese political leadership, such as Hu Jintao, even described the Sino-Cambodia relationship as one of "mutually trustworthy neighbors, friends and partners."[56] As Cambodia is extremely reliant on foreign trade, China has invested huge resources in Cambodia in terms of infrastructure, low interest loans and trade. Driven by its "Going Out" strategy,[57] China has encouraged many of its state-owned enterprises (SOEs) to invest in Cambodia. Consequently, it became Cambodia's largest foreign investor in 2005 and biggest aid donor in 2009.

The Chinese government understands that economic and political ties between China and Cambodia cannot endure without solid mutual trust. It is important for China to project a friendly image to Cambodians to ease worries about its presence in Cambodia and its rise in the region. The CI project has thus become an important vehicle for China's soft diplomacy in Cambodia.

Guanxi with Cambodian Elites

The support from Cambodia's national leaders is important to the operation of the CI at the Royal Academy of Cambodia. At the 2013 Confucius Institutes Conference in Asia held in Cambodia, Prime Minister Hun Sen acknowledged the importance of learning the Chinese language and the contribution of CIs in Asia. He then suggested that CIs in the region further implement the Confucius Institutes Action Plan (2012–5) set by the Hanban with a specific focus on training local teachers of Chinese language.[58] With Prime Minister Hun Sen's support, the CI in Cambodia was awarded the Confucius Institutes Award of 2013. The Chinese director, Wang Xianmiao, and Cambodian director, Chea Munyrith, were respectively awarded the Confucius Institute Individual Performance Excellence Award of the Year in 2011 and 2012.[59]

Guanxi with Cambodian Government Units

The CI at the Royal Academy of Cambodia was jointly established in 2009 by the Royal Academy of Cambodia, Canadia Bank, Ruitai Stone Co. Ltd., and the Jiujiang University of Jiangxi Province in 2009. It is the only CI in Cambodia and it receives fiscal support from both the Hanban and local overseas Chinese. As mandated by China, the main focus of this CI is the promotion of Chinese language and culture. As such, it is used as a platform for enhancing economic cooperation bilaterally. China attaches great importance to this CI, as evidenced by Xi Jinping's presence at its opening ceremony in 2009.[60]

In addition to the CI and its Chinese Teaching Stations, since March 2013 three more CCs have been established in Cambodia—at Angkor High School, the 70th Brigade, and the Police Academy of Cambodia. The latter two are government units, showcasing the close ties between the CI and public sectors in Cambodia.

The CI project in Cambodia is innovative for several reasons. First, it seeks to create a new Chinese language teaching system which is supported by the Cambodian government. Thus, it mobilized government units and students from local Chinese schools to participate in CI activities, such as the Chinese Proficiency tests conducted by the Cambodian-Chinese Association. For example, a Chinese language program provided by the CI at the Royal Academy of Cambodia was conducted on January 21, 2010. The majority of participants came from various government sectors, including the Prime Minister's Office and the Ministries of Defense, Home Affairs, Education, and News.[61] Such programs and courses are frequently held to showcase the friendship between China and Cambodia.

Moreover, the Cambodian CI is tasked to organize conferences and workshops that highlight bilateral relations. On July 8, 2015, the CI organized a symposium titled "One Belt One Road: New

Opportunities for Cambodia-China Cooperation." It was held in the Cambodian Senate, and representatives from key government units such as the Ministry of Foreign Affairs and International Cooperation, Ministry of Commerce, and the Council for the Development of Cambodia (CDC) attended and discussed the future of bilateral relations under China's grand strategy.[62]

Another important strategy to establish guanxi with Cambodian government units is the establishment of Chinese Teaching Stations (CTSs), a distinctive feature of the CI project in Cambodia. This pioneer project is installed in government units or local schools in those provinces where there is no CI or CC. These CTSs get support from the CI or CC, including teaching materials and teachers, and their flexible design facilitates the spread of influence in the localities. Currently, there are 18 CTSs collaborating with local universities, high schools and key government sectors, such as the Prime Minister's Office and the Ministry of Public Works and Transport.

Guanxi with Educational Institutions in Cambodia

The CTS project is crucial for engaging the localities in Cambodia. The salaries of its Chinese teachers, the expenses of the CTSs, and scholarships are sponsored by the CI project. To date, there are 18 CTSs in Cambodia. They are located in Phnom Penh, Sihanouk Province, Kandal Province, Banteay Meanchey Province and Siem Reap Province. They support the teaching of the Chinese language within Cambodia's education system.[63]

As part of its efforts to promote Chinese culture, the CI in Cambodia organized competitions among high school students such as "How much do you know about China?" and "Chinese Bridge" in May 2010 and May 2011. These were broadcast via local mainstream media such as the Byron TV station, CTN TV station, and published in *The Cambodian Daily*.[64]

The contribution of local overseas Chinese to establishing partnerships with local Chinese schools cannot be ignored. There are approximately 56,000 students studying in local Chinese schools, which are managed by the Cambodian-Chinese Association (known as Jian Hua) and its affiliated units. The association also manages the *Jian Hua Daily*, a newspaper which serves as its propaganda tool.[65] By establishing a favorable relationship with the Cambodian-Chinese Association and taking advantage of the existing resources of overseas

Chinese communities and schools, China's goals of promoting culture and language can be met.

Guanxi with Local Overseas Chinese in Cambodia

The CI also aims to strengthen relations with the Cambodian-Chinese Association which underwent profound changes in 1950–69 as a result of government suppression. In this regard, China provides direct assistance to the Cambodian-Chinese Association by conducting training classes for Chinese teachers in primary schools.

Cambodian CIs have become a venue for communication between the Chinese government and local overseas Chinese. Before the CI was established in Phnom Penh, this communication was made possible by the Chinese embassy in Cambodia. Currently, some (cultural) functions of the embassy have been assumed by the CI, enabling China to use the learning of language and culture as a tool for its political ends.

Table 5 summarizes how the CIs in Thailand, Singapore and Cambodia have created new guanxi and reinforced existing ones as they implemented their goal of promoting Chinese language and culture.

Table 5 Comparison of CIs and CCs in Thailand, Singapore and Cambodia

	Thailand	Singapore	Cambodia
National/ Local Elites	Thai Princess Sirindhorn	Minister Mentor Lee Kuan Yew, Prime Minister Lee Hsien Loong	Prime Minister Hun Sen
Government Units	Thai Royal Family, Ministry of Defense, Ministry of Foreign Affairs	Ministry of Manpower, Ministry of Education	Prime Minister's Office, Ministry of Defense, Ministry of Home Affairs, Ministry of Education and the News Ministry
Educational Institutions	Leading universities, i.e. Chulalongkorn University	Nanyang Technological University	The Royal Academy of Cambodia
Local Overseas Chinese	Local Chinese Associations	Local Chinese Associations, Singapore Chinese Teacher's Union	Cambodian-Chinese Association

Conclusion

The CIs and their related activities are stamping the soft footprint of China in Southeast Asia by establishing new and reinforcing existing guanxi with national/local elites, government units, educational institutions and local overseas Chinese. The examples of Thailand, Singapore and Cambodia show that China's CI project goes beyond promoting Chinese language and culture. It aims to establish new guanxi to reshape the perception of China as a peaceful and responsible great power and consequently enhance its bilateral relations with its Southeast Asian neighbors.

By focusing on the CIs in Thailand, Singapore and Cambodia, this chapter has shown how the CIs in these host countries have marked China's soft footprint in these areas. Thailand, an enthusiastic supporter of China's CI project, serves as the role model for other CI host countries. CIs and CCs in Thailand have successfully formed a network for government-to-government communication and institute-to-locality interaction. The cultural activities of these CIs help to project an attractive and favorable image of China to its Southeast Asian neighbors. Cultural affinity is the key feature in the case of Singapore, where China's soft diplomacy is facilitated by the high proportion of ethnic Chinese in the population. Significantly, the strategic concerns of the Singapore government and the integration of the CI project into the country's education system are also evident. For Cambodia, the full endorsement by the government, the innovative network of the CI project, and the acceptance of China's soft power at the grassroots level enhance the capacity and soft influence of the Cambodian CI. These three cases show the different responses of host countries to China's CI project and how these responses have facilitated China's soft diplomacy in their localities.

Nevertheless, the authenticity of the CIs in providing an authoritative representation of current China has also been viewed with increasing skepticism. Critics have been quick to point out the CIs' political mission and negative influence on campus politics,[66] attacking the CIs for trying to sanitize China's reputation via the classroom. Others regard the CI project as an attempt to mobilize China's friends and supporters while isolating dissenters, or even accuse the CIs of espionage.[67] For example, some worry that the CIs will be used to collect criticisms of China. It is also a concern that discussions of certain topics, such as Taiwan independence, Tiananmen, or Tibet are not allowed in the CIs. Most of these suspicions are directed primarily at the CIs' underlying supporter, the Chinese government, for its authoritarian regime and continuous violation of human rights.

The global expansion of the CI project will undoubtedly continue, as will the criticism of its academic integrity. As long as discussions of human rights and democracy as well as other sensitive and controversial issues are banned in CI classes, the focus on the CI's threat to freedom of thought and education will remain. The CI project will need more political will and resources if it is to succeed in remaking China into a global role model.

Notes

1. Yiwei Wang, "Public Diplomacy and the Rise of Chinese Soft Power," *The Annals of the American Academy of Political and Social Science* 616, no. 1 (2008): 257–73; Trefor Moss, "Soft Power? China Has Plenty," *The Diplomat*, June 4, 2013, <http://thediplomat.com/2013/06/soft-power-china-has-plenty/> (accessed August 25, 2015).
2. Ian Hall and Frank Smith, "The Struggle for Soft Power in Asia: Public Diplomacy and Regional Competition," *Asian Security* 9, no. 1 (2013): 1–18.
3. Pan Su-Yan, "Confucius Institute Project: China's Cultural Diplomacy and Soft Power Projection," *Asian Education and Development Studies* 2, no. 1 (2013): 22–33, 5; Alan Hao Yang and H.H. Michael Hsiao, "Confucius Institutes and the Question of China's Soft Power Diplomacy," *China Brief* 12, No. 13 (2012): 10–3.
4. Xinhua News Agency, "The 6th Confucius Institute Conference is Held in Beijing Opening Ceremony Attended by Li Changchun," *Hanban News*, December 21, 2011, <http://english.hanban.org/article/2011-12/21/content_396561.htm/> (accessed August 25, 2015).
5. Hanban [Confucius Institute Headquarters], "Liu Yandong Gives Keynote Speech at the Opening Session of the 8th Confucius Institute Conference," *Hanban News*, December 12, 2013, <http://english.hanban.org/article/2013-12/12/content_518317.htm/> (accessed August 25, 2015).
6. A contributor to *The New Yorker* magazine stated that the children in poor neighborhoods in Chicago are "compelled to learn that China will be a plausible part of their lives." See Evan Osnos, "Why Is Hu Jintao Going to Chicago?," *The New Yorker*, January 20, 2011, <http://www.newyorker.com/online/blogs/evanosnos/2011/01/why-is-hu-jintao-going-to-chicago.html/> (accessed August 28, 2015).
7. The Hanban in Beijing was chosen as one of the "distinguished governmental units" in May 2014 in terms of "staying firm with the political

direction," i.e. being loyal to the state and upholding political belief in the Party and the government, and "excellent performance and organized framework of the headquarters," i.e. working closely with CPC. See Work Committee of Central Government Departments, "*Chung Jian Wen Ming Ji Guan, Zheng Zuo Ren Min Man Yi Gong Wu Yuan Yun Dong, Xian Jin Ji Ti Ping Xuan*" [Evaluation of Distinguished Group for Constructing Civilized Institutions, Struggling for Civil Servant], Zi Guang Ge Wang Zhan, May 2014, <http://www.zgg.gov.cn/cjwmjgxjjtpx/xjjtpx/201405/t20140509_439363.html/> (accessed December 5, 2015).

8. Steven W. Mosher, "Confucius Institutes: Trojan Horses with Chinese Characteristics," Population Research Institute, March 28, 2012, <http://pop.org/content/confucius-institutes-trojan-horses-chinese-characteristics/> (accessed November 22, 2014).

9. "Concerns Grow Over China's Confucius Institutes," *Radio Free Asia*, July 25, 2014, <http://www.rfa.org/english/news/china/confucius-07252014111157.html/> (accessed November 22, 2014).

10. The CI project is politically supported by the Chinese leadership, such as Hu Jintao, Wen Jiabao, and Xi Jinping (see Erin Meyer and Andrew L. Wang, "Hu Jintao Pays Visit to Payton Prep," *Chicago Tribune*, January 21, 2011, <http://articles.chicagotribune.com/2011-01-21/news/ct-met-china-visit-0122-20110121_1_chinese-president-hu-jintao-chinese-companies-payton-students/> (accessed November 22, 2014); Hanban, "Highlights of Chinese Premier Wen Jiabao's Visit to Confucius Institute at the University of Al-Azhar, Indonesia," *Hanban News*, May 10, 2011, <http://english.hanban.org/article/2011-05/10/content_257863.htm/> (accessed December 5, 2015); Hanban, "Chinese President Xi Jinping Attends Signing Ceremony of Establishment of Confucius Institutes in Brazil," *Hanban News*, July 25, 2014, <http://english.hanban.org/article/2014-07/25/content_546267.htm/> (accessed December 5, 2015).

11. The discussion is based on the authors' fieldwork and interviews at CIs in the Philippines (2014), Myanmar (2013), Laos (2013), Indonesia (2013), Cambodia (2012), Singapore (2011), Malaysia (2010) and Thailand (2010 and 2015).

12. Xu Lin, Director-General of Hanban and Chief Executive of Confucius Institute Headquarters, stated that "the year 2011 witnesses stable expansion and development of Confucius Institutes in both size and strength ... the Confucius Institute has played an increasingly prominent role as a comprehensive platform for cultural exchanges, and its international influence has been enhanced further," (see Hanban, *2011 Annual Report* (Beijing: Hanban, 2012), 5.

13. Almost every Chinese director of CI commented on the development of the CI as "crossing the river by feeling the stone." Interview at the

Confucius Institute at Ritsumeikan University, Kyoto, Japan in September 2009.
14. Hanban, "About Confucius Institutes/Confucius Classrooms," *Hanban News*, March 31, 2014, <http://english.hanban.org/node_10971.htm/> (accessed November 22, 2015).
15. Maria Wey-Shen Siow, "China's Confucius Institutes: Crossing the River by Feeling the Stones," *Asia-Pacific Bulletin*, no. 91 (January 6, 2011): 1.
16. The Office of Chinese Language Council, *International Annual Report 2006* (Beijing: The Office of Chinese Language Council, 2006), 7.
17. The Belt and Road Initiative is the grand strategy intiated by Chinese President Xi Jinping. It has two strategic components—"The 21st-Century Maritime Silk Route" and the "Silk Road Economic Belt"—as roadmaps for spreading Chinese investment and influence. For example, in infrastructure, the "21st-Century Maritime Silk Route" emphasizes the importance of sealane neighbors, while the "Silk Road Economic Belt" models the ancient business route in the Han dynasty to enhance the relations with Central Asian countries.
18. Hanban, *2014 Annual Report* (Beijing: Hanban, 2014), 51.
19. This is the annual budget of the CI at Western Kentucky University in the United States. See WKU, "The Confucius Institute Staff-Terrill Martin," <http://www.wku.edu/ci/staff/terrill_martin/> (accessed March 10, 2014).
20. This is the annual budget for the CI at Melbourne University in Australia. See Geoff Maslen, "Australia: Warning – Be Wary of Confucius Institutes," *University World News*, December 2, 2007, <http://www.universityworldnews.com/article.php?story=20071130094503100/> (accessed March 10, 2014).
21. Hanban (Confucius Institute Headquarters), *2010 Annual Report* (Beijing: Hanban, 2010), 13, 51.
22. Hanban, "Liu Yandong Gives Keynote Speech at the Opening Session of the 8th Confucius Institute Conference," *Hanban News*, December 12, 2013, <http://english.hanban.org/article/2013-12/12/content_518317_3.htm/> (accessed December 22, 2014).
23. Interview at the Renmin University, Beijing, China, December 2010.
24. "A Message from Confucius: New Ways of Projecting Soft Power," *The Economist*, October 22, 2009, <http://www.economist.com/node/14678507/> (accessed December 12, 2014).
25. Renmin Chubanshe, *Zhonggong Zhongyang Guanyu Shenhua Wenhua Tizhi Gaige Tuidong Shehui Zhuyi Wenhua Dafazhan Dafanrong Ruogan Zhongda Wenti De Jueding* [The Decision of Deepening Reformation of Cultural Institution and Promoting the Development and Prosperity of Socialism] (Beijing: Renmin Chubanshe, 2011), 35–6.

26. Hanban, *2013 Annual Report* (Beijing: Hanban, 2013), 72–3.
27. Ian Storey, *Southeast Asia and the Rise of China: The Search for Security* (New York: Routledge, 2011) and François Gipouloux, *The Asian Mediterranean: Port Cities and Trading Networks in China, Japan and Southeast Asia, 13th–21st Century* (Cheltenham, UK: Edward Elgar, 2011).
28. Ho Khai Leong, ed., *Connecting & Distancing: Southeast Asia and China* (Singapore: Singapore Society of Asian Studies and Institute of Southeast Asian Studies, 2009).
29. "Xinhua Insight: Xi Urges China-ASEAN Economic Ties, Peaceful Dispute Settlements," *Xinhua News*, September 21, 2012, <http://news.xinhuanet.com/english/indepth/2012-09/21/c_131865664.htm/> (accessed March 14, 2013).
30. Wang Qian and Zhang Yunbi, "Xi Vows to Protect Maritime Interests," *China Daily*, August 1, 2013, <http://usa.chinadaily.com.cn/epaper/2013-08/01/content_16861678.htm> (accessed September 2, 2013).
31. Interview at the Confucius Institute in the Ateneo de Manila University, Manila, Philippines, August 2014; interview at Chulalongkorn University, Bangkok, Thailand, August 2010.
32. Chulacheeb Chinwanno, "Rising China and Thailand's Policy of Strategic Engagement," in *The Rise of China: Responses from Southeast Asia and Japan*, ed. Jun Tsunekawa (Tokyo: The National Institute for Defense Studies, 2009), 81–109.
33. Consulate of the People's Republic of China in Laoag, "President Hu Jintao Meets with Thai Prime Minister Samak," July 1, 2008, <http://laoag.chineseconsulate.org/eng/lgxw/t471411.htm> (accessed April 25, 2016).
34. Xinhua News Agency, "Xi Jinping Visits the Confucius Institute at Chulalongkorn University, Thailand on December 24," *Hanban News*, December 25, 2011, <http://english.hanban.org/article/2011-12/25/content_399472.htm> (accessed April 25, 2016).
35. Ministry of Foreign Affairs of the People's Republic of China, " Li Keqiang Meets with Prime Minister Prayut Chan-o-cha of Thailand," March 23, 2016, <http://www.fmprc.gov.cn/mfa_eng/zxxx_662805/t1350711.shtml> (accessed April 22, 2016).
36. "Princess Sirindhorn: Among the Top 10 International Friends of China," *Asian Correspondent*, December 6, 2009, <http://asiancorrespondent.com/25980/princess-sirindhorn-one-of-top-10-international-friends-of-china/> (accessed December 11, 2014).
37. Interview at the CI in Chiang Mai University, Chiang Mai, Thailand, December 2011.
38. Interview at the CI in Chulalongkorn University, Bangkok, Thailand, August 2010.

39. The Office of Chinese Language Council International Annual Report, 2006, 32.
40. Hanban, *2013 Annual Report*, 81 and 83.
41. Interview at the CI in Chulalongkorn University, August 2010.
42. Ku Shih-Hung and Huang Che-Yu, "Shilintong Gongzhu Chuxí Taiquo Zhuda Juban de Xin Zhongguo 60 Nian Yantao Hui" (Princess Sirindhorn Attends Thailand Chulalongkorn University's New China 60th Anniversary Conference), *China News*, October 23, 2009, <http://www.chinanews.com/hr/hr-yzhrxw/news/2009/10-23/1926115.shtml> (accessed September 22, 2015); Ku Shih-Hung, "Taiquo Gongzhu Shilintong Wei Dongfang Daxue Kongzi Xueyuan Jiepai" (Thai Princess Sirindhorn Unveils New Confucius Institute at Burapha University), *China News*, September 16, 2009, <http://www.chinanews.com/hwjy/news/2009/09-16/1868560.shtml> (accessed September 22, 2015).
43. "Confucius Institutes Organize Celebratory Activities on the PRC's 60th Anniversary," www.people.com.cn. October 3, 2010, <http://chinese.people.com.cn/GB/10153534.html> (accessed April 4, 2013).
44. Ku Shih-Hung, "Taiguo Kongzi Xueyuan Qingzhu Xin Zhongguo Liushi Huadan Huodong Huo Haoping" [Confucius Institutes in Thailand Celebrate New China's 60th Anniversary, Events Receive Praise], *China News*, October 2, 2009, <http://www.chinanews.com/hwjy/news/2009/10-02/1897504.shtml> (accessed September 22, 2015).
45. Chong Koh Ping, "Bilateral Trade and Investment Going Strong," *Straits Times*, November 6, 2015, <http://www.straitstimes.com/business/bilateral-trade-and-investment-going-strong> (accessed November 10, 2015).
46. SPH Razor, "Mandarin in Japan (MM Lee at Confucius Institute Pt 6)," Youtube, July 25, 2013, <https://www.youtube.com/watch?v=j3xyat8YtGo> (accessed April 30, 2016).
47. Prime Minister's Office, Singapore, Speech by Mr. Lee Kuan Yew, Minister Mentor, at Speak Mandarin Campaign's 30th Anniversary Launch, March 17, 2009, <http://www.pmo.gov.sg/content/pmosite/mediacentre/speechesninterviews/ministermentor/2009/March/speech_by_mr_leekuanyewministermentoratspeakmandarincampaigns30t.html#.VAL7iNgcSP8/> (accessed November 10, 2015).
48. Prime Minister's Office Singapore, Speech by PM Lee Hsien Loong at launch of Speak Mandarin Campaign 2014, June 11, 2014, <http://www.pmo.gov.sg/mediacentre/speech-pm-lee-hsien-loong-launch-speak-mandarin-campaign-2014> (November 10, 2015).
49. Memorandum of Understanding on Cultural Cooperation Between the Ministry of Culture of the People's Republic China and the Ministry of Information and the Arts of the Republic of Singapore, 1996, <http://www.fmprc.gov.cn/eng/wjb/zzjg/yzs/gjlb/2777/2778/t16195.htm/> (accessed December 22, 2015).

50. Agreement on Cultural Cooperation between the Government of the People's Republic of China and the Government of the Republic of Singapore, 2006, <http://tradeinservices.mofcom.gov.cn/en/b/2006-08-25/63711.shtml/> (accessed December 22, 2015).
51. "About Us," Confucius Institute, Nanyang Technological University, <http://ci.ntu.edu.sg/eng/aboutus/Pages/default.aspx> (accessed October 22, 2015); "Business Chinese," Confucius Institute, Nanyang Technological University, <http://ci.ntu.edu.sg/eng/Programme/aclp/Programmes/Pages/Programmes-Detailed.aspx?event=94ee1762-bc2c-4ff0-a168-0a791aef455f> (accessed October 22, 2015).
52. Hanban, *2010 Annual Report*, 80; *2011 Annual Report*, 82; *2013 Annual Report*, 76.
53. Interview at the CI in Nanyang Technological University, Singapore, 2010.
54. Hanban, "Confucius School in Singapore," 2014, <http://210.40.3.82/en_US/2/58/read/893;jsessionid=3B20DF6907574EE0348E05999059DAFF/> (accessed December 22, 2015).
55. "Teaching Sun Tzi in Confucius Institute," *China News*, September 26, 2011, <http://www.chinanews.com/hwjy/2011/09-26/3351946.shtml/> (accessed May 10, 2014).
56. "Hujintao Huijian Jianpuzhai Shouxiang Hun Sen" [Hujintao Meets Cambodian Prime Minister Hun Sen], *China Daily*, March 31, 2012, <https://www.chinadaily.com.cn/hqzx/2012-03/31/content_14962186.htm> (accessed April 5, 2013).
57. The "Going Out" strategy is promoted by the Chinese government to encourage its state-owned enterprises (SOEs) to explore emerging markets regionally and globally.
58. Speech of Prime Minister Hun Sen at the Opening of the Conference of Confucius Institute, Asia 2013 (PM), *Cambodia News Vision*, May 29, 2013, <http://cnv.org.kh/en/?p=3620/> (accessed May 23, 2014).
59. Hanban, *2010 Annual Report*, 82; *2012 Annual Report*, 74; *2013 Annual Report*, 72.
60. Interview at the CI in the Royal Academy of Cambodia, Phnom Penh, Cambodia, 2012.
61. Zhang Ruiling and Lei Bosong, "Confucius Institute Opens Chinese-language Class in Cambodia," China Central Television, January 22, 2010, <http://english.cctv.com/20100122/101597.shtml> (accessed March 20, 2015).
62. Song Yazhou, "Confucius Institute at Royal Academy of Cambodia Hosts a Symposium Entitled 'One Belt One Road: New Opportunities for Cambodia-China Cooperation,'" *Hanban News*, July 22, 2015, <http://english.hanban.org/article/2015-07/22/content_610463.htm> (accessed September 22, 2015).
63. Ibid.

64. Fieldwork in Phnom Penh, Cambodia, December 2012.
65. Interview at Cambodian Chinese Association, Phnom Penh, Cambodia, December 2012.
66. Marshall Sahlins, *Confucius Institute: Academic Malware* (Chicago: The University of Chicago Press, 2015); Christopher R. Hughes, "Confucius Institutes and the University: Distinguishing the Political Mission from the Cultural," *Issues & Studies* 50, no. 4 (2014): 45–83.
67. Daniel Golden, "Sex, Lies and Espionage: Did a Professor Spy for the FBI?" Bloomberg, <http://www.bloomberg.com/news/articles/2015-02-25/sex-lies-and-espionage-did-a-professor-spy-for-the-fbi-/> (accessed September 20, 2015).

References

"A Message from Confucius: New Ways of Projecting Soft Power." *The Economist*, October 22, 2009. <http://www.economist.com/node/14678507/> (accessed December 12, 2014).

Agreement on Cultural Cooperation between the Government of the People's Republic of China and the Government of the Republic of Singapore, 2006. <http://tradeinservices.mofcom.gov.cn/en/b/2006-08-25/63711.shtml/> (accessed December 22, 2015).

Chinwanno, Chulacheeb. "Rising China and Thailand's Policy of Strategic Engagement." In *The Rise of China: Responses from Southeast Asia and Japan*, edited by Jun Tsunekawa, 81–109. Tokyo: The National Institute for Defense Studies, 2009.

Chong, Koh Ping. "Bilateral Trade and Investment Going Strong." *Straits Times*, November 6, 2015. <http://www.straitstimes.com/business/bilateral-trade-and-investment-going-strong> (accessed November 10, 2015).

"Concerns Grow Over China's Confucius Institutes." *Radio Free Asia*, July 25, 2014. <http://www.rfa.org/english/news/china/confucius-07252014111157.html/> (accessed November 22, 2014).

Confucius Institutes at Nanyang Technological University. "About Us." <http://ci.ntu.edu.sg/eng/aboutus/Pages/default.aspx> (accessed October 22, 2015).

———. "Business Chinese." <http://ci.ntu.edu.sg/eng/Programme/aclp/Programmes/Pages/Programmes-Detailed.aspx?event=94ee1762-bc2c-4ff0-a168-0a791aef455f> (accessed October 22, 2015).

"Confucius Institutes Organize Celebratory Activities on the PRC's 60th Anniversary," www.people.com.cn. October 3, 2010. <http://chinese.people.com.cn/GB/10153534.html> (accessed April 4, 2013).

Consulate of the People's Republic of China in Laoag. "President Hu Jintao Meets with Thai Prime Minister Samak," July 1, 2008. <http://laoag.chineseconsulate.org/eng/lgxw/t471411.htm> (accessed April 25, 2016).

Gipouloux, François. *The Asian Mediterranean: Port Cities and Trading Networks in China, Japan and Southeast Asia, 13th–21st Century.* Cheltenham, UK: Edward Elgar, 2011.

Golden, Daniel. "Sex, Lies and Espionage: Did a Professor Spy for the FBI?" Bloomberg, February 25, 2015. <http://www.bloomberg.com/news/articles/2015-02-25/-lies-and-espionage-did-a-professor-spy-for-the-fbi-/> (accessed September 20, 2015).

Hall, Ian and Frank Smith. "The Struggle for Soft Power in Asia: Public Diplomacy and Regional Competition." *Asian Security* 9, 1 (2013): 1–18.

Hanban [Confucius Institute Headquarters]. *2009 Annual Report.* Beijing: Hanban, 2009.

———. *2010 Annual Report.* Beijing: Hanban, 2010.

———. *2011 Annual Report.* Beijing: Hanban, 2011.

———. *2012 Annual Report.* Beijing: Hanban, 2012.

———. *2013 Annual Report.* Beijing: Hanban, 2013.

———. *2014 Annual Report.* Beijing: Hanban, 2014.

———. "About Confucius Institutes/Confucius Classrooms." *Hanban News*, March 31, 2014. <http://english.hanban.org/node_10971.htm/> (accessed November 22, 2015).

———. "Chinese President Xi Jinping Attends Signing Ceremony of Establishment of Confucius Institutes in Brazil." *Hanban News*, July 25, 2014. <http://english.hanban.org/article/2014-07/25/content_546267.htm/> (accessed December 5, 2015).

———. "Confucius School in Singapore," 2014. <http://english.hanban.org/node_10683.htm> (accessed December 22, 2015).

———. "Highlights of Chinese Premier Wen Jiabao's Visit to Confucius Institute at the University of Al-Azhar, Indonesia." *Hanban News*, May 10, 2011. <http://english.hanban.org/article/2011-05/10/content_257863.htm/> (accessed December 5, 2015).

———. "Liu Yandong Gives Keynote Speech at the Opening Session of the 8th Confucius Institute Conference." *Hanban News*, December 12, 2013. <http://english.hanban.org/article/2013-12/12/content_518317_3.htm/> (accessed December 22, 2014).

Ho, Khai Leong (ed.). *Connecting & Distancing: Southeast Asia and China.* Singapore: Singapore Society of Asian Studies and Institute of Southeast Asian Studies, 2009.

Hughes, Christopher R. "Confucius Institutes and the University: Distinguishing the Political Mission from the Cultural," *Issues & Studies* 50, no. 4 (2014): 45–83.

"Hujintao Huijian Jianpuzhai Shouxiang Hun Sen" [Hujintao Meets Cambodian Prime Minister Hun Sen]. *China Daily*, March 31, 2012. <https://www.chinadaily.com.cn/hqzx/2012-03/31/content_14962186.htm> (accessed April 5, 2013).

Ku, Shih-Hung. "Taiquo Gongzhu Shilintong Wei Dongfang Daxue Kongzi Xueyuan Jiepai" [Thai Princess Sirindhorn Unveils New Confucius Institute at Burapha University]." *China News*, September 16, 2009. <http://www.chinanews.com/hwjy/news/2009/09-16/1868560.shtml> (accessed September 22, 2015).

Ku, Shih-Hung. "Taiguo Kongzi Xueyuan Qingzhu Xin Zhongguo Liushi Huadan Huoping Huo Haoping" [Confucius Institutes in Thailand Celebrate New China's 60th Anniversary, Events Receive Praise]. *China News*, October 2, 2009. <http://www.chinanews.com/hwjy/news/2009/10-02/1897504.shtml> (accessed September 22, 2015).

Ku, Shih-Hung and Huang Che-Yu. "Shilintong Gongzhu Chuxí Taiquo Zhuda Juban de Xin Zhongguo 60 Nian Yantao Hui" [Princess Sirindhorn Attends Thailand Chulalongkorn University's New China 60th Anniversary Conference]. *China News*, October 23, 2009. <http://www.chinanews.com/hr/hr-yzhrxw/news/2009/10-23/1926115.shtml> (accessed September 22, 2015).

Maslen, Geoff. "Australia: Warning—Be Wary of Confucius Institutes." *University World News*, December 2, 2007. <http://www.universityworldnews.com/article.php?story=20071130094503100/> (accessed March 10, 2014).

Memorandum of Understanding on Cultural Cooperation Between the Ministry of Culture of the People's Republic China and the Ministry of Information and the Arts of the Republic of Singapore, 1996. <http://www.fmprc.gov.cn/eng/wjb/zzjg/yzs/gjlb/2777/2778/t16195.htm/> (accessed December 22, 2015).

Meyer, Erin and Andrew L. Wang. "Hu Jintao Pays Visit to Payton Prep." *Chicago Tribune*, January 21, 2011. <http://articles.chicagotribune.com/2011-01-21/news/ct-met-china-visit-0122-20110121_1_chinese-president-hu-jintao-chinese-companies-payton-students/> (accessed November 22, 2014).

Ministry of Foreign Affairs of the People's Republic of China. "Li Keqiang Meets with Prime Minister Prayut Chan-o-cha of Thailand," March 23, 2016. <http://www.fmprc.gov.cn/mfa_eng/zxxx_662805/t1350711.shtml> (accessed April 22, 2016).

Mosher, Steven W. "Confucius Institutes: Trojan Horses with Chinese Characteristics." Population Research Institute, March 28, 2012. <http://pop.org/content/confucius-institutes-trojan-horses-chinese-characteristics/> (accessed November 22, 2014).

Moss, Trefor. "Soft Power? China Has Plenty." *The Diplomat*, June 4, 2013. <http://thediplomat.com/2013/06/soft-power-china-has-plenty/> (accessed August 25, 2015).

Osnos, Evan. "Why Is Hu Jintao Going to Chicago?" *The New Yorker*, January 20, 2011. <http://www.newyorker.com/online/blogs/evanosnos/2011/01/why-is-hu-jintao-going-to-chicago.html/> (accessed August 28, 2015).

Pan, Su-Yan. "Confucius Institute Project: China's Cultural Diplomacy and Soft Power Projection." *Asian Education and Development Studies* 2, no. 1 (2013): 22–33.

Prime Minister's Office, Singapore. Speech of Mr. Lee Kuan Yew, Minister Mentor, at Speak Mandarin Campaign's 30th Anniversary Launch, March 17, 2009. <http://www.pmo.gov.sg/content/pmosite/mediacentre/speechesninterviews/ministermentor/2009/March/speech_by_mr_leekuan yewministermentoratspeakmandarincampaigns30t. html#.VAL7iNgcSP8/> (accessed November 10, 2015).

———. Speech of Prime Minister Lee Hsien Loong at launch of Speak Mandarin Campaign 2014," June 11, 2014. <http://www.pmo.gov.sg/mediacentre/speech-pm-lee-hsien-loong-launch-speak-mandarin-campaign-2014> (November 10, 2015).

"Princess Sirindhorn: Among the Top 10 International Friends of China." *Asian Correspondent*, December 6, 2009. <http://asiancorrespondent.com/25980/princess-sirindhorn-one-of-top-10-international-friends-of-china/> (accessed December 11, 2014).

Renmin Chubanshe. *Zhonggong Zhongyang Guanyu Shenhua Wenhua Tizhi Gaige Tuidong Shehui Zhuyi Wenhua Dafazhan Dafanrong Ruogan Zhongda Wenti De Jueding* [The Decision of Deepening Reformation of Cultural Institution and Promoting the Development and Prosperity of Socialism]. Beijing: Renmin Chubanshe, 2011.

Sahlins, Marshall. *Confucius Institute: Academic Malware*. Chicago: The University of Chicago Press, 2015.

Siow, Maria Wey-Shen. "China's Confucius Institutes: Crossing the River by Feeling the Stones." *Asia-Pacific Bulletin* 91 (January 6, 2011): 1.

Song, Yazhou. "Confucius Institute at Royal Academy of Cambodia Hosts a Symposium Entitled 'One Belt One Road: New Opportunities for Cambodia-China Cooperation.'" *Hanban News*, July 22, 2015. <http://english.hanban.org/article/2015-07/22/content_610463.htm> (accessed September 22, 2015).

Speech of Prime Minister Hun Sen at the Opening of the Conference of Confucius Institute, Asia 2013. *Cambodia News Vision*, May 29, 2013. <http://cnv.org.kh/en/?p=3620/> (accessed May 23, 2014).

SPH Razor. "Mandarin in Japan (MM Lee at Confucius Institute Pt 6)," Youtube, July 25, 2013. <https://www.youtube.com/watch?v=j3xyat8YtGo> (accessed April 30, 2016).

Storey, Ian. *Southeast Asia and the Rise of China: The Search for Security*. New York: Routledge, 2011.

"Teaching Sun Tzi in Confucius Institute." *China News*, September 26, 2011. <http://www.chinanews.com/hwjy/2011/09-26/3351946.shtml/> (accessed May 10, 2014).

The Office of Chinese Language Council. *International Annual Report*. Beijing: The Office of Chinese Language Council, 2006.

Wang, Qian and Zhang Yunbi. "Xi Vows to Protect Maritime Interests." *China Daily*, August 1, 2013. <http://usa.chinadaily.com.cn/epaper/2013-08/01/content_16861678.htm> (accessed September 2, 2013).

Wang, Yiwei. "Public Diplomacy and the Rise of Chinese Soft Power." *The Annals of the American Academy of Political and Social Science* 616, no. 1 (2008): 257–73.

Western Kentucky University. "The Confucius Institute Staff-Terrill Martin." <http://www.wku.edu/ci/staff/terrill_martin/> (accessed March 10, 2014).

Work Committee of Central Government Departments. "Chung Jian Wen Ming Ji Guan, Zheng Zuo Ren Min Man Yi Gong Wu Yuan Yun Dong, Xian Jin Ji Ti Ping Xuan" [Evaluation of Distinguished Group for Constructing Civilized Institutions, Struggling for Civil Servant], Zi Guang Ge Wang Zhan, May 2014. <http://www.zgg.gov.cn/cjwmjgxjjtpx/xjjtpx/201405/t20140509_439363.html/> (accessed December 5, 2015).

"Xinhua Insight: Xi Urges China-ASEAN Economic Ties, Peaceful Dispute Settlements." *Xinhua News*, September 21, 2012. <http://news.xinhuanet.com/english/indepth/2012-09/21/c_131865664.htm/> (accessed March 14, 2013).

Xinhua News Agency. "The 6th Confucius Institute Conference is Held in Beijing Opening Ceremony Attended by Li Changchun." *Hanban News*, December 21, 2011. <http://english.hanban.org/article/2011-12/21/content_396561.htm/> (accessed August 25, 2015).

──────. "Xi Jinping Visits the Confucius Institute at Chulalongkorn University, Thailand on December 24." *Hanban News*, December 25, 2011. <http://english.hanban.org/article/2011-12/25/content_399472.htm> (accessed April 25, 2016).

Yang, Alan Hao and H.H. Michael Hsiao. "Confucius Institutes and the Question of China's Soft Power Diplomacy." *China Brief* 12, no. 13 (2013): 10–3.

Zhang, Ruiling and Lei Bosong. "Confucius Institute Opens Chinese-language Class in Cambodia," China Central Television, January 22, 2010. <http://english.cctv.com/20100122/101597.shtml> (accessed March 20, 2015).

About the Contributors

Teng-chi Chang is Associate Professor of Political Science at the National Taiwan University, and executive editor of the journal, *Asian Ethnicity*. His area of research includes Chinese international relations and foreign policy, the politics of the Communist Party of China, and cross-strait relations.

Ian Tsung-yen Chen is an Assistant Professor at the Institute of Political Science at National Sun Yat-Sen University (Taiwan). His research interests range across the fields of international relations, international and comparative political economy, and international organizations in the Asia-Pacific region.

Maria Serena I. Diokno is a Professor of History at the University of the Philippines and former chairperson of the National Historical Commission of the Philippines. Her research interests span across Philippine history (19th and 20th centuries) and historiography, public history and heritage, contemporary politics, and Southeast Asian studies.

Hsin-Huang Michael Hsiao is a Distinguished Research Fellow at the Institute of Sociology, Academia Sinica; Professor of Sociology at the National Taiwan University and National Sun Yat-Sen University; and Chairman of Taiwan-Asia Exchange Foundation. His areas of specialization include middle class, civil society and democratization in Asia; environmental movements, sustainability and risk society as well as Hakka studies in Taiwan and Southeast Asia.

Yumi Kitamura is Associate Professor at the Kyoto University Library. She works on contemporary Indonesian society, with focus on the

Chinese language in Indonesia, the culture of Chinese Indonesians, and life histories of Chinese-Indonesian migrants in the Netherlands.

Ngeow Chow-Bing is Acting Director of the Institute of China Studies at the University of Malaya. His research interests include China's political reforms, organization and management of the Communist Party of China, China's minority communities, and China-Southeast Asia relations.

Natalia Soebagjo is the Executive Director of the Centre for Chinese Studies, an independent body founded in 1999 to address the issue of a rising China and Indonesia's response. The centre also looks at developments within Chinese communities of Indonesia, particularly post-1998.

Dennis D. Trinidad is an Associate Professor and Coordinator for the Japanese Studies Program in the International Studies Department at De La Salle University, Manila. He specializes in the field of international political economy, such as Japanese and Chinese foreign aid and the politics of economic reform.

Alan Hao Yang is Deputy Director of the Institute of International Relations, Executive Director of the Center for Southeast Asian Studies, and an Associate Professor of the Graduate Institute of East Asian Studies at the National Chengchi University, Taiwan. His research interests cover ASEAN regionalism, border politics and resistance politics in Southeast Asia, and China-ASEAN relations.

Index

Note: Page locators in bold and italics represents tables and figures, respectively.

30 September Movement in 1965 (G30S), Indonesia, 174

Abalos, Benjamin, 157
Academy of International Business Officials, China, 149
Afro-Asian Conference, 40, 147, 160
Afro-Asian solidarity movement, 146
aid diplomacy of China, *see* China's aid diplomacy
Air Defense Identification Zone (ADIZ), 6, 46
American Association of University Professors, 12
American Dream, 37, 48–9
Angat Water Utilization and Aqueduct Improvement project, Philippines, 151
Angeles University Foundation (AUF), Philippines, 201
Annual Report on China's Cultural Soft Power Research, 15
anti-Chinese movement, 176–7
anti-communist movement, 2
Aquino, Corazon, 143

Aquino III, Benigno "Noynoy," 157, 161
Asian Development Bank, 7–8, 123
Asian financial crisis (1997), 5, 33, 45, 92
Asian Infrastructure Investment Bank (AIIB), 51
  China's leadership in, 51
Asia-Pacific Economic Cooperation (APEC), 40
  Bali Summit (2009), 44
  Informal Leadership Meeting (6th) of, 5
Association of Southeast Asian Nations (ASEAN)
  China's distrust of, 3
  China's strategy toward, 5
  Chinese investments in, 118
  creation of, 3
  relation with China, *see* China–ASEAN relations
Aung San, Suu Kyi, 69, 80–1

"back to Asia" strategy (United States), 44
Badawi, Abdullah, 4, 109
Bahasa Indonesia, 185
balance of power, 39, 50, 173
Bali-Hinduism, 178
Bandar Malaysia project, 102

Bank Negara Malaysia, 95
Bank of China, 19, 94, 95, 127, 129, 148
Bank of Finland, 134
Bansomdejchaopraya Rajabhat University, Thailand, 201, 206
Beibu Gulf Economic Region, 104
Beijing Consensus, 10, 37
Beijing Urban Construction Group, 102
Belt and Road Initiative, 21–3, 101, 199, 217n17
Biden, Joe, 49
BRIC countries, 36, 50–1
　China's leadership in, 51
　currency reserve assets, 51
Buddhism, 174, 177–8
Burmese Freedom and Democracy Act (2003), 69
Bush, George W., 34, 36–7
Business Chinese Program, 208

Cambodia
　Angkor High School, 211
　under China's grand strategy, 212
　Chinese investments in, 17
　Chinese language teaching system in, 211
　Chinese Teaching Stations (CTSs) in, 212
　CI project in, 210–13
　　distinctive feature of, 212
　Guanxi networks in, 203–4
　　with educational institutions, 212–13
　　with elites, 210–11
　　with government units, 211–12
　　with local overseas Chinese, 213
　Police Academy of, 211
　political relationship with China, 210
　Royal Academy of, 210–11
Cambodian-Chinese Association, 211–13
Cambodian Daily, The, 212
Campbell, Kurt, 82
Canadian Association for University Professors, 12
Cheng, Yen, 184
Chiang Mai University, Thailand, 205–6
China
　21st-Century Maritime Silk Route, 199
　ascendancy as a super power, 14
　diplomatic isolation of Taiwan, 160
　economy-based diplomatic charm offensive, 92
　foreign aid in 2011 and 2014, 148
　foreign policy, *see* foreign policy, of China
　Going Global Strategy, 13
　identity as a "great power," 45
　Ministry of Commerce, 98
　outward investment flows from, 117
　peaceful rise of, 14
　policy to safeguard sovereignty and territorial integrity, 202
　political and economic goals of, 134
　Qualified Domestic Institutional Investor (QDII) scheme, 94
　regional leadership ability, 150
　rising "indirect influence," 37
　status and global trajectory, 13
　strategy toward countries of ASEAN, 5
　Southeast Asia, 5
　theories of Old, 13–14

230 Index

UN voting pattern, 38
war with Vietnam, 3–4
Western Development Strategy, 150–1
as world's second-largest economy, 90
"China-as-a-threat" perception, 148, 160
China–ASEAN Expo, 5
    in Guangxi, 202
China–ASEAN Free Trade Agreement (2010), 5
China–ASEAN relations
    aggressive diplomacy, 5–6
    development of, 5
    diplomatic ties, 4
    foreign direct investment, 118
    Good Neighbor Policy, 3, 5
    Joint Declaration on Strategic Partnership and Prosperity, 150
    mutual suspicion and diplomatic relations, 2–4
    New Security Concept, 5
    normalization of, 4
    phases of, 2
    softening up and Chinese assertiveness toward, 4–5
    territorial disputes over, 5
    South China Sea, 5
    Treaty of Amity and Cooperation (TAC), 150
China Banking Regulatory Commission, 94
China Communications Construction Company (CCCC), 110
China Development Bank, 19, 127, 128, 134
China Enterprises Association of Malaysia, 100, **101**
China Export and Credit Insurance Corporation, 19

China General Nuclear Group, 102
China Harbour Engineering Corporation (CHEC), 102, 110
China Huadian Corporation (CHD), 120
China-in-siege mentality, 42
China International Center for Economic and Technical Exchanges, 149
China–Malaysia Qinzhou Industrial Park (CMQIP), 91, 101, 103–5
China National Machinery and Equipment Corporation Group (CNMEG), 156, 159, 161
China National Machinery and Equipment Import and Export Corporation (CMEC), 120
China National Machinery Import and Export Corporation (CMC), 120
China National Technical Import and Export Corporation (CNTIC), 120–1
China North Industries Corporation, 80
China North Locomotive and Rolling Stock Corporation (CNR), 102
China Power Investment Corporation (CPIC), 79
China Railway and Rolling Stock Corporation, 102
China Railway Construction Corporation (CRCC), 102, 110
China Railway Engineering Corporation (CREC), 102, 109–10
China Road and Bridge Construction (CRBC), 110
China's aid diplomacy
    aid-effectiveness paradigms, 142
    allotments of aid, 144
    Chinese aid to South Asia, *see* Chinese aid to South Asia

continuity and changes in, 146–50
core principles of, 147
effectiveness of, 144
evolution of, 144
foreign policy objectives of, 146
formation of aid institutions, 142
formulation of, 149
interest-free loans, 149
limits of, 141–61
loans to developing countries, 148
memoranda of understanding, 141
mismatch of Chinese Aid Institutions and DAC-conforming aid recipient, *158*
in North Korea, 146
in North Vietnam, 146
official development assistance (ODA), 142
in Philippines, 150–1
practices and modality of administering, 142
priority to infrastructure development, 148
recipient countries, 142
sectoral distribution of, 148
as soft-power tools, 141, 144–6
in Southeast Asia, 150–1
stages of foreign aid process, 150
suspension of, 144
in Third World countries, 147
unrestricted aid transfers, 142
China South Locomotive & Rolling Stock Corporation, 102
China threat theory, Western proponents of, 37, 40
China Youth Daily, 8
Chinese aid to South Asia, 9–10
allocation of, 9
contrasting principles of, 19–20
factors determining, 9
focus on infrastructure projects, 10
ideological agenda of, 9
impact on recipient societies, 9
for strategic reasons, 9
Chinese construction companies and banks
economic and political culture of, 18
practices of, 119, 132–4
Chinese culture, 10
in Indonesia, *see* Chinese culture, in Indonesia
internationalization of, 201
public displays of, 174
public manifestations of, 174
Chinese culture, in Indonesia
30 September Movement in 1965 (G30S), 174
historical background of, 173–5
prohibition of public displays of, 174
public expression of, 173
state-recognized religion, 174
Chinese currency, importance of, 95
Chinese Dream discourse, 33, 41
Beautiful China discourse, 48
Civilized China discourse, 48
discourse power of, 48–9
Harmonious China discourse, 48
increasing hegemonism, 47–8
link with Latin American Dream, 49
parts of, 48
shared future of, 49
Strong China discourse, 48
Chinese education, 176, 203, 209
Chinese GDP
doubling of, 48
overtaking of US, 47

Chinese-Indonesian cooperation project, 18
Chinese companies' investment motives in, 118
coal-fired plants, 119, 121
construction of, 127
Coordinating Team for the Acceleration of Power Plant Construction, 122, 124–5
engineering, procurement and contract (EPC) agreements, 122, 130
environmental impact assessments, 121
Fast Track Program Phase I (FTP-I), 18, 118
completion of, 123
cross-conditionality of using loans, 134
government's guarantees for loans, 131
implementation of, 120
planning of, 119–23
power plants, 131
procurement process, 123–7
for providing power, 123
PT PLN's assessment of, 131
technical standards, 123
Yudhoyono's FTP-I, 127
financing problems, 118, 127–9
finding solutions for, 131–2
foreign direct investments, 118
implementation of, 119–20
land procurement, 121
logistical problems of, 129–30
memorandums of understanding, 120
number of bids submitted for the Java projects, **125**
oil-fired plants, 119
operational strategies of, 118
practices of Chinese construction companies and banks, 132–4
rationale, goals and organization of, 119–23
technical aspects of, 129–30
tendering process in, 123
Chinese Indonesians, 21
celebration of Imlek, 183
change of names to Indonesian-sounding names, 174
Confucian teachings among, 175
contribution to the economic sector by, 183
cultural identity of, 183
cultural practices within Indonesia, 173
laws to separate from their native culture, 174
Pentecostal-Charismatic movement, 174
in post-Suharto era, 175
religious conversion to Christianity, 174
religious landscape of, 175
religious practices of, 175
relisting of Confucianism, 175
re-Sinicization movement, 176
rights of, 183
state-instigated discrimination against, 181
strategic mobilization of Chinese soft power by, 186
Chinese investments
Heinrich Böll Stiftung et al. report (2008) on, 8
motives of, 118
outward direct investment (ODI), 6–7
shifts in, 8–9
in Southeast Asia, 6–7

Chinese language
  credit/non-credit language courses, 202
  Mandarin, 185
  proficiency tests, 211
  teaching programs for, 201
  in Cambodia, 211
  in Thailand, 205
Chinese Malaysian culture, 20
Chinese-medium schools, 174
Chinese Nationalist Party, 2
Chinese Proficiency Test, 201, 211
Chinese religion and rituals, 176
  Buddhism, 175, 177, 178
  Confucianism, see Confucianism
  Imlek Nasional (New Year event), 183
  new streams of, 184–5
  Taoism, 41, 175–7
Chinese revolution, 177
Chinese superiority, ancient notion of, 14
Chinese Teaching Stations (CTSs), 201, 202, 211
  establishment of, 212
Chinese tourists, visiting Malaysia, 95–6
Chulalongkorn University, Thailand, 205–7
civilian diplomats, 203
civil society organizations, 21
Clinton, Hillary, 22, 44, 45, 57n50
club of great powers, 36
CNR Changchun Railway Vehicles, 103
coal-fired plants, 119, 121, 127
  construction of, 127
Cold War, 9, 38, 40, 49, 146
color revolutions, 49
commercial liberalism, theory of, 65
Commission on Audit (COA), 144
Communist Party of China (CPC), 2, 32

14th National Congress of, 148
15th National Congress of, 117
18th Congress Report, 32, 39
Central Committee (11th) of, 3
opening-up policy, 3–4
peaceful engagement with external powers, 3
Politburo of, 194
political and economic reforms, 46
Xi's public speeches on mission of, 47
community of common destiny, 21
Composite Index of Economic Influence (CIEI), 73–5
Composite Index of National Capability (CINC), 73
Confucianism, 41
  among Chinese Indonesians, 175
  and China's soft footprint, 175–7
  as delisted religion, 20
  delisting of, 180
  development of, 184
  followers of, 183
  history of, 175
  in Indonesia, 21, 175, 177–9
  and MATAKIN during the Suharto years, 179–80
  monotheistic form of, 177
  re-establishment of, 184
  re-recognition of, 180–1
  rise of, 176
  in school curriculum, 180, 183
  as state religion in China, 20, 176, 184
  status of, 184
  Tien (Heaven), concept of, 177
  Wahid's support for reinstating, 182
Confucius China Studies Program (CCSP), 200

234 Index

Confucius Classrooms (CCs), 195, **198**
  annual growth rate of, 199
  comparison of, **213**
  number of countries by region that host, 197
  Sawang Boriboon Wittaya School, 206
  in Southeast Asia, **203**
  Srinakorn School, 206
  in Thailand, 204
  worldwide operation of, 200
  Xingmin Phitsanulok School, 206
Confucius Institute Conference, 195, 201, 215n4, 217n22
Confucius Institutes (CIs), 10–11, 43
  Action Plan (2012–5), 211
  actual budget of, 199
  annual growth rate of, 199
  authenticity of, 214
  awards of, 201
  on bilateral relations between China and host countries, 202
  for China's overseas propaganda, 12
  as China's soft footprints in Southeast Asia, 202–3
  Chinese language programs, 201, 205
  Chinese Teaching Stations, 211
  closure of, 12
  comparison of, **213**
  Conference in Asia (2013), 210
  Confucius Institute Conference (2011), 195
  cost of running, 199
  cultural activities of, 214
  Development Plan, 200
  effect on academic freedom, 12
  establishment of, 11, 194
  expansion of, 12
  fiscal support from the Chinese government, 199–200
  going global, 12–13
  government-sponsored, 173
  and host countries, 196–9
  and its Guanxi networks, 204
  Khong Kauw Hwee, 177
  language schools, 173
  Lyon Confucius Institute, 12
  major expenditures of, **199**
  middle and primary schools, 12
  number of, **198**
  number of countries by region that host, **197**
  operational budget of, 200
  overseas, 145
  overview of, 196
  performance assessment of, 201–2
  performance evaluation of, 201
  in Philippines, 141
  Preliminary Study of Contemporary Mainland China, 209
  recruitment of students and teachers, 207
  Sam Kauw Hwee, 177
  in Seoul, Korea, 196
  soft diplomacy based on, 195, 202
  in Southeast Asia, 21, 195, **203**
  spread of, 195
  in Thailand, 204–7
  Thiong Hua Hui Guan (THHK), 176–7
  worldwide operation of, 200
constructive partner, idea of, 4
cooperative power, 172
"core interests" policy discourse, 32, 45–6
credibility, issue of, 35–6, 125, 134, 145
cross-border economic activities, 64, 65

cultural and language programs, 14
cultural footprints of China, 20-1, 173
cultural outreach, by China, 11-12
cultural soft power, idea of, 15
currency exchange rate, 128
    IDR-to-USD, 128
currency swap agreement, 95, 129

Declaration on the Conduct of Parties in the South China Sea (DOC), 46
Deng, Xiaoping, 3, 31, 38-9, 50, 204
    "hiding light" principle, 32, 43, 45, 51
dependency, politics of, 1
Development Assistance Committee (DAC), 19, 142
Diaoyu (Senkaku) Islands dispute, 45-6
diplomatic relations, between China and Southeast Asia, 2-4
domestic economic reform policy, 4
Dongfang Electric Corporation, 121
Dream of Northeast Asia, 49
dual industrial parks, 101
Dulles, John Foster, 45
Dutch East Indies, 175-7, 185

East China Sea dispute, 32
    Air Defense Identification Zone (ADIZ), 6, 46
East Coast Economic Region (ECER), 105-6, 109
Eastphalian order, 1
economic benefits, of China's investments, 63
economic bonds, 65
economic offensive of China, 66
    and China's economic presence in Myanmar, 69-73
    community-based opposition to, 79-82
    Composite Index of Economic Influence (CIEI), 73-5
    crucial-case research design to study, 66-8
    influence of, 64-6
    Sino-Myanmar interdependent relationship and, 68-9
economic role, of China in Southeast Asia, 6-7
economic sanctions, 69-71, 76, 82
Economist, The, 11, 22
Eight Principles for Economic Aid and Technical Assistance to Other Countries (China), 147
electrified double-track railway project (EDTP), 109-11
engineering, procurement and construction (EPC) contracts, 19, 130
engineering, procurement and contract (EPC) agreements, 19, 122, 130
environmental impact assessments, 121
established power, idea of, 49, 123
European Association for Chinese Studies (EACS), 12
Executive Bureau of International Economic Cooperation, China, 149
export credits, 5, 124, 127, 142
Export-Import Bank of China, 19, 127, 148
    concessional loans from, 150

Fast Track Program Phase I (FTP-I), 18, 118
    completion of, 123
    cross-conditionality of using loans, 134

government's guarantees for
loans, 131
implementation of, 120
planning of, 119–23
power plants, 131
procurement process, 123–7
for providing power, 123
PT PLN's assessment of, 131
technical standards, 123
Yudhoyono's FTP-I, 127
Five Principles of Peaceful
Coexistence, 2
Five-Year Program for Economic
and Trade Cooperation between
China and Malaysia (2013–17),
97
Foreign Affairs, 40
foreign aid institutions, 148
foreign direct investment (FDI), 6,
10, 65–6, 71, 97, *see also* outward
direct investment (ODI)
in ASEAN, 118
China's outward, 117
in Indonesia, 118
in Malaysia, 97–8, 107
short-term investment, 98
foreign policy, of China, 32
core interest, defence of, 45–6
at crossroads, 51–2
engagement with other
countries, 38
Good Neighbor Policy, 43–4
hard balancing against
America's "rebalancing,"
43–4
multipolarity, idea of, 39
from "multipolarity" to the
"harmonious world," 42–3
over-involved, 38–9
in response to US's new policy
initiatives, 45
"soft" power diplomacy, *see*
"soft" power

"Stand with the Third World"
causes, 38
trend and model of, 39–42
on US rebalancing and "forward
deployment," 44–5
before Xi Jinping, 38–46
"Forest City" project, 103
forward deployment diplomacy
(United States), 44–5, 47
Fuhua Group Ltd, 154

G2, concept of, 43
Gemas-Johor Bahru project, 109–11
global financial crisis (2008), 43, 128
global governance, China's proposals
for, 51
"Going Out" strategy (China),
13, 117, 134, 148–9, 151, 157,
159–60, 210
good governance, principles of, 123,
131
Good Neighbor Policy (China), 3, 5,
43, 44, 46, 148, 160, 202
government-owned or controlled
corporations (GOCCs), 143
government-to-government
industrial park, 104
Great Cultural Revolution, 47
Great External Propaganda
(*dawaixuan*), 21, 195
great power diplomacy (China), 32,
45
Guangxi Beibu International Port
Group, 106
Guanxi networks
in Cambodia, 210–13
establishment of, 203–4
in Singapore, 207–10
in Thailand, 204–7
Guided Democracy in Indonesia,
173
Guito, Lany, 180–1

Habibie, Bacharuddin Jusuf, 182
Haksu Tjhie Tjay Ing, 178
Halal food industry, 97
Han culture, acceptance of, 13
Hanyu Shuiping Kaoshi (HSK), 201
Harbin Power Equipment Co. Ltd., 121
"hard power" of economic strength, 10
harmonious society, notion of, 4
harmonious world, concept of, 14, 40–1, 51
He, Qinglian, 10
"hiding light" principle, 32, 45–7, 51
high-speed railway (HSR) project
diplomatic battle between China and Japan, 102
in Malaysia, 102–3, 109
Hinduism, 178
Hock, Kiat Koh, 208–9
Hokkien Kong Tik Soe, 176
Holland-Chinese schools, 177
Huangyan/Scarborough Shoal, 46
Hu, Jintao, 8, 17, 31, 32, 210
  on China's peaceful rise/development, 41
  "harmonious world" policy, 32
  leadership style, 47
  official visit to Thailand, 204
  Sino-Russian Joint Statement on the International Order for the 21st Century (2004), 40
  soft power approach to foreign policy, 32
human rights violation
  China's positions on, 64, 75
  exploiting for political purposes, 77
  in Iran, 77
  in Myanmar, 67–8, 77
Hurrell, Andrew, 36, 54n20

Imlek Nasional (New Year event), 182–3
Indonesia
  30 September Movement in 1965 (G30S), 174
    suppression of, 174
  anti-Chinese movement, 176
  Bahasa Indonesia, 185
  ban of discrimination against ethnic Chinese, 182
  Chinese culture in, see Chinese culture, in Indonesia
  Chinese expansion of soft power in, 173
  Chinese FDI in, 118
  Chinese-Indonesian cooperation project, see Chinese-Indonesian cooperation project
  Chinese influence on political thinking in, 173
  coal-fired power plants, 18, 119, 121
  construction of, 127
  Confucianism in, 21, 177–9
  contracts awarded for the Java projects, **126**
  depoliticization of religious groups, 174
  diplomatic relationships with China, 175
  electrical power plants, 134
  energy crisis, 120
  engineering, procurement and construction (EPC) contracts, 19
  fall of Suharto, 182–4
  Fast Track Program Phase I, see under Chinese-Indonesian cooperation project
  government's preference for Chinese companies, 123
  Guided Democracy, 173

independence of, 173
industrial policies, 133
Islamic rebellions in Sumatra and Sulawesi, 173
Komisi Pemberantasan Korupsi (KPK), 127
loan for power plants, 129
Majelis Tinggi Agama Khonghucu Indonesia (MATAKIN), 178
mass killings in, 174
Ministry of Finance, 131
Ministry of Religion, 178
newspapers and magazines, 183
oil-fired plants, 119
power sector, 134
Presidential Decree No. 59/1972, 127
Presidential Regulation No. 8/2006, 125
Presidential Regulation No. 59/2009, 122
Presidential Regulation No. 71/2006, 121, 127
Presidential Regulation No. 86/2006, 127
Procurement of Public Goods and Services, 125
PT Truba Alam Manunggal Engineering Tbk, 125
Reform Era, 182–3
re-recognition of Confucianism in, 180–1
rise of China and being Chinese in, 182–4
rising demand for electricity, 123
state-recognized religion, 174, 184
supra-regulatory institutions, 133
Western influence on, 174
Indonesian Communist Party, 173
Indonesian Stock Exchange, 125
Indrawati, Mulyani, 127
Industrial and Commercial Bank of China, 94
industrial park, 107
  government-to-government, 104
information and communications technology (ICT), 97, 100
initial public offerings (IPOs), 95
International Monetary Fund (IMF), 5, 50, 85n26
international relations theory (IRT), 34, 39
intra-industry trade, phenomenon of, 94
Iraq war, 36, 43
Irawan, Bingky, 181
Ircon International, 109

Japan
  diplomatic battle with China over HSR project, 102
  official development assistance, 9
Japan Bank for International Cooperation (JBIC), 155
Japan International Cooperation Agency (JICA), 159
Jiang, Zemin, 5, 31, 45, 148
  great power diplomacy, 32, 45
Jian Hua Daily, 212
Jin, Canrong, 41
joint ventures, 80, 98, 103, 105, 109
  Sino-Malaysian, 105

Kachin Independence Army (KIA), 80
Kalla, Jusuf, 120, 127–8
Kang You Wei's movement, 176
Keohane, Robert O., 33
Khong Kauw Hwee, 177

Khor, Yu Leng, 91
kickbacks and corruption, allegations of, 156
Koh, Hock Kiat, 209
Komisi Pemberantasan Korupsi (KPK), Indonesia, 127
Kongzi Institute for the Teaching of Chinese Language (University of Malaya), 201
Korean Dream, 49
Kuala Lumpur International Airport (KLIA), 103
Kuantan Pahang Holdings Sdn Bhd, 105
Kyoto Protocol, 38

Lampton, David M., 34
language education, promotion of, 173, 206
Latin American Dream, 49
Lee, Gregory B., 12
Lee, Hsien Loong, 208
Lee, Kuan Yew, 208
Letpadaung copper mine projects, Myanmar, 64
  protests against, 79
Liberal Greater West, 36
Li, Keqiang, 94, 103
  Lancang-Mekong Cooperation Leaders' Meeting, 204
Li, Peng, 4
Liu, Su Mei, 184
Liu, Yandong, 194
loans, 66, 122, 127–9, 157–8, 210
  concessional, 17, 19, 73, 134, 141, 149, 151
  difficulties with the Chinese banks, 129
  government's guarantees for, 131
  interest-free, 73, 149
  low-interest, 85n27, 148, 150
  pledges from China, 151
  RMB-denominated, 129
  soft loan, 102
  US dollar-denominated, 129
local government units (LGUs), 143, 145, 208
Lyon Confucius Institute, 12

Macapagal-Arroyo, Gloria, 142, 153, 161
Majelis Tinggi Agama Khonghucu Indonesia (MATAKIN), 178, 182
  Boen Bio branch of, 181
  Confucianism and, 179–80
  Imlek Nasional (New Year event) hosted by, 183
  on official status of religions in Indonesia, 183
  regional branches, 184
making friends instead of making enemies, idea of, 5
Malacca dilemma, 8
Malacca Straits, 8
Malaysia
  Bandar Malaysia project, 102
  Bank Negara Malaysia, 95
  Barisan Nasional coalition, 112
  Barisan Nasional government in, 106
  bilateral trade with China, 92–4
  capital market, 94
  central-local (state) dynamics in, 108–9
  China Enterprises Association of Malaysia, **101**
  China-Malaysia Qinzhou Industrial Park (CMQIP), 91, 101, 103–5
  China's economic footprint and recent developments in, 101–3

China's economic presence in, 18, 97–8
  construction projects, **100**
  politics of, 107–8
  projects approved and implemented, **99**
  statistical data of, 98–100
China's investment in, 91, 98, **99**, 106
China's property developers in, **104**
Chinese investors/enterprises in, 100
Cross-Border Collateral Agreement, 95
currency swap agreement with China, 95
economic growth of, 94
economic relations with China, 92
electrified double-track railway project (EDTP), 109
financial sector, 94–5
Five-Year Program for Economic and Trade Cooperation between China and Malaysia (2013–17), 97
foreign direct investment (FDI), 97
  China's annual investment, **98**, 107
  short-term investment, 98
"Forest City" project, 103
Gemas-Johor Bahru Double-Track Railway Project, 110, **111**
government-linked companies (GLCs) in, 91
high-speed railway (HSR) project, 102
  operated by Kuala Lumpur International Airport (KLIA), 103
investments in China, 96–7
  annual and accumulated, **96**
Kuala Lumpur International Airport (KLIA), 103
Malacca Gateway project, 103
Malaysia-China Kuantan Industrial Park (MCKIP), 18, 91, 101
  development of, 103–7
  estimated cost for building, 105
  examination of, 91, 92
Malaysia Development Berhad (MDB), 95, 102
Malaysian Investment Development Authority (MIDA), 98
MH370 incident (2014), 95
political-bureaucratic nexus, 91
political-business collusion, 109–11
purchase of government bonds by China, 94
RMB bonds, 94
Securities Commission of, 94
statistics of Malaysia's trade with China
  Chinese, **93**
  Malaysian, **93**
Stock Exchange, 95
tourism sector in, 95–6
urban redevelopment project, 102
visa-waiver policy, 96
Xi Jinping's visit to, 102
Malaysia-China Business Council (MCBC), 107
Malaysian Embassy, in China, 96
Mandarin language, 185
maritime corridor, 8
Maritime Silk Road initiative, 5, 103
material (hard) power, 35
Mattern, Janice B., 35, 36

memorandum of understanding (MOU), 79, 95, 120, 141, 151, 208
Mertha, Andrew, 91
MH370 incident (2014), 95
military-economic containment, 51
Millennium Development Goals (MDGs), 148
Ministry of Commerce (MOFCOM), China, 149
Mischief Reef
　Philippines claim over, 150
Missile Technology Control Regime (MTCR), 38
MMC Gamuda, 109, 110
Mochtar, Fahmi, 123
moderately well-off society, goal of, 48
Mohamad, Mahathir, 10, 90
　visit to China, 92
Mongolia's "Third Neighbor Diplomacy," 45
Muslim festivals, celebration of, 176
Myanmar
　ASEAN trading partners, 69
　bilateral trade with US, 69
　Burmese Freedom and Democracy Act (2003), 69
　China's FDI in, 71–2
　China's loss of influence in, 83
　civilian-led government, 75
　Composite Index of Economic Influence (CIEI), 73–5
　dissatisfaction with China's investments, 64
　economic sanctions by US on, 69–70
　external debts, 74
　human rights violations in, 67–8, 77–8
　international economic sanctions against, 69
　intra-ASEAN trade volume, 69
　investments of Japan and India in, 71
　inward FDI from the World and China, 72
　Japanese aid to, 82
　Kachin Independence Army (KIA), 80
　Letpadaung copper mine projects, 64, 75
　major trading partners, 70
　military junta, 75
　Ministry of Electric Power, 79–80
　Myitsone Dam, 64, 75, 79
　National League for Democracy (NLD), 69
　political prisoners, release of, 80
　political reform in, 78
　relation with China, see Sino-Myanmar relations
　repression of domestic opposition parties, 69
　State Peace and Development Council (SPDC), 69
　sunk investments in, 71
　support for China's positions on human rights, 75
　top ten countries' CIEI relative to, 74
　top trading goods of, 71
　total trade with the world, 74
　UNGA "Situation of Human Rights in Myanmar" resolution, 76

Nabi (prophet), 177
Nahdlatul Ulama, 174, 181
Nanyang Technological University (NTU), 208
　Confucius Institute Foundation, 210
　Nanyang Chinese Youth Literature Award, 210

Nanyang Xunmeng Guang (Chinese school), 176
Nasution, Abdul Haris, 179
National Development and Reform Commission (NDRC), 133
National People's Congress, 47
Nguyen, Van Chinh, 19
no-conditionality, principles of, 142
non-material (soft) power, 34–5
non-Western countries, 50, 173
normal China, identity of, 42
North Luzon Railway Corporation (NLRC), 155
North Luzon Railway (Northrail) project, Philippines, 19, 151, 154–7, 159, 161, 166n54
  allegations of kickbacks and corruption, 156
  completion of, 155
  corruption charges against the Arroyo administration, 166n54
  financial assistance for, 155–6
  government's handling of the relocation issues, 156
  legal and constitutional violations in, 155
  legality of supply deal with CNMEG, 156
  phases of, 155
  suspension of, 157
Northrail, see North Luzon Railway (Northrail) project, Philippines
North-South aid relations, 146
nuclear-weapon-free world, 64, 75–6, 78
Nye, Joseph S., 6, 32, 35, 37, 90, 144
  Bound to Lead, 172
  notion of soft power, 36, 64, 145

Obama, Barrack, 16, 37, 43–5, 49, 82
offensive realism, idea of, 3

Office of Chinese Language Council International, 196
official development assistance (ODA), 9, 85n27, 142
  DAC's definition of, 143
oil-fired plants, 119
"opening up" diplomacy, 3–4
  four pillars of, 4
Organisation for Economic Co-operation and Development (OECD), 19, 85n27
  Development Assistance Committee (DAC) of, 142
  definition of ODA, 143
other official flows (OOFs), 142, 161
outward direct investment (ODI), 6–7

Panetta, Leon, 44, 47
Park, Geun-hye, 49
Partai Komunis Indonesia (PKI), 173–4
peaceful coexistence, Chinese principle of, 2, 41
peaceful rise of China, 14, 40
People's Bank of China, 95
People's Daily, The, 13
People's Liberation Army (PLA), 32
Permanent Court of Arbitration, The Hague, 6
Pheng, Yin Huah, 109
Philippine-Eastern China Business Forum, 157
Philippines
  aid management in, 143
  Angat Water Utilization and Aqueduct Improvement project, 151
  Angeles University Foundation (AUF) in, 201
  challenges to Sino-Philippines aid relations, 151–9

China's foreign aid diplomacy
  in, 150–1
  factors influencing
    underutilization of aids,
    155
  patterns of, 154
  public perception of, 155
Chinese-assisted loan projects,
  157
Commission on Audit (COA),
  144
completed China-assisted loans
  and grants in, **152**
Confucius Institutes in, 141
Congressional Oversight
  Committee on ODA Law,
  144
Department of Finance (DOF),
  158
Department of Transportation
  and Communication
  (DOTC), 156
Development Plan, 158
dispute with China over
  Mischief Reef, 150
Framework Agreements and
  MOUs with China, **153–4**
interactions with DAC donors,
  142
Investment Coordination
  Committee (ICC), 158–9
National Economic and
  Development Authority
  (NEDA), 144, 151, 158
nationwide telecommunications
  network, 156
North Luzon Railway (Northrail)
  project, 151, 159
  allegations of kickbacks and
    corruption, 156
  completion of, 155
  corruption charges
    against the Arroyo
    administration, 166n54
  financial assistance for,
    155–6
  government's handling of
    the relocation issues,
    156
  legal and constitutional
    violations in, 155
  legality of supply deal with
    CNMEG, 156
  phases of, 155
  suspension of, 157
Official Development Assistance
  Act (1996), 143
Philippine National Broadband
  Network (NBN) projects,
  151
  cancellation of, 157
  legal and constitutional
    violations in, 155
relation with China, 151
Republic Act (RA) 8182, 143
Senate blue ribbon committee,
  157
South China Sea dispute, 151
  appeal to Hague tribunal,
    46, 151
University of the Philippines
  (UP) Law Center, 156
"pivot to Asia" strategy (United
  States), 32, 43–5, 47
political leadership of China, 2
"powerful enemy" syndrome, 4
Prayuth, Chan-ocha, 204
project management, 130
Protestantism, 178
PT Perusahaan Listrik Negara (PT
  PLN), 119
  assessment of the FTP-I
    program, 131
PT Truba Alam Manunggal
  Engineering Tbk, 125
Putin, Vladimir, 40
  Xi's joint statement with, 50

Qian, Qichen, 4
Qinzhou City, 105
Qinzhou Jingwu Investment Co, Ltd., 105
Qualified Domestic Institutional Investor (QDII) scheme, 94
Qu, Xing, 52n1

Razak, Najib, 102–3
"rebalancing" strategy (United States), 32, 43–4, 51
recipient economies, welfare losses for, 142
Red Second Generation, 47
Reformed Evangelical Church of Indonesia, 185
rejuvenation, quest for, 1, 48
religious groups, depoliticization of, 174
Rendao (way of humans), 41
Renminbi Qualified Foreign Institutional Investor (RQFII) scheme, 94
representational force, 36
re-Sinicization movement, 176–7
responsibility, idea of, 45
responsible stakeholder, 39
Rhodes, Ben, 44
Rimbunan Hijau, 105
rising power, idea of, 4, 49, 148
rogue aid, by China in South Asia, 9–10
Roque, Harry, 156
Royal Academy of Cambodia (RAC), 201, 211
Rumsfeld, Donald, 34
Russia-China relations, 50

Sahlins, Emeritus Marshall, 12–13
Sam Kauw Hwee, 177
Sarekat Islam, 177

Securities Commission of Malaysia, 94
security architecture, principles of, 50
self-identity reformation, 42
severe acute respiratory syndrome (SARS), 43
Shanghai Electric Corporation Ltd., 121, 129
Silk Road Economic Belt, 5, 22, 101, 199, 217n17
Singapore
  academic interactions with China, 209
  Agreement on Cultural Cooperation, 208
  Business Chinese Program, 208
  China's soft diplomacy in, 209
  CI project in, 207–10
  cooperation with China, 208
  ethnic Chinese in, 207
  Guanxi networks in, 203–4, 207–10
    with educational institutions, 209
    with elites, 208
    with government units, 208
    with local overseas Chinese, 209–10
  Memorandum of Understanding on Cultural Cooperation, 208
  political and economic relationship with China, 207
  Speak Mandarin Campaign, 208
  Workforce Development Agency (Workplace Singapore), 208
Sinicized charm offensive, 38
Sino-"barbarian" dichotomy, 13
Sino-centralism, concept of, 13
Sino-Myanmar relations, 63
  affinity score, 76
  aid relationship, 72–3

community-based opposition to, 79–82
Composite Index of Economic Influence (CIEI), 73–5
crucial-case method to investigate, 66–8
dissatisfaction with China's investments, 64
economic exchanges, 66
economic presence of China in Myanmar, 69–73
external and internal security, 68
foreign direct investments (FDI), 71–2
growing divergence between, 75
on human rights violations, 67–8
interdependent relationship, 68–9
Letpadaung copper mine projects, 64
protests against, 79
Myitsone Dam project, 64, 79
security relationship, 67
on sense of legitimacy and need for support, 68
on voting patterns in UN General Assembly, 75–8
Sino-Russian Joint Statement on the International Order for the 21st Century (2004), 40
Sino-US relations, 49
small and medium enterprises (SMEs), 97
social equality and justice, 4
socialist market economy, 147–8
soft border, concept of, 13
"soft" power
China's soft footprints to Southeast Asia, 64–5, 172
concept of, 34, 145, 172
Confucianism and, 175–7
constructivist theories of, 34
cultural and economic aspects of, 173
cultural asset of the US, 172
debate on, 33–8
definition of, 35
diplomacy, 10–11, 32
effective use of, 145
efficacy of, 145
foreign policy discourse and, 36–8
human ideation and constructivism, 34–5
in Indonesia, 173
info-tech based trend of, 35
institutionalist theories of, 33
limits of foreign aid as a tool of, 144–6
material capabilities of, 33
as non-material power, 35
Nye's notion of, 36, 64
role in foreign policy, 34
scope of, 33–4
as sociolinguistically constructed "truth," 35–6
sociolinguistic nature of, 33–8
sources of, 64
state-to-state affairs, 173
struggle for, 35
style and paradox of, 33
Xi's readjustment of, 33
South China Sea dispute, 32
blockade of Huangyan/Scarborough Shoal, 46
between China and ASEAN countries, 1, 5
China's claim to historic rights, 6
China's military presence, 45
Declaration on the Conduct of Parties in the South China Sea (DOC), 46
'nine-dash line' demarcation, 6

as part of China's "core interests," 46
Philippines appeal to Hague tribunal, 46, 151
ruling of the Permanent Court of Arbitration on, 6
Southeast Asia
  bilateral economic relationship with China, 65
  China's application of soft power in, 65
  China's economic offensive and influence in, 64-6
  China's foreign aid diplomacy in, 150-1
  China's soft footprints to, 64-5
  Chinese investments and aid to, 63-4
  cross-border economic activities, 64
  economic benefits of China's investments in, 63
  exploitation of natural resources by China, 63
  foreign direct investment (FDI), 66
  personal and economic exchanges with China, 66
South-South cooperation, 146, 160
Soviet Union, 39, 49
  economic aid to Southeast Asia, 9
  Vietnam policy toward, 2
spaces of contestation, 17-18
Speak Mandarin Campaign (Singapore), 208
sphere of influence, 1-2, 202
Spratly Islands, 46
S P Setia, 105
standards of living, 48
State-Owned Assets Supervision and Administration Commission (SASAC), China, 120, 133

state-owned enterprises (SOEs), 18, 95, 102, 107, 117, 120, 149, 158-9, 161, 210
Strezhnev, Anton, 75
Suharto, 174-5
  fall of, 182-4
  suppression of the G30S, 174
Sukarno
  overthrow of, 2
  presidency of, 173
  presidential decree, 178
  suppression of Muslim political groups, 174
Sukarnoputri, Megawati, 182
supra-regulatory institutions, 133
Surabaya Chinese, 176
Suzhou Industrial Park, 104
Syrian humanitarian crisis, 38

Taiwan, 20, 22, 46
  Buddhist sect from, 175
  China's objectives of isolating, 147
  diplomatic isolation of, 160
  expulsion from United Nations, 147
  soft power, 175, 184-5
Taman Mini Indonesia Indah, 183
Tan-Zam railway project, 147
Taoism, 41, 175-7
Thailand
  Chiang Mai University, 206
  Chinese language training programs in, 205
    for Thai Chinese teachers, 205
  Chulalongkorn University, 205-7
  CI project in, 204-7
  Guanxi networks in, 203-4
    with educational institutes, 206

with elites, 205
with government units, 205
with local overseas Chinese, 206-7
Hu Jintao's official visit to, 204
Ministry of Education, 205
number of CIs and CCs in, 204
relation with China, 204-5
teaching framework agreement, 205
Thein, Sein, 79-80, 82
theories of Old, 13-14
Thiong Hua Hui Guan (THHK), 176-7
Third Neighbor Diplomacy (Mongolia), 45
Third World
  idea of, 50
  unity, 40
"three faces" of Chinese power, 34
Thucydides' Trap, 52
Tiananmen Square incident (1989), 31, 52n1, 145
Tiandao (way of heaven), 41
Tianjian Eco-city projects, 104
Tibet, unrest in, 43
Tien (Heaven), concept of, 177
Tjoa Djien Ho, 175-6
Tong, Stephen, 185
trade gap, between China and Southeast Asian countries, 7
traditional culture, elements of, 172
Treaty of Amity and Cooperation (TAC), 150
tributary system, of ancient China, 2, 14, 35
trust deficit, 16, 49, 52
Two Corridors, One Economic Belt, 8
Tzu Chi (Buddhist sect from Taiwan), 175, 184
  in post-Suharto Indonesia, 185
  teachings of, 185

UN Convention on the Law of the Sea, 6
Union of Myanmar Economic Holdings Limited (UMEHL), 80
United Nations General Assembly (UNGA), 68, 75, 147
  China and Myanmar voting patterns in, 75-8
  expulsion of Taiwan from, 147
  Sino-Myanmar affinity score, 76
  "Situation of Human Rights in Myanmar" resolution, 76
  "Situation of Human Rights in the Islamic Republic of Iran" resolution, 77
  "Situation of Human Rights in the Syrian Arab Republic" resolution, 77
  "Towards a Nuclear-Weapon-Free World" resolution, 78
United Nations Security Council (UNSC), 38, 68
United States
  "back to Asia" strategy, 44
  foreign policy, 45
  forward deployed diplomacy, 44-5
  "pivot to Asia" strategy, 16, 32, 43-4, 45, 47
  "rebalancing" strategy, 32, 43, 44-5, 51
  relation with Vietnam, 45
  War on Terror, 34, 36
University of Maryland, 37
UN Resolution 1441 on weapons inspections in Iraq (2002), 38
unrestricted aid transfers, 142
urban redevelopment project, 102
U Zaw Min, 80

value-added goods, 94
victim mentality, concept of, 42

Vietnam
   Chinese investments in, 7, 19
   Exclusive Economic Zone, 6
   invasion of Cambodia, 2
   policy toward the Soviet Union, 2
   relation with China, 2
      dispute over oil rigs, 6
   relation with United States, 45
      on embargo on arms sales, 45
   war with China, 3–4
visa-waiver policy, 96
Voeten, Erik, 75, 86n30

Wahid, Abdurrahman
   "looking toward Asia" policy, 182
   policy toward Chinese Indonesians, 182
   support for reinstating Confucianism, 182
Waltz, Kenneth N., 33–4
Wanbao Mining, 80
War on Terror, 34, 36
Washington Consensus, 37
wealth and power, quest for, 1
welfare losses, for recipient economies, 142
Wen, Jiabao, 103, 112, 153
Wen Mian (God of Literature), 176
Western Development Strategy (China), 150–1
Western industrialized donor countries, 147
Western theories and concepts, Sinicization of, 15
Widodo, Joko, 119, 127
Wijaya, Budi, 180
Wong, Danny, 20
world communist system, collapse of, 9
World Trade Organization, 150

Xiamen University, 107, 207
Xiao, Qian, 155
Xi, Jinping, 32
   Belt and Road Initiative, 21–3, 101
   China-ASEAN Expo in Guangxi, 202
   Chinese Dream discourse, 33, 41
      parts of, 48
   Chinese foreign policy before, 38–46
   countermeasures to deal with US's rebalancing plan, 49
   foreign policy discourse, 36
   joint statement with Vladimir Putin, 50
   leadership style, 47
   Maritime Silk Road project, 5
   new leverage, 49–50
   on Sino-Thai political relationship, 204
   soft power offensive, 33
   speeches on
      China's goal, 47
      CPC's mission, 47
   visit to Malaysia, 102
Xinhua (state-run news agency), 48
Xinjiang, unrest in, 22, 43, 46

Yao, Xinzhong, 41
Yoshihiko, Noda, 45, 82
Young Confucius Cultural Camp, 209
Yudhoyono, Susilo Bambang, 121, 129, 183

Zenith Construction, 102
Zhao, Haiqing, 41, 56n40
Zheng, Bijian, 40, 54n24
Zheng, Da, 100

Zhou, Enlai, 147, 160
  Eight Principles for Economic Aid and Technical Assistance to Other Countries, 147

Five Principles of Peaceful Coexistence, 2
Zhu, Rongji, 148
Zoellick, Robert B., 39
ZTE-National Broadband Network, 19, 156